VOLKSWAGEN 411 1968–72 AUTOBOOK

Workshop Manual for
Volkswagen 411 1968–69
Volkswagen 411L 1968–69
Volkswagen 411E 1969–70
Volkswagen 411LE 1969–72

by

Kenneth Ball G I Mech E

and the

Autopress team of Technical Writers

AUTOPRESS LTD   GOLDEN LANE   BRIGHTON   BN1 2QJ   ENGLAND

The AUTOBOOK series of Workshop Manuals is the largest in the world and covers the majority of British and Continental motor cars, as well as all major Japanese and Australian models. For a full list see the back of this manual.

CONTENTS

Acknowledgement

Introduction

Chapter 1   The Engine   9

Chapter 2   The Fuel System   29

Chapter 3   The Ignition System   45

Chapter 4   The Cooling System   53

Chapter 5   The Clutch   59

Chapter 6   The Gearbox and Differential   65

Chapter 7   Automatic Transmission   77

Chapter 8   Rear Suspension and
Drive Shafts   83

Chapter 9   Front Suspension and Hubs   89

Chapter 10   The Steering System   97

Chapter 11   The Braking System   107

Chapter 12   The Electrical System   119

Chapter 13   The Bodywork   131

Appendix   137

ISBN 0 85147 353 9

First Edition 1972

© Autopress Ltd 1972

Printed and bound in Brighton England for Autopress Ltd by G Beard & Son Ltd

ACKNOWLEDGEMENT

My thanks are due to Volkswagen Motors Ltd for their unstinted co-operation and also for supplying data and illustrations.

I am also grateful to a considerable number of owners who have discussed their cars at length and many of whose suggestions have been included in this manual.

Kenneth Ball G I Mech E
Associate Member Guild of Motoring Writers
Ditchling Sussex England.

INTRODUCTION

This do-it-yourself Workshop Manual has been specially written for the owner who wishes to maintain his car in first class condition and to carry out his own servicing and repairs. Considerable savings on garage charges can be made, and one can drive in safety and confidence knowing the work has been done properly.

Comprehensive step-by-step instructions and illustrations are given on all dismantling, overhauling and assembling operations. Certain assemblies require the use of expensive special tools, the purchase of which would be unjustified. In these cases information is included but the reader is recommended to hand the unit to the agent for attention.

Throughout the Manual hints and tips are included which will be found invaluable, and there is an easy to follow fault diagnosis at the end of each chapter.

Whilst every care has been taken to ensure correctness of information it is obviously not possible to guarantee complete freedom from errors or to accept liability arising from such errors or omissions.

Instructions may refer to the righthand or lefthand sides of the vehicle or the components. These are the same as the righthand or lefthand of an observer standing behind the car and looking forward.

CHAPTER 1

THE ENGINE

1:1 Description
1:2 Removing the engine
1:3 Oil and filter changes
1:4 Torque wrench settings
1:5 The cylinder heads and valve gear
1:6 Setting the valve clearances

1:7 Cylinders and pistons
1:8 The lubrication system
1:9 Clutch and flywheel
1:10 The crankcase assembly
1:11 Reassembling a stripped engine
1:12 Fault diagnosis

1:1 Description

All the models covered by this manual follow the standard Volkswagen practice of having a flat four air-cooled engine mounted in the rear of the car. The engine is bolted to and mounted directly behind the combined transmission and final drive unit.

Sectioned views of the engine are shown in **FIG 1:1**. The crankcase is made up of two light-alloy castings bolted together in the vertical plane. The lower portion of the castings forms the oil pan and there is no separate sump. The castings are machined to take the four main bearing crankshaft as well as the camshaft immediately below it. One crankcase casting, the crankshaft and connecting rods, camshaft and associated parts are shown in **FIG 1:2**. The crankshaft has four throws and each piston therefore has its own throw. The cylinders and cylinder heads are bolted down on studs to the crankcase and by offsetting the pairs of cylinders adequate clearance is given between the connecting rods. Renewable bearing inserts are used for the crankshaft and camshaft bearings. The design gives a very short crankshaft which, combined with the four main bearings, gives a very rigid structure.

Individual cylinders are fitted, deeply finned to allow for cooling, and each pair of cylinders is fitted with a single cylinder head. Overhead valves are fitted and these are operated using rocker arms (pivoting on a rocker shaft), pushrods, and tappets from the centrally mounted single camshaft. The tappets (cam followers) move in machined bores in the crankcase casting while the push-rods operate in tubes between cylinder head and crank-case. The camshaft is driven directly by gears from the crankshaft.

A schematic view of the lubrication system is shown in **FIG 1:3**. The oil is contained in the lower portion of the crankcase castings. Note that the base is deeply finned to allow for oil cooling. A gear type oil pump draws the oil from the oil pan and supplies it under pressure to the engine. Oil to the pump passes through a strainer, accessible from under the engine, to ensure that large particles are not drawn into the pump. The oil under pressure passes from the pump through a fullflow filter element, which is renewable, before passing to the engine or oil cooler. A ball valve is fitted to the oil filter so that in the event of the element becoming choked a supply of oil will still pass to the engine. Relief valve assemblies are fitted, which serve the double purpose of controlling the oil flow through the oil cooler and limiting the maximum pressure in the system. When the engine is cold and the

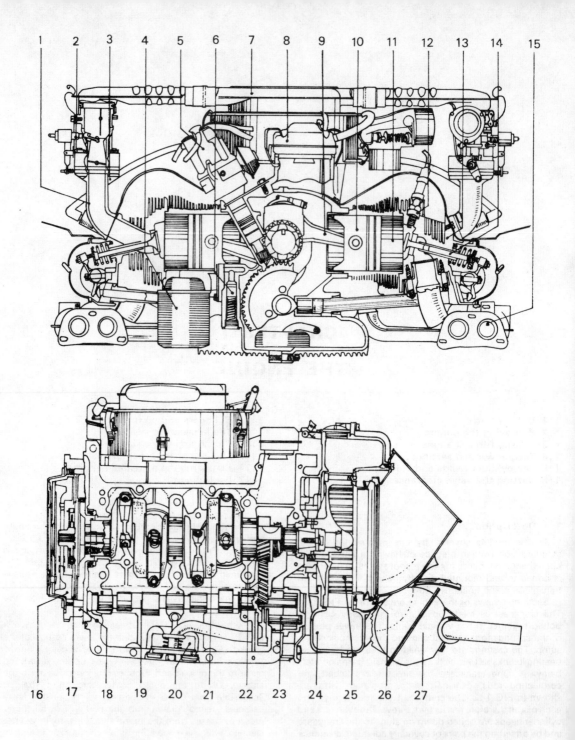

FIG 1:1   Sectioned views of the engine

Key to Fig 1:1   1 Air intake pipe   2 Carburetter   3 Balance pipe   4 Oil filter   5 Ignition distributor   6 Oil pressure relief valve   7 Air cleaner   8 Crankcase breather   9 Connecting rod   10 Piston   11 Cylinder   12 Spark plug   13 Cylinder head   14 Valve   15 Heat exchanger   16 Clutch   17 Clutch driven plate   18 Flywheel   19 Camshaft   20 Oil strainer   21 Crankshaft   22 Camshaft drive gear   23 Oil pump   24 Fan housing   25 Fan   26 Fan belt pulley   27 Silencer (muffler)

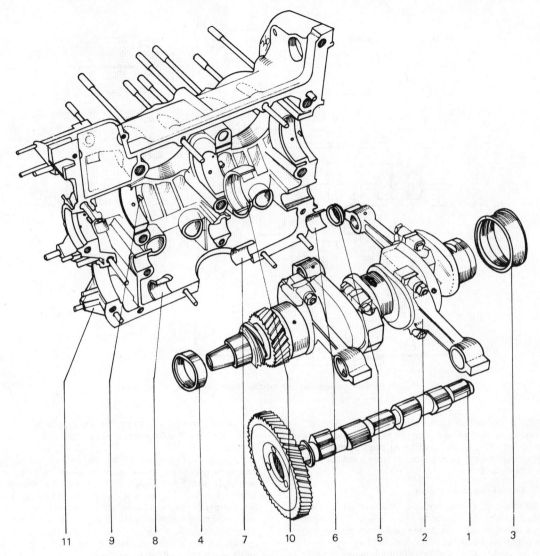

FIG 1:2 The crankshaft, camshaft and one crankcase casting

Key to Fig 1:2 1 Camshaft   2 Crankshaft with connecting rods   3 No. 1 main bearing   4 No. 4 main bearing   5 Camshaft bore end cover   6 No. 1 camshaft bearing shell   7 No. 2 camshaft bearing   8 Lefthand shell for No. 3 camshaft bearing   9 Crankshaft bearing dowel   10 No. 2 crankshaft bearing shell   11 Lefthand crankcase half

pressure is high, both relief valves have their pistons pressed down against their springs by the oil pressure. The upper valve allows the oil to bypass the oil cooler to ensure more rapid warming-up of the engine. The lower relief valve allows surplus oil to return directly to the oil pan and limits the maximum pressure in the system. As the oil warms up the pressure drops and allows the upper valve to close, so that the oil passes through the oil cooler. The lower valve will still limit the maximum pressure in the system. Oil galleries and internal passages then lead the oil to the crankshaft main bearings, camshaft bearings and cam followers. The front main bearing is lubricated by a

tapping from No. 2 bearing and the big-end bearings are lubricated from the main bearings by passages drilled through the crankshaft. A metered supply of lubricant passes up the hollow pushrods to lubricate the rocker assembly, the oil then returning down the pushrod tubes. The remainder of the parts are lubricated by oil splash.

The oil pump is driven by the rear of the camshaft. The distributor is driven by gears from the crankshaft.

A cooling air impeller mounted on the rear of the crankshaft draws in air from outside and blows it over the engine. The engine is enclosed, as shown in **FIG 1:4**, and deflector plates guide the air over the fins. Thermo-

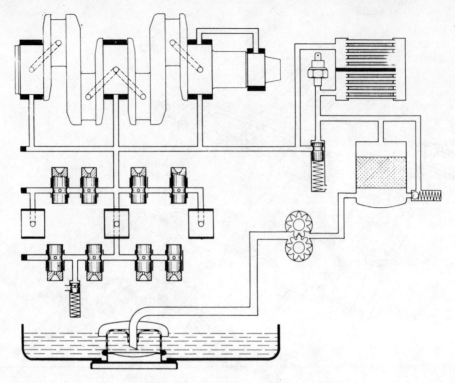

FIG 1:3   Schematic diagram of the engine lubrication system

statically controlled ducts control the amount of air drawn in, so that when the engine is cold rapid warm-up is ensured. Part of the cooling air passes through heat exchangers on the exhaust and is then used for heating the interior of the car.

1:2   Removing the engine

Removal of the engine on Volkswagen models is comparatively easy. Because of the design of the engine it will be found essential to remove it for many operations, more than are usual on a conventional engine.

If the owner is not a skilled automobile mechanic he is advised to read the **Hints on Maintenance and Overhaul** section in the **Appendix**, as this contains much useful information.

The car must be raised for the removal of the engine so **make sure that all supports used are strong enough and firmly based.** A trolley jack should be used for supporting the engine and for wheeling it out from under the car. A suitable adaptor, VW.612/4, is made for supporting the engine but if this is not available use a suitable plate and pieces of wood as packing to prevent damage to the engine. An assistant is required to steady parts and help in difficult operations.

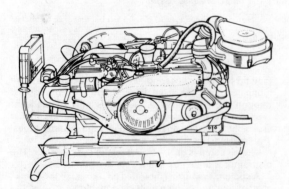

FIG 1:4   External view of the engine fitted with fuel injection

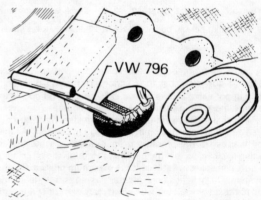

FIG 1:5   Removing the circlip from the drive shaft

Removal:

1 Disconnect both battery cables from the battery. The ground cable should be disconnected first and connected last to prevent any danger of shortcircuits. Note that the battery is under the front lefthand seat.

2 On all models remove the air cleaner. Disconnect all fuel system connections from the engine, noting that fuller details of both carburetter and fuel injection systems are given in **Chapter 2**. On models fitted with carburetters, disconnect the inlet line to the fuel pump (plugging it with a suitable plug to prevent fuel syphoning through) and disconnect the leads to the automatic chokes and idle valve solenoids. Label the leads and lay them safely out of the way. On models fitted with fuel injection, disconnect the electrical leads, after labelling any that are not obvious, and also disconnect the fuel ring main. On all models, disconnect the throttle linkage from the engine.

3 Disconnect the electrical leads to all other components on the engine. These components include the starter motor, alternator, ignition coil and oil pressure warning switch. Disconnect the primary lead and the HT lead from between the ignition coil and distributor. Unless the connections are perfectly obvious, leads should be labelled as they are disconnected. Too often only a mental note is made as they are disconnected, and if the colours have faded or become obscured with dirt there is great uncertainty about the correct connections when it comes to reassembly.

4 Remove the rear seat and take out the cover over the drive shaft. Remove the nut with the aid of the special wrench VW.796. Tap lightly on the tool to dislodge the circlip, as shown in **FIG 1 : 5**. Pull the shaft forward by approximately 100 mm (4 inch).

5 Remove the cooling air intake duct, warm air fan and associated parts such as cooling air intake valves and bellows, as well as hoses. Remove the engine compartment seal. Remove the shield for the silencer (muffler). Disconnect the heat exchanger control boxes and their hoses and cables so that the control boxes can be removed. Remove the heater booster exhaust pipe.

6 On models fitted with automatic transmission, remove the dipstick as well as the filler tube. Disconnect the vacuum line from the intake manifolds balance pipe. It will also be necessary to remove the cover so that the three bolts securing the torque converter to the engine drive plate can be removed. Once the engine has been removed it is essential to fit a strap, or thick wire, across the converter housing to prevent the converter from falling out.

7 Remove the nuts from the upper engine securing bolts. Fit the transmission support VW.785 into the mountings of the diagonal arms so as to support the transmission. A jack may be used to support the transmission, but be sure to fit a pad of wood between jack and transmission to prevent damage to the castings or automatic transmission oil pan.

8 Support the engine on the trolley jack and adaptor. Remove the nuts from the lower engine supports and take out the four bolts securing the engine to the transmission. Draw the engine back until the transmission input shaft is clear of the clutch and then lower the engine so that it can be wheeled out from under the

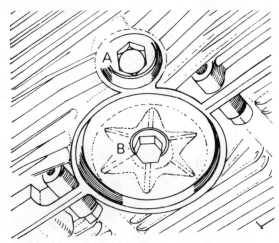

FIG 1 : 6   The engine drain plug and oil strainer

FIG 1 : 7   Removing or installing the oil filter

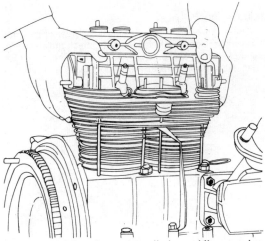

FIG 1 : 8   Holding down the cylinders while removing the cylinder head

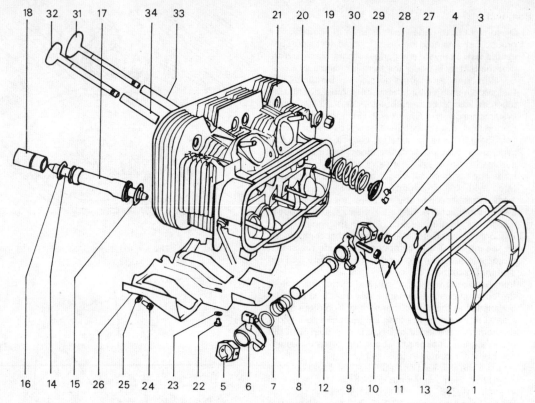

FIG 1:9 The cylinder head and its components

Key to Fig 1:9 1 Cylinder head cover 2 Cover gasket 3 Nut 4 Spring washer 5 Support 6 Exhaust valve rocker arm 7 Thrust washer 8 Spring 9 Inlet valve rocker arm 10 Valve adjusting screw 11 Locknut 12 Rocker shaft 13 Retaining wire for pushrod tubes 14 Pushrod 15 Seal 16 Seal 17 Pushrod tube 18 Tappet 19 Nut 20 Washer 21 Cylinder head 22 Cheese head screw 23 Washer 24 Cheese head screw 25 Washer 26 Deflector plate 27 Valve cotter halves 28 Spring cap 29 Valve spring 30 Oil deflector ring 31 Inlet valve 32 Exhaust valve 33 Inlet valve guide 34 Exhaust valve guide

vehicle. Do not forget to fit a retaining plate to hold the torque converter in place on automatic transmission models.

Installation:

The engine is installed in the reverse order of removal. Before installing the engine, visually check the clutch for damage (it may well be worth while removing the clutch so that it can be fully examined, to save work later). Check

that the input shaft pilot bearing is in good condition. Check that the clutch release bearing is in good condition and not excessively worn.

Lightly lubricate the clutch release bearing guide with molybdenum disulphide paste. Check the splines of the input shaft of the transmission and rub some molybdenum disulphide powder onto them with a clean piece of rag. Apply a little lithium-based grease to the starter motor shaft.

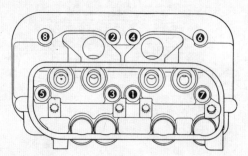

FIG 1:10 The correct sequence for slackening or finally tightening the cylinder head nuts

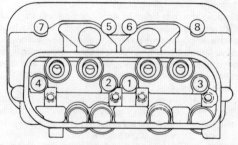

FIG 1:11 The correct sequence for the preliminary tightening of the cylinder head nuts

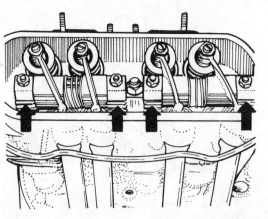

FIG 1:12   The correct installation of the rocker shaft clamps

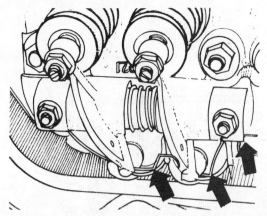

FIG 1:14   The wire clip for the pushrod tubes correctly engaged

Check the mating flanges of the engine and transmission for dirt or damage. Hard deposits should be softened with a suitable harsh solvent and then scraped off with a piece of perspex or hardwood. Light damage or nicks should be smoothed down with an oilstone, scraper or fine file.

When installing the engine, be sure not to allow it to hang on the transmission input shaft, otherwise the clutch will be damaged. Secure the engine fully into place before removing the supports. New self-locking nuts should be used to secure the engine carrier to the bonded mountings. Tighten them to a torque of 2.5 kg m (18 lb ft).

Slide in the drive shaft with the special wrench VW.796 in place, turning the shaft slightly as required. Engage the circlip by tightening the nut.

The remaining parts are then installed in the reverse order of removal. Set the throttle linkage in the full throttle position and make engine idling adjustments as required.

1:3 Oil and oil filter changes

When running-in a new or reconditioned engine, the oil and oil filter should be changed after the first 1000 kilometres (600 miles). After this first oil change, the oil should be changed at intervals of 5000 kilometres (3000 miles) and the filter element at intervals of 10,000 kilometres (6000 miles). This means that the oil filter is changed at every other oil change after the engine has been run in.

The drain plug for the engine is shown at **A** in **FIG 1:6**. Take the car for a short run to warm the oil and stir any loose dirt up into suspension. Remove the drain plug and allow the oil to drain out into a suitable container. While the oil is draining, remove the bolt **B** shown in the figure, take off the cover and withdraw the oil strainer. Wash the oil strainer in clean fuel and dry it with compressed air. Discard the old gaskets and assemble the strainer parts in the reverse order of removal. Tighten the bolt **B** to a torque of 1.0 to 1.3 kg m (7 to 9 lb ft). Refit the drain plug **A** using a new seal.

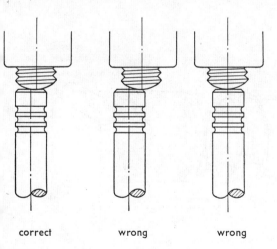

correct   wrong   wrong

FIG 1:13   The correct and incorrect positioning of the rocker arms in relation to the valve stems

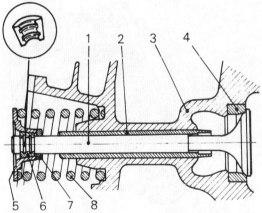

FIG 1:15   Sectioned view through a typical valve

Key to Fig 1:15 1 Valve 2 Valve guide 3 Cylinder head
4 Valve seat insert   5 Valve cap   6 Split collet (lock)
7 Oil seal   8 Valve spring

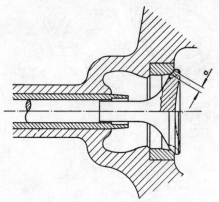

FIG 1:16   The valve seat width

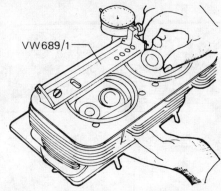

FIG 1:17   A method of checking the wear in the valve guides and valve stems

A special wrench or tool is required for removing the oil filter. One type of tool is shown in **FIG 1:7** and this has slots for a tommy bar so that the filter can be undone if it is stiff. Another type of tool is like a large C-spanner with teeth that fit into notches in the housing. It is just possible to use a conventional strap spanner to turn the filter. Unscrew the old element and discard it, without attempting to clean it in any way. Check the gasket on the new element and smear it lightly with engine oil. Fit the new element by hand until the gasket can be felt to contact the engine, then tighten the element by a further half turn.

Filling:

The engine dipstick has two marks on it, indicating the maximum and minimum levels. The minimum quantity of oil should be $2\frac{1}{2}$ Litres ($4\frac{1}{2}$ Imp pints, $5\frac{1}{4}$ US pints).

For an oil change only, 3 Litres (5.25 Imp pints, 6.3 US pints) of oil will be required but for an oil and filter change 3.5 Litres (6.1 Imp pints, 7.3 US pints) of oil are needed.

Fill the engine with just less than the correct amount of oil and start it up. Check for oil leaks around the filter or

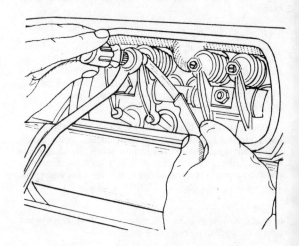

FIG 1:18   Setting the valve clearances

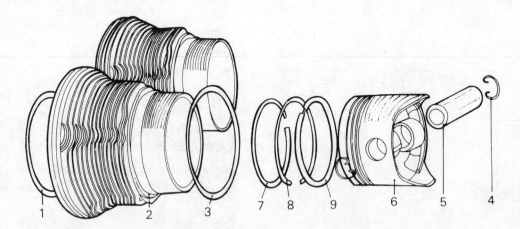

FIG 1:19   The pistons and cylinders

Key to Fig 1:19   1 Sealing ring   2 Cylinder   3 Sealing ring   4 Circlip   5 Piston pin   6 Piston   7 Upper compression ring   8 Lower compression ring   9 Oil scraper ring

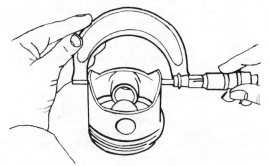

FIG 1:20   Measuring the piston diameter

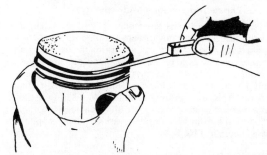

FIG 1:22   Checking the side clearance of the piston rings in the piston

strainer. Drive the car onto level ground and stop the engine. Leave for five minutes to allow the oil level to settle and then top up to the full mark on the dipstick. Do not overfill the engine as this can lead to oil leaking past oil seals, excessive consumption, and frothing of the oil by the big-end bearings thrashing in it.

In use, topping up to the upper mark is only essential when the level has fallen to the lower mark on the dipstick.

Extreme condition:

If the oil remains cold there is little chance of contaminants and water (products of combustion) evaporating from the oil, which will quickly become too dirty to use. If the car is only used for city driving or short distances in wintry conditions the oil should be changed at intervals of 2500 kilometres (1500 miles). If the car is used in Arctic conditions with the average temperature around —25°C (—15°F) the oil should be changed at intervals of 1250 kilometres (750 miles).

In temperate climates any good grade of HD SAE.30 oil may be used. In normal winter conditions SAE.20W/20 oil may be used.

For average temperatures between 5°C (40°F) and —30°C (—20°F) an SAE.10 oil should be used. For average temperatures below —10°C (25°F) an SAE.5 oil should be used. Note that there is an overlap for the different grades of oil and that the figures are a guide and not mandatory.

The use of a thinner oil as the temperature drops will ensure easier starting.

1:4 Torque wrench settings:

A torque wrench is nearly as essential a tool for working on the engine and transmission as a set of spanners. Light-alloy is used extensively in the construction of the engine and that 'extra pull on the spanner for luck' can easily strip threads or damage components. Main torque wrench settings are given throughout in the relevant sections and a consolidated list is also given in the **Appendix.**

Stripped threads can be repaired using Heli-coil inserts. The task is best left to a service garage but basically the stripped thread is tapped out with the appropriate tap for the size. The Heli-coil insert is then screwed into place down these tapped threads, using the special tool for the purpose, and the tang broken off. The attachment bolt will then run up and down using the Heli-coil insert as the threads.

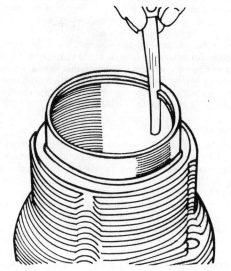

FIG 1:21   Checking the fitted gap of the piston rings

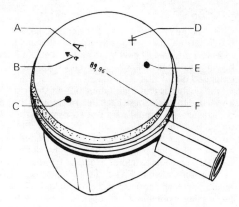

FIG 1:23   Typical piston crown markings

Key to Fig 1:23   **A** Part number and identification mark **B** Arrow or word VORN   **C** Blue, Pink or Green paint mark showing grade   **D** Weight grading mark   **E** Paint mark showing weight grading (Brown=—, Grey=+)   **F** Piston size in millimetres

1 : 5 The cylinder heads and valve gear

The cylinder heads are made of light-alloy, so great care must be taken not to damage them or to score the joint faces. The nuts and studs securing the cylinder heads also keep the cylinder heads in place so care must be taken not to allow the cylinders to move once the head is off. One method of holding down the cylinders is shown in **FIG 1 : 8**, though thick wire may be used in a similar manner. Take care not to break off or damage the cooling fins on the cylinders. Typical cylinder head components are shown in **FIG 1 : 9**.

Removal:

The cylinder heads should not be removed when the engine is hot as this can be a cause of distortion.

1 With the manifolds and deflector plates removed, pull down the spring that secures the rocker cover in place and remove the cover with its gasket. Evenly slacken and then remove the nuts securing the rocker shaft assembly to the head. Slide off the rocker shaft assembly. If both cylinder heads are being removed, mark the rocker assemblies so that they cannot become interchanged.

2 Free the wire clips securing the pushrod tubes. Progressively and evenly slacken the cylinder head attachment nuts in the order shown in **FIG 1 : 10**. Make sure that both (or all four) cylinders are held down by some form of clamp (see **FIG 1 : 8**).

3 Carefully pull off the cylinder head by hand, making sure that it is kept square. If the head sticks assist it with light blows from a hide-faced or rubber mallet. Take great care to hit squarely and not to hit at one point only but work evenly around the base. The fins are of light-alloy and can easily be damaged. Do not crank the engine as there is a danger of the cylinders moving or the head tilting.

4 Remove the pushrods, their tubes, and related parts. Discard all old gaskets and seals. It is essential that pushrods are stored in the correct order as they must be installed back into their original positions.

Installation:

1 Check all the parts and service the components. Make sure that all parts are scrupulously clean before assembly and use all new seals and gaskets. Lubricate bearing surfaces liberally with clean engine oil or graphited oil.

2 Fit the pushrods and their tubes, noting that care will be needed to guide these back into position as the head is installed. Take great care not to damage the seals on the pushrod tubes.

3 Fit the cylinder head back into place and secure it with all the nuts fingertight. Progressively tighten the cylinder head nuts to a torque load of 1.1 kg m (7 lb ft) in the order shown in **FIG 1 : 11**, making sure that the head is seating correctly and not cocked. When the preliminary tightening has been completed tighten the bolts to the correct final torque of 3.2 kg m (23 lb ft) in the order shown in **FIG 1 : 10**.

4 Install the rocker arm assembly back into place, tightening the nuts to 1.4 kg m (10 lb ft) making sure that the slots in the shaft clamps face in the original direction. Take care to make sure that the pushrods are correctly seated in the tappets and rocker arms during

this operation. Typical correct positioning of the clamps is shown in **FIG 1 : 12**. The rocker assembly should be set so that the ends of the rocker arms are very slightly offset in relation to the ends of the valve stems, so that they impart a slight rotation to valves as they operate. A typical set-up is shown in **FIG 1 : 13**.

5 The wire clips for retaining the pushrod tubes are fitted as shown in **FIG 1 : 14**, so that they are in the slots of the rocker shaft bearings and enter the bottom edge of the pushrod tubes.

6 Set the valve clearances as described in the next section and refit the remainder of the parts in the reverse order of removal.

Decarbonizing:

Sharp metal tools must not be used for removing carbon or deposits. Scrapers should be made up from hardwood, perspex or solder. Shape the end to a suitable chisel point. Similarly wire brushes, hand or rotary, must not be used. A special rotary wire brush, with wire enclosed at both ends, is made for cleaning valve guides and it is permissible to use this.

Leave the valves fitted while cleaning the combustion chambers as the valves will protect the head seats. Scrape out carbon and deposits, taking great care not to damage or score the cylinder head seating faces (including those for the manifolds). If desired, a light polish can be given using worn emerycloth dipped in paraffin (kerosene). Once the chambers have been cleaned, the the valves can be removed and the ports cleaned out in a similar manner, taking great care not to damage the valve guides or head seats. If the special rotary wire brushes are not available, clean the valve guides by pulling strips of cloth soaked in solvent through them. Thoroughly clean the cylinder head with a suitable solvent after decarbonizing.

Make sure that the cylinders are held down firmly in place and carefully crank the engine until the piston is near TDC. Scrape off deposits from the crown in a manner similar to that for cleaning the combustion chambers. The light polish with worn emerycloth must only be carried out on the piston crown if the piston is removed from the engine, otherwise abrasive particles cannot be satisfactorily removed.

Examine the fins on the cylinder head for cracks or damage. An attempt should be made to straighten slightly bent fins but do not use such force that they snap. Nicks or breaks should be blended in smoothly by the use of a file. If an excessive number of fins are damaged, a reconditioned cylinder head should be fitted.

Valve removal:

A conventional valve spring compressor should be used for removing the valves and their associated parts. A typical sectioned valve and its related parts are shown in **FIG 1 : 15**. Fit the compressor so that its end holds the head of the valve and press down so that valve cap 5 is pressed down the stem and the spring 8 compressed. If the cap sticks, give it a light tap with a hammer to free it. Lift out the spring collets using tweezers, long-nosed pliers, or a piece of magnetic rod. Release the tool slowly and remove it. Remove the valve cap, spring, and seal. Discard the oil seals, fitting new ones on reassembly. Slide the valve out through the combustion chamber.

Check and clean the parts then reassemble them in the reverse order of dismantling. Lubricate the valve stem liberally with clean oil. Once the parts have been fitted, give the end of the valve stem a sharp blow with a hammer to make sure that the split collets are fully seated.

Valves:

Remove deposits from the valve using a scraper or rotary wire brush. Take care not to damage the seating face of the ground portion of the stem.

Check the head of the valve for burning or excessive pitting of the seat. There must be at least .8 mm ($\frac{1}{32}$ inch) of head material left above the seating face and if there is less than this minimum, or the seat makes a sharp edge, the valve must be renewed.

Check the stem of the valve for scores, wear or bends. Use a steel straightedge to check the straightness of the stem. Light damage or wear on the end of the stem can be trued up by grinding or using an oilstone. Discard badly pitted, burnt valves or any which have defective stems.

Valve springs:

These should be checked by applying load to them and noting their length. If they are satisfactory a load of 81 to 93 kg (178 to 205 lb) will be required to compress them to a length of 29.9 mm (1.18 inch).

If a special rig for testing the springs cannot be borrowed or made up, obtain one new valve spring. Mount each old spring in turn end on to the new one and compress the pair between the jaws of a vice. If the old spring is weak, it will be appreciably shorter than the new one. If weak valve springs are found, the complete set should be renewed.

Pushrods:

Check the pushrods for bend, renewing any that are bent without attempting to straighten them. The pushrods can either be rolled along a true surface or they can be laid on V-blocks and rotated while using a dial indicator gauge to check for excessive runout.

Flush through the pushrods with paraffin, or suitable solvent, followed by compressed air.

Grinding valve seats:

If garage cutting or grinding equipment is used to cut the seats, note that the inlet valve angle is 30 deg. while that for the exhaust valves is 45 deg.

Check all seats for excessive pitting. Those which are badly pitted should be recut using garage equipment as the use of grinding paste will remove excessive metal from the mating seat.

Slide the valve back into its guide and smear a little grinding paste around the seat. Use medium-grade initially unless the seats are in good condition, in which case only fine-grade paste need be used.

Press the valve down into its seat using a suction cup tool and grind with a semi-rotary motion, spinning the handle of the tool between the palms of the hands. Regularly withdraw the valve partially, turn it through a quarter-turn and then press it back to carry on grinding. This ensures that concentric scores are not allowed to build up. Carry on with medium-grade paste until only very shallow pits are left. Wipe away all traces of paste

and repeat the process using fine-grade paste until both seats are matt-grey with no pits or scores. Wash the head and valve thoroughly to remove all traces of abrasive particles.

Check the seat width, shown in **FIG 1 : 16**. For exhaust valves the seat width in the head should be 2.0 to 2.5 mm (.078 to .098 inch) and that for the intake valves 1.8 to 2.2 mm (.070 to .086 inch). If the seats are too wide they should be narrowed using 75 deg and 15 deg. cutters. The 15 deg. cutter will lower the seat width into the head while the 75 deg. cutter will narrow the seat width out of the head. Lightly smear Prussian Blue on the seat, press the valve down and rotate the valve so that the area of contact will be shown on the valve. Use the cutters to set the cylinder head seat to the correct width and so that it meets the valve sealing face centrally. The Prussian Blue will also show that the valve is seating fully around its circumference.

Valve seats and valve guides:

These are a shrink fit into the light-alloy of the head and if they are defective a factory reconditioned cylinder head must be fitted. The owner cannot install new guides or valve seats.

Check the valve seats for cracks, or cracking of the light-alloy around them. If valve grinding has increased the diameter of the chamfer until it is very close to the diameter of the insert then a reconditioned cylinder head must be installed.

A typical method of checking the wear in the valve guides is shown in **FIG 1 : 17**. Use a new valve and fit it so that its stem is flush with the end of the guide. Rock the head of the valve backwards and forwards, noting the play on the dial indicator gauge. Excessive play denotes excessive wear and this in turn will lead to high oil consumption.

1 : 6 Setting the valve clearances

This should be carried out after cylinder head removal and installation, or if the valve train sounds noisy.

Remove sufficient cowling, free the clip, and take off the rocker cover on each cylinder head.

The engine must be cold when setting the valve clearances. The method of adjustment is shown in **FIG 1 : 18**. A feeler gauge of the correct thickness is inserted between the end of the valve stem and the adjusting screw on the rocker arm. Crank the engine until a pair of valves is fully closed. Slacken the locknuts on the adjusters with a ring spanner and slide the feeler gauge into place. Use a screwdriver to turn the adjuster until sliding drag is felt on the feeler gauges as it is moved. Hold the adjuster with the screwdriver and tighten the locknut. Check that the adjustment has not altered. Adjust the other valve on the cylinder in a similar manner.

Crank the engine through 180 deg. and the valves of the cylinder next in the firing order will be fully closed. Adjust the clearance and then repeat the procedure on the remaining two cylinders.

Refit the rocker covers, using new gaskets if required, and install cowling parts removed.

A special tool is made to assist in setting the clearances but this is basically a spanner and screwdriver combined and saves juggling with the various tools to try and keep them all in place.

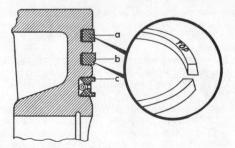

FIG 1:24 The piston rings installed

Key to Fig 1:24
b Lower compression ring

a Upper compression ring
c Oil scraper ring

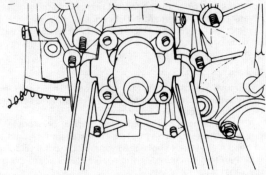

FIG 1:25 Typical method of removing the oil pump

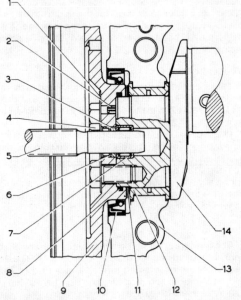

FIG 1:26 Sectioned view of the flywheel attachment and rear oil seal

Key to Fig 1:26   1 Washer   2 Split sleeve   3 Felt ring
4 Screw   5 Drive shaft   6 Spacer   7 Needle bearing
8 Sealing ring (rubber)   9 Flywheel   10 Oil seal   11 Shim
12 No. 1 crankshaft bearing   13 Crankcase   14 Crankshaft

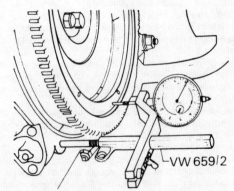

FIG 1:27 Measuring the crankshaft end play

Damaged valve stem ends, adjusting screws, or rocker arms will make it difficult to set the clearance accurately. If the end of a valve stem has spread at all, be sure to use an oilstone to remove any burrs before sliding the valve out of its guide otherwise the guide will become scored.

1:7 Cylinders and piston

The components are shown in **FIG 1:19**.

Removal:

It is possible to remove a cylinder head and both its cylinders as an assembly after the cylinder head nuts have been removed. This is not recommended for the average owner because of the danger of tilting a cylinder and jamming the piston, and the danger of the pistons and connecting rods dropping sharply as they come free from the bore.

Remove the cylinder head as described in **Section 1:5**. It is most advisable to mark the piston crowns, cylinders and equivalent mounting points on the crankcase with a code of different spots of coloured paint, as pistons and cylinders must not be interchanged in position once they are bedded-in.

Carefully pull each cylinder in turn away from the crankcase so that the piston slides out of it and the attachment studs do not catch in the cooling fins. As the piston starts to come free, support the connecting rod so that there is no danger of the piston and rod assembly falling and damaging the crankcase. Once the cylinders have been removed, take great care when cranking the engine as there is a danger of the connecting rods thrashing up and down, to the detriment of the crankcase, or the pistons catching on the studs.

Use circlip pliers to remove the circlips securing the gudgeon pins in the pistons. Try pressing the gudgeon pin out by hand pressure so that the piston can be freed from the connecting rod. If the gudgeon pin is stiff to press out, wrap the piston in rags and pour boiling water over it to heat the piston. Use sheets of tin or equivalent to prevent the water running into the engine. Once the piston has reached a temperature of approximately 80°C the gudgeon pin should slide out easily with hand pressure. It is advisable to discard the retaining circlips and install new ones on reassembly.

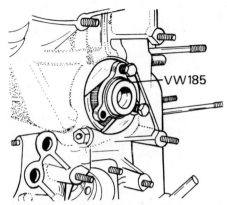

FIG 1:28   Removing the cooling fan hub

Cylinder bores:

These should be checked whenever the cylinder head is removed. A good guide to the amount of wear is given by judging the thickness of the unworn ridge around the top of the bore.

For accurate checks of bore wear and piston to bore clearance special gauges are required. The bore should be measured at several points to determine the ovality, taper, and wear. Measure with, and at right angles to, the thrust axis noting that the maximum wear will take place approximately 25 mm (1 inch) from the top of the bore. Measure the skirt of the piston with a micrometer gauge, as shown in **FIG 1:20**, so that the skirt to bore clearance can be calculated. Reboring and fitting an oversized piston or fitting new piston and cylinder should be carried out if the running clearance exceeds .20 mm (.008 inch).

The oil consumption of the engine will generally give a good guide to the state of the bore. New parts should be fitted when the oil consumption exceeds 1 Litre in 1000 kilometres (approximately 3 pints per 1000 miles). Check that high oil consumption is not due to external leaks or worn valve guides.

If the oil consumption is fairly high but not sufficient to warrant fitting new parts, new rings can be fitted to the pistons. Before fitting new rings, have the unworn ridge around the tops of the bores removed and the whole bore surface lightly honed. The ridge will have worn in with the old ring and the new ring, being unworn, will therefore hit the ridge and break up. Light honing or scuffing of the bore breaks the glaze and allows the new rings to bed-in better.

If a bore is found to be scored, the cylinder must be renewed and similarly defective pistons must also be renewed.

Piston rings:

Special ring clamps are made for removing and installing the rings on the piston. The tool gently parts the ends of the ring so that it can be lifted up over the piston crown. Failing the special tool, the rings can still be removed and installed using three steel shims (such as discarded feeler gauges). Carefully lift the end of the top ring out of its groove and slide one shim under it. Work the shim around under the ring, pressing the ring onto the piston land above it as the ring frees but taking care not to use force. Once all the ring is on the land, slide the other two

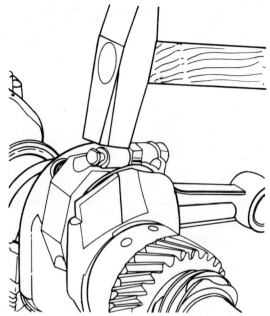

FIG 1:29   Tapping on the bearing to release any pretension

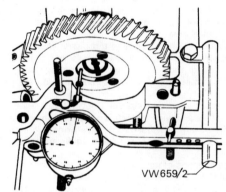

FIG 1:30   Measuring the camshaft end play

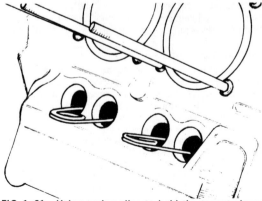

FIG 1:31   Using spring clips to hold the tappets (cam followers) in place

shims under the ring so that all three are equally spaced, and slide the ring up and off the piston using the shims to protect the piston. Gently parting the ends of the ring with the thumb nails will help, but take care not to score the back of the piston with the ring. Remove the remaining rings in a similar manner.

Before installing new piston rings, check their fitted gap. Spring the ring into the bottom of the cylinder and push it slightly down with a piston so that the ring is square in the bore. Measure the gap between the ends of the ring with feeler gauges, as shown in **FIG 1 : 21**. If the gap is incorrect, remove the ring and carefully file the ends to bring the gap within limits.

When the rings have been installed in the piston, check the side clearance with feeler gauges, as shown in **FIG 1 : 22**. It is possible to fit the outer edge of the ring into the groove, and check the side clearance, without actually installing the rings. If the clearance is excessive, try using a new ring and if the clearance is still excessive a new piston must be fitted.

Pistons:

Remove the piston rings before cleaning the pistons. The crowns can be lightly polished with worn emerycloth dipped in kerosene after deposits have been removed with a soft scraper. Clean the ring grooves with a piece of broken piston ring. Take great care to remove only carbon and dirt from the ring grooves as if metal is removed the oil consumption will be increased. Clean out the return holes behind the oil control ring with a piece of blunt-ended wire.

Lacquering on the sides of the piston should only be removed using a suitable harsh solvent to soften the deposit and then scrubbing with a proprietary non-metallic pot scourer. Do not use abrasives on the piston sides.

Check the piston skirt for uneven wear pattern or polished areas which indicate a distorted connecting rod.

When cleaning the pistons, take care not to interchange them as the identification paint marks may easily be washed off.

The selection of the correct grade and weight of piston is best left to a VW dealer. New pistons will have the marks as shown in **FIG 1 : 23** on their crowns. The main mark to note is the arrow or word 'VORN' and the piston must be installed so that this mark faces the flywheel end of the engine. The gudgeon pins are slightly offset in the pistons, to prevent piston slap, and it is for this reason that the pistons must be installed in the correct direction.

Connecting rods:

Thoroughly clean the connecting rods and check them for obvious damage. If it is suspected that a connecting rod is bent or twisted, because of the wear pattern on the piston or crankpin, the rod should be checked on special jigs. A slight amount of distortion can be straightened under a press or using a special jig.

Because the gudgeon pin can be pressed through the small-end bush or piston while the parts are cold this does not indicate excessive wear. If the piston bores are worn a new piston must be fitted. Renewable bushes are fitted to the small-ends of the connecting rods. A special jig is required to renew these bushes so again the work should be left to an agent.

Cooling fins:

Check the cooling fins on the cylinders for damage. Distorted fins should be straightened as much as possible without exerting sufficient force to snap them. Nicks or broken portions should be blended in smoothly using a file or small rotary grindstone.

Installation:

Thoroughly clean the mating surfaces of the cylinders and crankcase, as well as those of cylinders and head. Soften any old jointing compound using carbon tetra-chloride or trichlorethylene and then scrape off with a tool made from hardwood or perspex. Under no circumstances clean the light-alloy surfaces with a wire brush or hard metal scraper.

Wash the parts in suitable solvent to remove any dirt. The cylinders should have been cleaned on removal, but to protect the bores against corrosion they should be smeared with grease. It is this grease and dirt which must now be removed.

Install the piston rings in the reverse order of removal. The dimensions are given in **Technical Data** at the end of the manual. The upper compression ring is tapered and the lower compression ring stepped. Both of these rings must be fitted so that the marking 'TOP' on them faces towards the crown of the piston, as shown in **FIG 1 : 24**.

Fit the circlips on the flywheel side of Nos. 1 and 2 pistons and on the fan side of Nos. 3 and 4 pistons. Make sure that the circlips are fully seated in their grooves. Heat the pistons in boiling water. Take out each piston in turn, holding it with rags, and fit it to its correct connecting rod. Make sure that the arrow or word 'VORN' points towards the flywheel for all pistons. Press the gudgeon pin in fully by hand so that the piston is fitted to the connecting rod. Install the other circlip to secure the gudgeon pin, making sure that this too is fully in its recess.

Lightly oil the piston skirt and piston rings. Turn the oil control ring so that its gap is uppermost and turn the other two rings so that their gaps are evenly spaced at 120 deg. Fit a ring clamp so that the rings are compressed into their grooves. If the correct VW tool, or a proprietary equivalent is not available a large worm-driven hose clip may be used instead, but more care must then be taken.

Fit a new sealing ring and guide the cylinder onto its studs, aligning the previously made paint marks, and carefully press it down to the crankcase. Guide the piston into the bore and allow the ring clamp to slide off the rings as they enter the bore. Do not allow the rings to escape from the clamp before they are in the bore and do not use force. The whole operation is fairly tricky and it is advisable to have an assistant to support the parts and check that studs are not catching in fins.

Once a pair of cylinders is in place, install their cylinder head.

1 : 8 The lubrication system

A schematic layout of the lubrication system is shown in **FIG 1 : 3** and the general operation is described in **Section 1 : 1**. Draining and changing of the engine oil as well as the oil filter element is described in **Section 1 : 2**.

If the oil cooler is found to be leaking, check the main

pressure relief valve. If the piston of the main relief valve sticks closed, excessively high oil pressure will be built up and may cause damage to the oil cooler.

Oil cooler:

Free the attachments and remove the oil cooler. Discard the old seals, installing new ones on reassembly. Blank off the connections to prevent dirt from entering the engine or oil cooler.

Wash down the outside of the oil cooler using any suitable cleansing solvent. Blow through between the fins with compressed air to make sure that they are absolutely clear and clean. Once the exterior is clean, flush through the interior with clean solvent (such as fuel or trichlorethylene) and then blow through with dry compressed air.

A rough check for leaks can be made by partially filling the oil cooler with fuel or solvent (after the exterior is dry), blanking the inlet and outlet, and examining the outside surface.

Normally a leaking oil cooler should be exchanged and not repaired by the owner. If the leak is small and fairly accessible, and the metal can be thoroughly cleaned and degreased, the area can be covered with a catalytic type of epoxy glue, which will withstand the heat and pressure as well as being very hard when set.

If there is any doubt as to the condition of the oil cooler it should be pressure-tested to 6 kg/sq cm (85 lb/sq inch). Do not use compressed air for testing because if the unit ruptures it may do so explosively. Fill the unit with fluid and test it hydraulically, as any failure will allow an immediate drop in pressure with no danger of further rupturing.

Relief valves

Remove the plug and withdraw the spring and plunger. If the plunger sticks in position, thread in a suitable tap and use the tap to withdraw the plunger.

Sticking of the upper relief valve plunger in the out position will cause all the oil to flow through the oil cooler and give a prolonged warm-up period, while sticking in the inner position may cause overheating.

Sticking of the lower relief valve plunger in the closed position will raise the oil pressure and may cause the oil cooler to fail, while sticking in the open position will cause a drop in oil pressure.

The plunger should be discarded if it is scored or worn. Light damage or high spots may be smoothed down with Crocus paper to make sure that the plunger slides freely in its bore.

Check the springs for weakening or corrosion and renew them if they are defective. The data for the springs is given in **Technical Data**.

Oil pump:

The cooling fan and ducts must be removed before the oil pump is accessible. Take off the four nuts attaching the oil pump and then withdraw it with the aid of two levers, used in a similar manner to the one shown in **FIG 1 : 25**. Removal of the cover from the pump is best carried out by using the special tool VW.803.

The pump should give long service without appreciable wear as it carries the full oil flow through the engine. The

most likely cause of oil pump wear is failing to change the engine oil at the stipulated intervals so that dirt particles are drawn through.

Check the gears for undue wear marks on their teeth faces and check that the driven gear revolves freely on its pin. Check that the pin is securely in place.

Check the housing and cover for wear or scores. Light scoring on the coverplate may be lapped down on fine-grade grinding paste spread onto plate glass, but if the wear or scoring is excessive a new cover or new pump should be fitted, as a worn pump can be one of the causes of low oil pressure.

After washing the parts and examining them, liberally oil the gears and fit them back into the pump body. Lightly oil the sealing ring and refit it together with the cover. Check that the gears rotate freely. Set the tab on the pump shaft so that it aligns with the slot in the end of the camshaft and push the pump back into position. Slowly crank the engine through two complete revolutions so as to centralize the pump and then tighten the attachment nuts.

1:9 Clutch and flywheel

Full details of the clutch, its maintenance, and servicing are given in **Chapter 5**. This section deals only with the removal and installation of the clutch.

The engine must be removed from the car before the clutch and flywheel are accessible.

Clutch:

If the clutch is to be used again, make light aligning marks across clutch cover and flywheel so that the balance will not be lost when the clutch is installed.

Slacken the six bolts securing the cover to the flywheel, one or two turns at a time and in a diagonal sequence. It is essential that the bolts are slackened in this sequence otherwise the pressure of the clutch spring may distort the cover. Once all the bolts are removed, lift off the cover assembly and carefully collect the driven plate (without allowing it to drop). Do not handle the clutch driven plate with dirty or greasy hands and keep oil or grease away from the linings.

Check the clutch for wear or defects (see **Chapter 5**). Fit the driven plate back into place, holding it there with a special mandrel. The mandrel fits accurately through the hub of the driven plate and has a spigot which fits into the needle roller bearing in the end of the crankshaft. It is essential that this mandrel is used as it centralizes the driven plate, allowing the transmission input shaft to be inserted. Fit the cover back into place, aligning the previously make marks. Progressively tighten the attachment bolts in a diagonal sequence to a torque of 2.5 kg m (18 lb ft).

Flywheel:

A sectioned view of the flywheel attachment and crankshaft rear oil seal is shown in **FIG 1 : 26**.

The flywheel starter ring gear is integral with the flywheel and if the teeth are broken or badly worn, a new flywheel must be fitted. Slight damage to the teeth can be removed by having a maximum of 2.0 mm (.08 inch) skimmed off the clutch side of the teeth but the edges should then be lightly chamfered to give a lead-in for the starter motor pinion. Small burrs or light damage should be smoothed down with a file and oilstone.

If the clutch face of the flywheel is scored or burnt, it may be machined down to provide a flat surface again, though if the damage is deep a new flywheel must be fitted.

The shims 11 fitted between the flywheel and crankshaft control the end play of the crankshaft. The method of checking the crankshaft end play is shown in **FIG 1 : 27**. When making adjustments, such as after reassembling the engine, omit the oil seal and felt ring. The full procedure will be dealt with later.

The flywheel can be removed after removing the clutch and taking out the attachment bolts.

Before installing the flywheel, thoroughly clean the shims and mating faces of the crankshaft and flywheel. Check the spigot needle roller bearing and renew if defective. Extract the old bearing with a suitable internal-legged extractor and impact hammer, then drive the new bearing carefully back into place with a suitable drift. If the bearing is satisfactory, lubricate it lightly with lithium-based grease. Check the condition of the oil seal 10 and renew it if defective or worn. Moisten the felt ring 3 with clean engine oil and wipe away the surplus. Lightly oil the running surface on the flywheel where it will contact the oil seal. Install the flywheel, with shims in place, and tighten the attachment bolts to a torque of 12.5 kg m (90 lb ft).

It is advisable to check the runout on the flywheel after it has been installed. Mount a dial indicator gauge as shown in **FIG 1 : 27** and press the crankshaft fully forward to take up the end play, then check the runout by slowly cranking the engine over. Excessive runout can be caused by specks of dirt between crankshaft and flywheel but if it cannot be cured by cleaning or light skimming a new flywheel should be installed.

1 : 10 The crankcase assembly

One side casting together with the crankshaft, camshaft and related parts are shown in **FIG 1 : 2**. The engine must be removed from the car, and the cylinder heads as well as cylinders removed before the castings can be parted to gain access to the crankshaft, crankshaft bearings, camshaft, camshaft bearings and cam followers (tappets). It will also be necessary to remove the air ducts, cooling fan, and its hub. The cooling system parts are dealt with in **Chapter 4** and the cooling fan is secured to the hub by three bolts.

Oil seals:

The rear end of the camshaft is sealed by the bore end cover while the front end is sealed by the attachment of the oil pump and its gasket.

The rear oil seal for the crankshaft is dealt with in the previous section and can be renewed after the removal of the flywheel.

To gain access to the front oil seal it is necessary to remove the cooling air ducts. Press off the cooling fan hub, preferably using the special tool VW.185 as shown in **FIG 1 : 28**, after removing its attachment bolt and washer. Prise out the old oil seal, taking care not to damage the castings. Slightly chamfer the outer edge of the bore to remove any burrs, and clean out the bore. Lightly smear the periphery of the new seal with sealing compound, lubricate the lips with grease, and drive it back

into position, preferably using the special drift VW.191. Install the cooling fan hub and tighten its bolt to a torque load of 2.8 kg m (20 lb ft). Install the cooling parts.

Parting castings:

Remove all the parts mentioned earlier in this section. It is advisable to remove the flywheel as well. To prevent damage, the pistons should also be removed and great care taken not to allow the connecting rods to fall heavily against the castings. Rags wrapped around the connecting rods will protect the castings.

Evenly slacken all the nuts securing the two castings and remove the nuts. Do not pry between the castings in an effort to part them, as this will cause damage to the mating faces. Tap gently and evenly all round the joint with a rubber mallet to dislodge the righthand half casting. When the castings have been parted, remove the components.

Clean the castings with a suitable solvent and blow through all oilways and passages with compressed air. Clean and check the mating faces of the crankcase castings. Soften any jointing material with trichlorethylene or similar solvent and then scrape it off with a tool made of perspex or hardwood. Slight chips or burrs should be smoothed down with an oilstone or by careful use of a scraper. The two castings are a matched pair and if either one is defective, both must be renewed as a set.

Before finally assembling the engine, bolt the two castings together and check the bores of the crankshaft main bearings and camshaft bearings for wear, ovality or taper.

Tappets (cam followers):

When the castings have been parted, withdraw the tappets from their bores and store them in their correct order.

Check each tappet in turn for scoring or wear on the cylindrical surface or chipping or other damage on the flat surface. Check that the tappet slides freely in its bore. Discard any defective tappets and fit new ones in their place.

Crankshaft bearings:

Remove the crankshaft from between the castings. Each connecting rod and its cap should be marked with a numeral indicating position or a code of dots. The connecting rods must be installed back into their original positions so note the directtion in which the markings face.

Slacken both nuts on each connecting rod, then remove them and take off the bearing cap. Ease the cap off with light hammer blows if it sticks in place. Leave the bearing inserts in place and temporarily refit the caps loosely to the connecting rods so that there is no danger of intermixing inserts or caps.

Measure each crankpin at several points to determine wear, ovality or taper. If there is excessive wear or scoring, the crankshaft will have to be reground and new under-sized bearing inserts fitted.

Similarly check the crankshaft journals and have them reground if necessary.

Thoroughly clean the crankshaft. Blow through the oilways with paraffin under pressure followed by compressed air (use a syringe and tyre pump if nothing else is available). This is particularly important if the crankshaft has been reground or a bearing has run, as swarf or metal may otherwise remain and be forced into the bearings by the oil pressure when the engine is running. If the engine is to be left dismantled for any length of time, wipe over the journals and crankpins with an oily rag (or smear them lightly with grease) to prevent corrosion.

Examine the bearing inserts. If any show signs of cracking, pitting, wearing or cracking on the surface, renew the complete set. Check the big-end bearing inserts for signs of undue wear which could indicate connecting rod distortion.

New bearing inserts are fitted as received, apart from cleaning, and do not require boring or scraping to make them fit. Under no circumstances should shims be fitted or parts filed to alter the clearance of the bearings, in an attempt to take up wear.

The old connecting rod nuts and bolts should be discarded and new ones installed on reassembly. Clean the crankpin thoroughly again and make sure that the bore in the connecting rod and cap is scrupulously clean. Wipe the bearing inserts with a piece of leather and insert them back into their respective positions, making sure that the tag is correctly located. Lubricate the crankpin with clean engine oil or graphited-oil and fit the connecting rod back into place, tightening the nuts to a torque of 3.3 kg m (24 lb ft) and locking them by peening. Check that the connecting rod rotates freely about its crankpin, easing any tension by lightly tapping as shown in FIG 1:29. Lay aside the assembly, covering it over to stop it from becoming dirty, ready for reassembly of the engine.

Camshaft:

The camshaft driving gear is made of light-alloy and is riveted to the camshaft.

Wash the camshaft in solvent and check for wear or damage. Measure the journals and examine the bearing inserts in the same way as for the crankshaft bearings.

Slight pitting at the lobes of the cams is fairly common and light score marks can be polished off with an oilstone. If the cams are excessively scored install a new camshaft, but note that in some cases it is possible to have cams reground.

Mount the camshaft between the centres on a lathe and use a dial indicator gauge to check the runout at the centre journal. Normally the runout should be within the limit of .02 mm (.0008 inch) but the wear limit is .04 mm (.0016 inch).

The front bearing inserts for the camshaft are fitted with flanges which control the camshaft end play. Lay the bearings back into one crankcase casting, after careful cleaning, and use a dial indicator gauge to measure the end play, as shown in FIG 1:30. The normal limits are .04 to .13 mm (.0016 to .005 inch) and new thrust bearings must be fitted if the wear limit of .16 mm (.0063 inch) is exceeded.

Lay the crankshaft and its main bearings into the casting and check the backlash between the timing gears. The backlash limit is .05 mm (.002 inch) which is hardly perceptible. Various sized timing gears are available in $\frac{1}{100}$ mm variations to adjust the backlash. Markings —1, 0, +1 and +2 are made on the back of the gears (do not confuse with valve timing marks) to indicate the size of the gear.

Crankshaft gears:

The crankshaft timing drive gear is supplied in one size only. Both gears and spacer can be removed by pulling them off with a suitable extractor after the retaining clip has been removed.

Check for damage on the crankshaft and smooth down with an oilstone if required. The gears must be a tight press-fit and if they are loose it is possible to have the surface built up so that they are again a tight fit, without having to fit a new crankshaft. Such building-up should be left to a specialist firm.

Special tools VW.428 and VW.415A are made for pressing the gears back into position but a press and suitable spacers may be used. Before installing the gears it is essential to heat them in an oil bath to a temperature of at least 80°C (196°F). This can be done by immersing them in a tin of oil and heating the oil in boiling water. Once the gears have cooled, check that they are a tight fit.

Assembling the crankcase:

The connecting rods should already have been fitted to the crankshaft and checked for free rotation. Wipe off any protective from the crankshaft journals and clean them thoroughly.

Lubricate the bores for the tappets and slide the tappets back into place. To prevent the tappets from falling out it is advisable to hold them in place with clips made out of springy wire, as shown in FIG 1:31.

Refit any stud seals and check that the bearing dowels in the castings are secure. Give a final wipe to the bearing bores in the castings and to the bearing inserts with a piece of leather. Fit the crankshaft No. 3 main bearing insert shells and camshaft bearing inserts back into position in the castings. Wipe the Nos. 1 and 4 crankshaft main bearing inserts, lubricate them liberally with oil and slide them back onto the crankshaft. Lubricate the bearings in the lefthand side casting and lay the crankshaft and camshaft back into place. Smear a little jointing compound around the camshaft bore end cover and fit it back into position, as arrowed in FIG 1:32. The camshaft and crankshaft must be fitted so that the two dots on one of the gears are on either side of the circle on the other gear, as shown in FIG 1:33. This ensures that the valve timing is correct. Note that the marks are on the front of the gears, so do not confuse size marks on the back of the camshaft gear with timing marks.

Smear a little jointing compound evenly around the mating faces of the two crankshaft castings. Take great care not to put on so much compound that it creeps into bearings or blocks oilways.

Lower the other casting down into place and progressively tighten the nuts to a torque of 2 kg m (14 lb ft). Check that the crankshaft and camshaft rotate freely, taking care to support the connecting rods.

The remaining parts are then installed in the reverse order of removal.

Crankshaft end play:

Leave the crankshaft oil seals off and install the flywheel with two shims (items 11 shown in FIG 1:26). Mount a dial indicator gauge onto the crankcase, as shown in FIG 1:27 and lever the crankshaft firmly in and

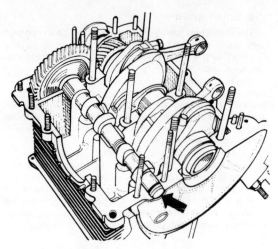

FIG 1:32 Fitting the camshaft bore end cover

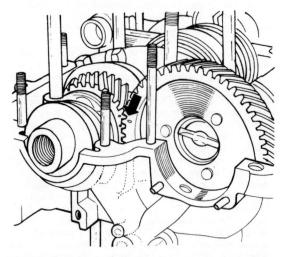

FIG 1:33 Correctly aligning the valve timing marks

out so that the end play can be measured. By noting the end play with two shims only, calculate the thickness of the third shim to give a total play of .07 to .13 mm (.0027 to .0051 inch). Shims are available in thicknesses of .24 mm, .30 mm, .32 mm, .34 mm, .36 mm and .39 mm and the size is etched on them (though it is advisable to check them with a micrometer if they have been used previously. If the end float is checked without dismantling the engine no action need be taken until the wear limit of .15 mm (.006 inch) is reached.

Excessive crankshaft end play can cause a knock in the engine, particularly at slow speeds, and the knock will stop when the clutch is operated.

Once the three shims have been selected to give the correct crankshaft end play, install the oil seals and felt ring, then finally install the flywheel.

1:11 Reassembling a stripped engine

Removal of the crankshaft and separation of the crank-case castings requires full dismantling of the engine so therefore most of the details have been covered in the previous section. Installation of the remainder of the parts is dealt with in the relevent sections. Fitting the distributor drive gearshaft is dealt with in **Chapter 4**.

This section will give the best order for reassembly as well as a few hints and tips that will save aggravation.

When the engine has been first removed from the car, blank off any apertures and wash down the exterior of the engine. Paraffin (or fuel) may be used to remove the worst of the dirt followed by another wash to thoroughly clean the exterior. Alternatively proprietary dirt-dissolving agents may be used followed by washing with water.

As parts are removed they should again be cleaned and any bright metal surfaces wiped over with grease to prevent corrosion. Have a small tin of fuel at hand so that nuts, bolts and small parts can be dropped straight into it for cleaning of threads. Sludge will accumulate in the bottom of the tin so either discard the dirty fuel regularly or have another tin in which the parts can be given a final swill.

Put the appropriate nuts, bolts and washers and small parts into bags and tie them to the main component. Note the positions of any special bolts or those that are longer or shorter than standard and if a sketch is used it can be taped to the bag. Usually all nuts, bolts, washers and odd little parts are dropped into one large cardboard box (which either breaks or gets knocked over) and there is a frantic search to find the appropriate size of nut or bolt when it comes to reassembly.

Have a special storage area where the parts can be laid out in order. Keep them in boxes and wrap them in newspaper to prevent them collecting dirt.

Before starting reassembly, clear the bench or working area and brush it clean. Lay clean paper over it so that parts can safely be laid down.

The components should have been checked as they are removed and cleaned but make sure that all threads are satisfactory, dowels and studs securely in place, flanges true, and castings not cracked.

All old seals and gaskets should have been discarded so new ones should be used throughout on reassembly. Metal parts may be safely washed in harsh solvents, such as trichlorethylene or carbon tetrachloride, and this type of solvent must be used to soften and remove traces of sealing or jointing compound. Scrape light-alloy castings with tools made of hardwood or perspex only.

All bearing surfaces should be liberally lubricated with engine oil or graphited oil as parts are installed. At the most, judicious tapping with a rubber mallet should be used (except when a press is required) for the assembly of parts. Do not use brute force if parts will not fit together, but dismantle them again so that the cause can be found. Check that parts move as they should after they have been fitted.

Start by fitting the connecting rods to the crankshaft. Slide the bearing back into place and then press on the crankshaft drive gears. Fit tappets and bearing inserts into place then bolt the crankcase halves together with the crankshaft and camshaft in place. Do not forget to align the valve timing marks when fitting crankshaft and camshaft.

Adjust the crankshaft end float by selectively fitting the shims under the flywheel. Fit the crankshaft oil seals and install the cooling fan hub and flywheel.

Fit the pistons to their correct connecting rods, making sure that the arrow points towards the flywheel end of the engine. Slide on the cylinders and install the cylinder heads. Adjust the valve clearances with the engine on the bench and then fit the rocker covers. Fit old sparking plugs to prevent dirt falling through the plug holes.

Install deflector plates and cooling system components. Accessories such as the oil filter, fuel pump and distributor should be left until last.

Once the engine has been assembled, install it back into the car and set the fuel system and ignition systems to their static settings. Fill the crankcase to the correct level with fresh oil and add a little extra for the oil filter and for filling the oilways, noting that the level must be topped up to the maximum mark after the engine has been run and the level settled.

While the engine is being reassembled, have the battery charged up so that it is at full capacity. Remove the old sparking plugs and crank the engine on the starter motor to prime the fuel system, oil system and to check that the engine rotates freely without binding.

Install the correct sparking plugs and start the engine. If the engine fails to start, work through systematically to check for faults. When the engine does start it will sound rough and will smoke as the excess lubricant is burnt out of the combustion chambers and bores. Smoke may also be produced as greasy marks burn off the cylinders and hot exhaust pipes.

Allow the engine to warm up before making final adjustments to ignition and fuel system.

1:12 Fault diagnosis

(a) Engine will not start

1 Defective ignition coil or distributor cap
2 Defective distributor capacitor
3 Dirty, pitted or incorrectly operating ignition contacts
4 Ignition wires loose or insulation faulty
5 Water or dirt on HT leads
6 Battery discharged, loose or dirty battery terminals
7 Faulty or jammed starter motor
8 HT leads incorrectly connected
9 Defective fuel pump
10 Vapour lock in fuel lines (hot weather only)
11 Over- or under-choking
12 Blocked pump filter, defective injectors or blocked jets
13 Leaking valves
14 Sticking valves
15 Valve timing incorrect
16 Ignition timing incorrect

(b) Engine stalls after starting

1 Check 1, 2, 3, 4, 5, 10, 11, 12, 13 and 14 in (a)
2 Defective or incorrectly set sparking plugs
3 Retarded ignition
4 Mixture too weak
5 Water in fuel system
6 Fuel tank breather pipe blocked
7 Incorrect valve clearances

(c) Engine idles badly

1 Check 2 and 7 in (b)
2 Air leaks at manifold joints
3 Fuel system incorrectly adjusted
4 Automatic choke not operating correctly
5 Too rich a mixture
6 Worn piston rings
7 Worn valve stems and guides
8 Weak exhaust valve springs

(d) Engine misfires

1 Check 1, 2, 3, 4, 5, 8, 9, 12, 13, 14, 15 and 16 in (a); 2, 3, 4 and 7 in (b)
2 Weak or broken valve springs

(e) Engine overheats (see Chapter 4)

(f) Compression low

1 Check 13 and 14 in (a); 6 and 7 in (c) and 2 in (d)
2 Worn piston ring grooves
3 Scored or worn cylinder bores
4 Dirty air cleaner or defective strangler valve
A high compression test pressure indicates excessive deposits in combustion chamber.

(g) Engine lacks power

1 Check 3, 10, 12, 13, 14, 15 and 16 in (a); 2, 3, 4 and 7 in (b); 6 and 7 in (c) and 2 in (d). Also check (e) and (f)
2 Leaking joints or gaskets
3 Fouled sparking plugs
4 Automatic ignition advance not operating

(h) Burnt valves or seats

1 Check 13 and 14 in (a); 7 in (b) and 2 in (d). Also check (e)
2 Excessive carbon or deposits in combustion chamber

(j) Sticking valves

1 Check 2 in (d)
2 Bent valve stems
3 Scored valve stems or guides
4 Incorrect valve clearance

(k) Excessive cylinder wear

1 Check 11 in (a) and also check (e)
2 Lack of oil
3 Dirty oil
4 Piston rings gummed up or broken
5 Piston rings badly fitted
6 Bent connecting rod
7 Dirt under cylinder seatings (causing cylinder to be tilted)

(l) Excessive oil consumption

1 Check 6 and 7 in (c); 3 in (f) and also check (k)
2 Ring gaps too wide
3 Oil return holes in piston blocked with carbon
4 Oil level too high
5 External leaks through loose attachments or poor gaskets
6 Defective oil seals
7 Oil level too high

(m) Bearing failure

1 Check 2, 3 and 6 in (k)
2 Restricted oilways
3 Worn journals or crankpins
4 Oval or tapered bearing bores
5 Loose big-end bearing caps
6 Extremely low oil pressure

(n) Low oil pressure

1 Check 2 and 3 in (k) and 2, 3 and 4 in (m)
2 Choked oil strainer
3 Defective relief valve
4 Faulty indicator or oil pressure gauge and connections

(o) High fuel consumption (see Chapter 2)

CHAPTER 2

THE FUEL SYSTEM

2:1 Description
2:2 Fuel tank
2:3 Evaporative emission control

PART 1 THE CARBURETTER FUEL SYSTEM
2:4 Maintenance
2:5 The fuel pump
2:6 Carburetter operation
2:7 Carburetter faults

2:8 Carburetter adjustments
2:9 Fault diagnosis

PART 2 THE FUEL INJECTION SYSTEM
2:10 Description
2:11 Maintenance
2:12 Adjustments
2:13 Components
2:14 Fault diagnosis

2:1 Description

All models are fitted with a fuel tank at the front of the car and an oil-bath type air cleaner is fitted as standard.

Twin carburetters, one per pair of cylinders, may be fitted or an electronically controlled fuel injection system installed in place of the carburetters. The fuel injection system does not offer any advantages in fuel consumption, power, or maximum speed but it does make for much easier starting in very cold weather and it brings the emissions from the engine within the current stringent legal requirements. For these reasons, fuel injection will be fitted mainly to those models destined for the North American and Scandinavian markets.

The amount of work that can be carried out by the owner on a fuel injection system is strictly limited, as accurate meters and special test equipment are required.

Part 1 of the chapter deals exclusively with the carburetter versions while Part 2 deals only with the fuel injection system, both parts being fully self-contained.

2:2 Fuel tank

This is the only component that is common to both types of fuel system.

If filters or lines clog regularly, the tank should be cleaned. In minor cases this can be carried out by draining and refilling with clean fuel (or straining the old fuel through a chamois leather) but if contamination is excessive the tank must be removed and swilled out or renewed. Special descaling solutions are made for cleaning the fuel tank after it has been removed.

The filler pipe and fuel tank sender unit are accessible after removing the covers at the rear of the luggage compartment but to remove the fuel tank it is necessary to take off the front axle carrier complete with related parts as well as removing the brake line between the master cylinder and T-piece.

2:3 Evaporative emission control

Some models, particularly those for the Californian market, may be fitted with a carbon canister to prevent fuel fumes evaporating from the fuel tank and escaping into the air.

The filler cap is sealed and the fuel tank vented to atmosphere through the carbon filled canister. Fuel fumes are adsorbed by the carbon and when the engine starts, the cooling fan blows air through the canister to purge it of fuel fumes. The air from the canister when the engine is running is then led into the air cleaner so that fuel fumes are burnt in the combustion chambers.

The carbon canister is designed to cope with fumes and not liquid fuel, so if liquid fuel accidentally passes through the canister it must be discarded and a new one fitted in its place.

PART 1 THE CARBURETTER FUEL SYSTEM

2:4 Maintenance

This is confined to cleaning the filter elements at regular intervals and checking that the throttle linkage operates fully and freely. Pivot points in the throttle linkage should be lightly oiled.

Air cleaner:

The air cleaner must be removed from the engine for cleaning purposes. No hard and fast rules can be laid down as to the servicing period and in extreme dusty conditions it may even be necessary to clean the air cleaner daily. The lower portion must be cleaned when there is only 4 to 5 mm of clean oil above the sludge layer.

Disconnect the crankcase breather hose then lift the spring clip so that the air intake hose may also be disconnected from the air cleaner. Release the two clips securing the air cleaner to the engine, free the spring clips securing the ducts to the carburetters and lift out the air cleaner assembly in a horizontal position.

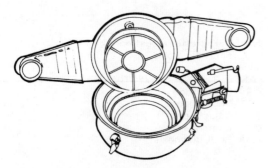

FIG 2:1 The air cleaner fitted with carburetters

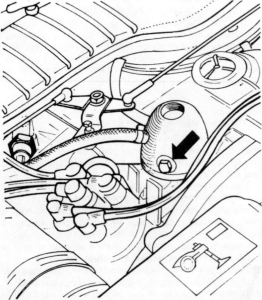

FIG 2:2 Typical fuel filter plug on mechanical fuel pump

The top portion of the air cleaner can be removed after freeing the three clips securing it to the base. **Do not lay the top portion so that the filter element is upwards.**

Clean out the lower portion of the air cleaner, removing all sludge and old oil. Fill it to the mark with fresh oil (approximately .45 Litre, .8 Imp pint). Normally SAE.30 oil should be used but oil as thin as SAE.10 may be used in arctic climates. The upper portion filter element should not normally require cleaning and if it does then scraping off dirt with a piece of wood is sufficient. Only in extreme cases should the filter element be swilled in paraffin (kerosene) or diesel fuel. The air cleaner with the top removed is shown in **FIG 2:1**.

Install the air cleaner in the reverse order of removal, making sure that all seals and hoses are in good condition as well as seating correctly. Check that the preheater valve in the inlet operates freely.

Fuel filter:

The access plug for a typical fuel filter is shown in **FIG 2:2**. Remove the plug arrowed in the figure and withdraw the filter element. Loosely refit the plug while cleaning the element to prevent fuel from syphoning out. Swill the element clean in fuel and dry it with gentle air pressure. Examine the element for tears or other damage before refitting it in the reverse order of removal.

2:5 The fuel pump

A mechanically operated diaphragm-type fuel pump is mounted on the engine for drawing the fuel from the tank and supplying it under slight pressure to the carburetter float chambers.

A sectioned view of the fuel pump is shown in **FIG 2:3**. The pushrod 1 is actuated by an eccentric cam on the engine camshaft. The movement of the pushrod actuates the operating lever 2 so that it pulls down on the diaphragm rod. The downward movement of the diaphragm draws fuel from the tank through the inlet 9, filter 10 and inlet valve into the chamber above the diaphragm. On the return stroke, the pressure of the diaphragm spring 5 and lever spring 7 press the diaphragm up to force the fuel out through the outlet valve 4 and outlet pipe 15 to the carburetters. When the needle valves in the carburetter float chambers close, the fuel pressure will overcome the pressure of the springs and the diaphragm will be held in the down position. As soon as fuel is used, the needle valves open and the drop in pressure allows the diaphragm to move up again and then be pressed down by the action of the operating lever 2. The cut-off valve 14 is opened by fuel pressure, so that when the engine stops the valve closes and prevents fuel from dribbling or syphoning through to the carburetters.

Testing:

A brief check can be carried out to see that the fuel pump is operating. Disconnect one line from one of the carburetters and point it into a suitable container. Crank the engine over on the starter motor and if the pump is operating and the lines are not blocked there will be a good spurt of fuel at every other revolution of the engine (camshaft rotating at half engine speed).

For full checks a pressure gauge is required. The pump

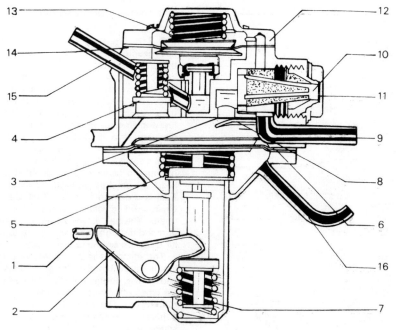

FIG 2:3   Sectioned view of the fuel pump

Key to Fig 2:3   1 Pushrod   2 Operating lever   3 Suction valve   4 Pressure valve   5 Diaphragm spring   6 Diaphragm
7 Spring for lever   8 Suction valve retainer   9 Fuel inlet   10 Filter   11 Plug with washer   12 Cover for upper part   13 Spring
14 Cut-off valve   15 Fuel outlet connection   16 Breather pipe

should maintain a fuel pressure of approximately .3 kg/sq cm (4.5 lb/sq inch) with the engine running at a 3800 rev/min. High fuel pressure will only be caused by a hardening diaphragm or having incorrect springs fitted, but low pressure can be caused by many defects ranging from general wear to partiallly blocked fuel lines.

If the pump is satisfactory, the fuel delivery pressure can be adjusted by altering the thickness of gasket between pump and engine.

If a graduated container, T-piece and suitable tap are available the fuel delivery flow should be checked. The pump should deliver 400 cc of fuel in one minute at an engine speed of 3800 rev/ min.

When testing the pump, take adequate precautions against fire.

Removal:

Usually it is possible, though difficult, to remove the fuel pump while the engine is installed in the car. Should difficulty be found then it is necessary to remove the engine (see **Chapter 1, Section 1:2**).

Disconnect the lefthand side heater control box from the heat exchanger on the exhaust system. Remove the lower air deflection plate. Disconnect both fuel lines from the pump, plugging the inlet line with a suitably sized bolt to prevent fuel syphoning through. Disconnect the breather pipe. Remove the attachment nuts using a spanner held at an angle. The pump can then be removed together with its gaskets.

Before installing the pump, pack the body with universal grease (noting that if grease has been washed out it is likely that the pump diaphragm is defective). Check the protrusion of the pushrod at the highest point and if necessary adjust it to 5 mm (.2 inch) by selectively fitting gaskets. Note that the end of the pushrod with the smallest diameter must be installed towards the camshaft. Install the pump in the reverse order of removal.

Servicing:

The components of the fuel pump are shown in **FIG 2:4**.

Remove the pump and wash down the exterior to remove road dirt. Make light file marks across the flanges to ensure that the parts will be reassembled in the correct alignment.

Take out the screws 1 so that the top cover and cut-off valve assembly parts can be removed. Remove the plug 6 and withdraw the filter 8 and washer 7. Remove the screws 9 securing the upper pump body half 10 and remove the upper body. The valves can then be removed from the upper body if required. Remove the clip 11 and pull out the lever spindle 12 so that the operating lever 13 can be removed. The diaphragm assembly complete with springs can now be removed.

Check the valves for damage, distortion or weak springs. They can be tested by gently sucking and blowing through them while fitted. **If the valves are removed it is essential to install them correctly,** with the machined side of the disc towards the valve seat, otherwise the pump will not operate.

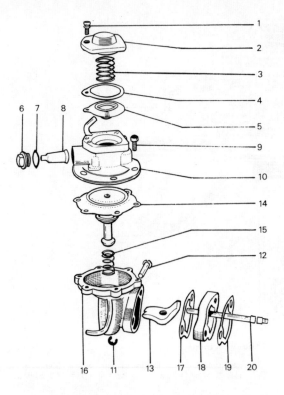

FIG 2:4 The components of the mechanical fuel pump

Key to Fig 2:4 1 Screw with spring washer
2 Pump cover   3 Spring for cut-off valve   4 Gasket for
cut-off valve   5 Cut-off valve   6 Plug   7 Sealing washer
8 Filter strainer   9 Screw with spring washer
10 Upper pump body half   11 Circlip   12 Lever spindle
13 Pump lever   14 Diaphragm and spring   15 Diaphragm
spring   16 Lower pump body half   17 Gasket
18 Intermediate flange   19 Gasket   20 Pushrod

Clean the interior of the castings and check them for
cracks or damaged flanges. Light damage to flanges
should be smoothed down with a file or scraper, making
sure that mating flanges meet squarely.

Check the diaphragm for hardening or any splits or
pinholes. Check the springs for distortion, corrosion or
weakening.

Renew all defective parts, noting that if there is
excessive general wear it will be simpler and more
efficient to install a new pump.

Reassemble the pump in the reverse order of dismantling,
making sure that the two valves are correctly fitted. The
special plate VW.797/3 should be bolted to the attachment flange, or push the operating lever arm in by 5 mm
(.2 inch) from the flange face to locate the diaphragm
correctly when tightening the screws 9. The screws
should be tightened progressively and in a diagonal
sequence.

Fill the pump body with universal grease before
installing the pump.

2:6 Carburetter operation

A sectioned view of a typical carburetter is shown in
FIG 2:5. The float 27 rides on the fuel to operate the
float needle valve 4 and 5 so that no more fuel enters when
the level is correct. At idling speed, the main suction is
in the bore beside the throttle valve 34 and the mixture is
drawn through the port controlled by the idle mixture
screw 29. Further ports are fitted to ensure a smooth
transition from idle to main jets. At full throttle opening
fuel and air emulsified together are drawn out through the
discharge arm 36 by the suction in the venturi.

When accelerating, the fuel flow lags behind the air
flow because of greater inertia of the fuel. A throttle
operated accelerator pump is fitted to inject extra fuel to
keep the mixture strength correct during acceleration.
Fuel is drawn in from the float chamber as the throttle
closes and injected into the air stream as the throttle
opens. The ball valves 25 and 26 make sure that fuel is
pumped through and not returned to the float chamber or
air drawn in on the return stroke.

The idling jet is controlled by a solenoid. When the
ignition is switched on the solenoid opens the idle jet and
allows the engine to idle. As soon as the ignition is
switched off, the solenoid closes the idle jet and prevents
running-on. The solenoid is fitted with a grubscrew for
adjustment. With the engine running at idle, set the grubscrew so that the engine cuts immediately the wire is
disconnected from the solenoid. The grubscrew can also
be used to hold the jet permanently open in case of
solenoid failure, though a new solenoid should be fitted as
soon as possible to prevent running-on after stopping the
engine.

An automatic choke is fitted to each carburetter. The
choke valve is held in the closed position by a bi-metallic
spring when the engine is cold and the ignition off. As
soon as the ignition is switched on, current flows through
the heating element in the choke housing cover. As the
bi-metallic spring heats up it loses its tension and allows
the air flow through the carburetter to open the choke
valve. A vacuum piston is also fitted and this partially
opens the choke valve against the action of the bi-
metallic spring as soon as the engine starts, thus weakening the very rich mixture required for start. The vacuum
piston also acts as an anti-stall device. If the engine
falters, the vacuum is reduced and the action of the
vacuum piston weakened so that the choke valve can
close and restore rich mixture strength temporarily.

Altitude corrector:

This is not standard equipment but it can be fitted on
cars that regularly travel between extremes of altitude.

To fit the corrector, remove the plug for the main jet
from the side of the float chamber as well as the main jet,
and thread the correct assembly back into their place.

The corrector contains an aneroid capsule which expands and contracts with changes of altitude and the
aperture of the main jet is correspondingly varied by a
needle attached to the capsule.

Starting:

By following the correct procedure, easy starting is
guaranteed (provided that there are no defects which
would cause the engine not to start).

When the temperature is below freezing and the engine

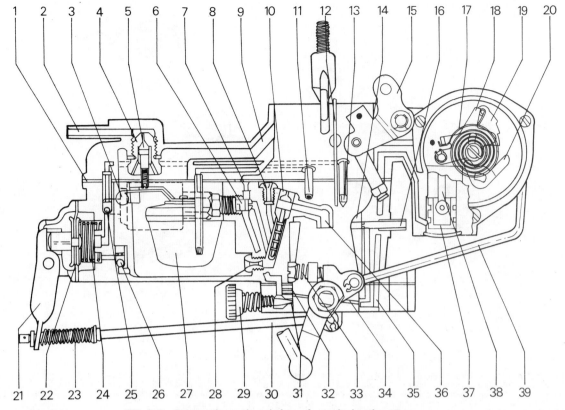

FIG 2:5 Schematic sectioned view of a typical carburetter

Key to Fig 2:5 1 Gasket 2 Fuel hose connection 3 Float hinge pin 4 Needle valve housing 5 Float needle 6 Pilot jet 7 Air bleed drilling 8 Air correction jet 9 Float chamber vent 10 Emulsion tube 11 Power fuel tube 12 Choke valve 13 Accelerator pump injector tube 14 Venturi 15 Relay lever 16 Distributor vacuum connection 17 Bi-metal spring 18 Intermediate lever 19 Fast-idle cam 20 Stop lever 21 Accelerator pump lever 22 Diaphragm 23 Spring 24 Diaphragm return spring 25 Pressure ball valve 26 Suction ball valve 27 Float 28 Main jet 29 Volume control screw 30 Connecting rod 31 Slow-running mixture outlet 32 Bypass port 33 Slow-running adjusting screw 34 Throttle valve 35 Vacuum drilling 36 Discharge arm 37 Vacuum piston 38 Piston rod 39 Operating rod

is cold, press the accelerator pedal fully down and then release it before operating the starter motor immediately after switching on the ignition.

If the engine is warm, slowly press down the accelerator pedal while operating the starter motor.

If the engine is hot, press the accelerator pedal fully down (without any pumping) and hold it there while operating the starter.

2:7 Carburetter faults

The components of the carburetter are shown in **FIG 2:6**. The carburetters should be removed and partially dismantled so that the parts can be cleaned. Special cleansing fluids are made for carburetter cleaning but many of them must be handled with care as they are caustic. Acetone or a similar suitable solvent will remove gum and deposits from parts. When cleaning the jets, swill them in clean solvent and then blow through them with compressed air. Similarly clean ports and passages. **Never poke through the jets with wire or bristle as this will wear the accurately calibrated jets.**

Service kits of spares and gaskets are available and these should be used when reassembling the carburetter.

Flooding:

Check that the appearance of flooding is not given by leaking gaskets or connections.

The most likely cause is dirt jamming the float chamber needle valve open, but it can also be caused by a worn needle, defective float, or high fuel delivery pressure.

Remove the air cleaner and take off the carburetter top cover, after disconnecting the choke operating rod and fuel supply line.

Use a box spanner to remove the needle valve assembly. It may be possible to clear dirt without removing the valve assembly, in which case leave the fuel line connected and crank the engine on the starter motor so that fuel flushes through the valve.

Check that the needle moves freely in the valve body. Hold the needle closed by light finger pressure and try to blow through the valve. If the valve leaks it must be renewed.

Withdraw the float and its pin, then check the float for punctures or defects. If the float is shaken and fuel is heard sloshing inside it then it is punctured. The point of puncture can be found by immersing the float in hot water, when the leak will show up as a stream of bubbles.

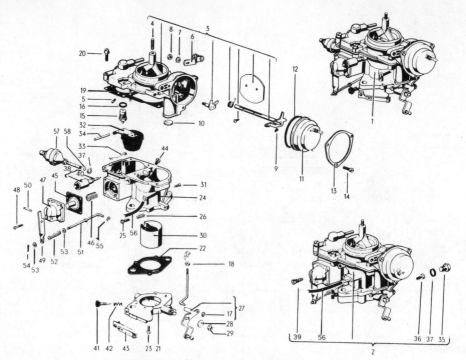

FIG 2:6 The carburetter components

Key to Fig 2:6 1 Carburetter, 34.PDSIT.2 (.3) 2 Carburetter, 34.PDSIT.2 (.3) 3 Carburetter top cover 4 Stud 5 Injector tube stud 6 Carburetter starter lever 7 Spring washer 8 Shaft nut 9 Circlip for piston rod 10 Closing washer for vacuum piston 11 Cover with bi-metal spring 12 Cover gasket 13 Cover retaining ring 14 Retaining ring screw 15 Float needle valve 16 Sealing washer 17 Connecting rod circlip 18 Connecting rod nut 19 Carburetter gasket 20 Cover screw 21 Throttle body 22 Gasket 23 Securing screw 24 Carburetter main body 25 Slow-running adjusting screw 26 Spring 27 Throttle valve lever with rod 28 Washer 29 Throttle valve shaft nut 30 Choke tube 31 Choke tube securing screw 32 Float 33 Float spindle leaf spring 34 Float spindle 35 Main jet plug 36 Main jet 37 Sealing washer 38 Idling shut-off valve 39 Slow-running fuel jet 40 Shut-off valve jet 41 Slow-running volume screw 42 Spring 43 Slow-running air valve 44 Air correction jet 45 Pump diaphragm 46 Diaphragm spring 47 Pump cover 48 Pump cover screw 49 Pump operating lever 50 Pump lever spindle 51 Pump connecting rod 52 Connecting rod spring 53 Washer 54 Splitpin 55 Circlip 56 Vacuum hose 57 Altitude corrector 58 Sealing washer

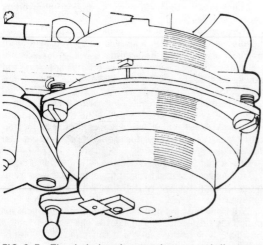

FIG 2:7 The choke housing attachments and alignment marks

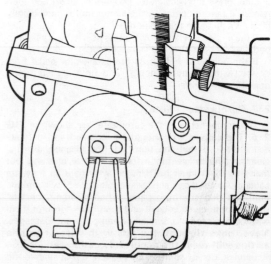

FIG 2:8 Checking the fuel level in the carburetter

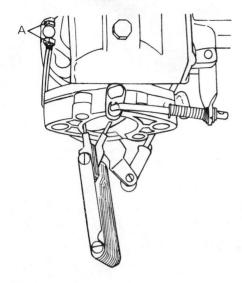

FIG 2:9   Setting the automatic choke linkage

Fuel can be driven out by alternately heating and cooling the float but solder on the float will alter its weight and it should therefore only be repaired by this method in an emergency.

Once the float and needle valve parts have been examined it is advisable to check the fuel level.

Starvation:

Starvation can be caused by similar faults to those causing flooding. The fuel delivery pressure should be checked as a low pressure can cause starvation at speed. Dirt or wear can cause the float chamber needle valve to stick in the closed position. Similarly dirt in the carburetter can block jets and cause starvation.

Check that the fuel lines are not blocked, blowing through them in a reverse direction with compressed air to clear them.

If the engine stalls after a period of running and then will not start again until some time has elapsed, remove the fuel tank filler cap as soon as possible after the engine stalls. If an inrush of air is heard and the engine will then start, the fuel tank vent system is blocked.

Poor idle may be caused by a defective idling valve solenoid valve, so check this.

Running-on:

If the fault has gradually built up over a period of time it is likely that the engine requires decarbonizing.

Check the operation of the idle jet solenoid. Use a test lamp to confirm that the wire is live when the ignition is switched on. Leaving the ignition on, brush the end of the wire across the terminal on the solenoid and if the solenoid is operating it will be heard to chatter or click as the contact is made and broken. If the solenoid does not operate, use the grubscrew to set the valve to full open so that the engine can be run.

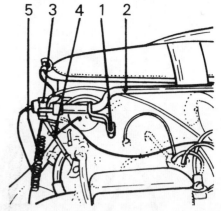

FIG 2:10   The throttle linkage at the carburetter

Key to Fig 2:10   1 Accelerator cable   2 Cross-shaft
3 Levers   4 Pullrod   5 Return spring

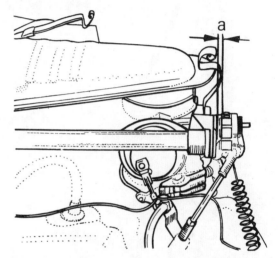

FIG 2:11   Setting the clearance 'a' for the throttle linkage

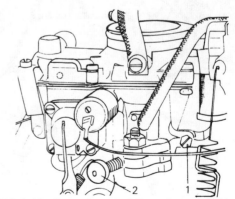

FIG 2:12   The carburetter idling adjustment points

Key to Fig 2:12   1 Idle speed adjusting screw
2 Volume control screw (mixture)

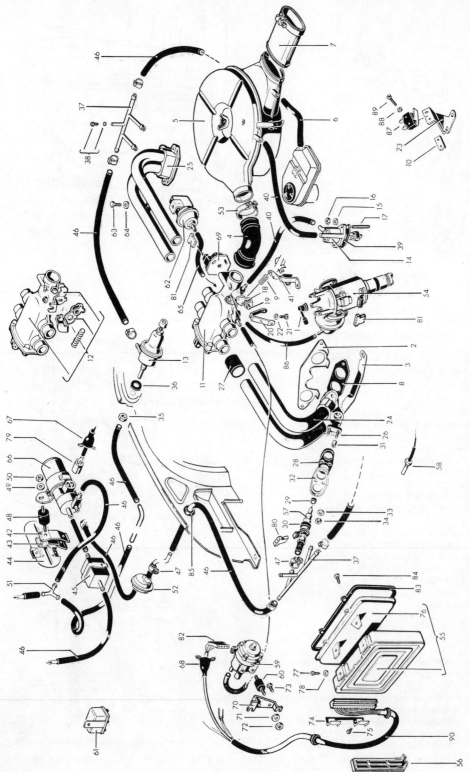

FIG 2:13   The components of a typical fuel injection system

Key to Fig 2:13   1 Connector   2 Inner cover   3 Outer cover   4 Elbow   5 Air filter   6 Hose to de-aerator   7 Intermediate piece   8 Gasket   9 Spring   10 Plate
11/12 Suction manifold assembly   13 Pressure regulator   14 Auxiliary air regulator   15 Washer   16 Nut   17 Stud   18 Pivot pin   19 Screw   20 Bracket   21 Screw
22 Washer   23 Bracket   24 Suction pipe (left)   25 Suction pipe (right)   26 Stud   27 Rubber hose   28 Valve support   29 Bush   30 Bush   31 Bush   32 Retainer plate
33 Washer   34 Nut   35 Nut   36 Insulating washer   37 Fuel injection piece   38 Screw and washer   39 Gasket   40 Rubber hose   41 Return spring bracket   42/43 Clamp
44 Protection plate   45 Fuel filter   46 Fuel flexible pipe   47 Clip   48 Flexible mounting   49 Washer   50 Nut   51 Y-piece   52 Noise damper   53 Clip   54 Distributor
55 Control unit   56 Sliding cover   57 Injector   58 Temperature sensor   59 Pressure sensor   60 Rubber bush   61 Relay   62 Pressure switch   63 Screw   64 Washer
65 Rubber pipe   66 Fuel pump   67 Rubber boot   69 Throttle switch   70 Pressure sensor bracket   71 Washer   72 Nut   73 Screw   74 Handle   75 Cover   76 Cover
77 Screw   78 Washer (shakeproof)   79 Connector cover   80 Two-way connector   81 Three-way connector   82 Four-way connector   83 Gasket   84 Screw
85 Screw   86 Grommet   87 Kick-down switch   88 Washer   89 Screw   90 Cable harness

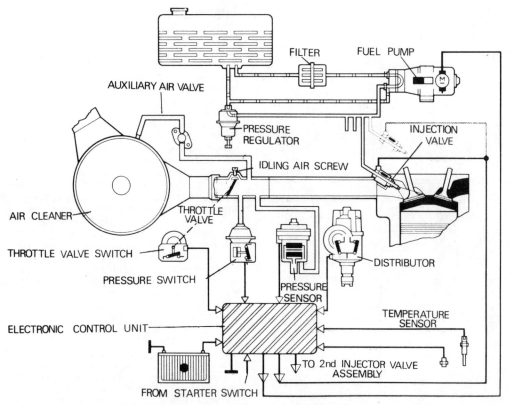

FIG 2:14   The schematic layout of a fuel injection system

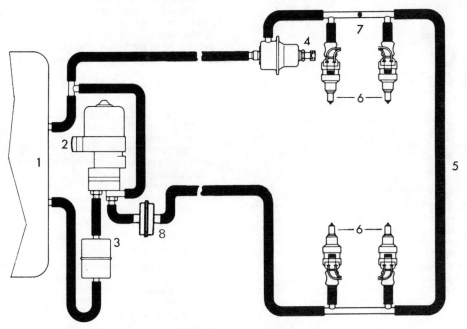

FIG 2:15   The fuel circuit

Key to Fig 2:15   1 Fuel tank   2 Fuel pump   3 Fuel filter   4 Pressure regulator   5 Fuel loop line   6 Injectors
7 Sealing screw for pressure gauge connection   8 Damper

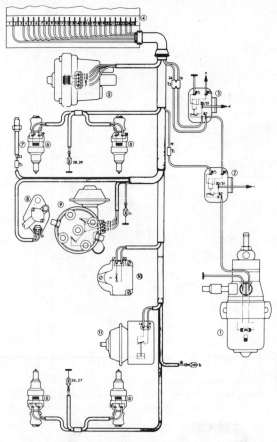

FIG 2:16   The electrical circuit

Key to Fig 2:16   1 Fuel pump   2 Pump relay
3 Voltage supply relay   4 Electronic control unit
5 Pressure sensor   6 Injectors   7 Cylinder head temperature
sensor   8 Crankcase temperature sensor   9 Ignition
distributor with trigger contacts   10 Throttle valve switch
11 Pressure switch   **a** Wire to ignition/starter switch
b Wire to starter solenoid terminal 50   **c** Wire to terminal 30
d Wire to positive battery terminal   **T**   Wire connector
T₂ Wire connector

Choke operates incorrectly:

Check that the leads to the automatic chokes are both
live when the ignition is switched on. If the choke does
not release itself within five minutes it is likely that either
the bi-metallic spring or the heater element is defective.
In both cases the complete choke housing cover must be
renewed as neither of the components is repairable. The
attachments are shown in **FIG 2:7**. Remove the air cleaner
to gain access and then remove the three screws securing
the cover in place. Remove the cover, gasket and securing
ring.

When installing the cover, make sure that the tang on
the choke lever engages in the eye of the bi-metallic
spring. Set the cover so that the marks shown in **FIG
2:7** are in alignment before fully tightening the screws.

Difficulty in adjusting:

Mechanical wear and damage will make it difficult to
adjust the carburetters satisfactorily. The most likely
points of wear are the idle volume adjusting screw itself
or the throttle valve assembly. Wear on the choke valve
assembly may make cold starts difficult but generally will
not affect the running of the engine once warm, unless
the wear is such as to jam the choke valve in the closed
position.

The volume control screw has a tapered tip so that as
it is turned in or out, the effective area of the port is
smoothly altered. If the screw is tightened down onto its
seat, or has seen long service, the tip may wear to a
stepped portion. Once a step has worn into the tip, adjustment will be erratic and turning the screw will make dis-
proportionate variations in idle mixture. **Never tighten
the screw firmly down onto its seat.**

A worn throttle valve or throttle valve spindle will also
make adjustment difficult. The spindle and valve can be
removed after taking off the throttle linkage parts. Take
out the two screws securing the throttle valve to the
spindle, slide the valve plate out of its slot and withdraw
the spindle. If fitting a new spindle does not take up the
wear then it will be necessary to install a new carburetter.
Install the parts in the reverse order of removal but before
fully tightening the screws securing the valve plate to the
spindle, check that the valve operates freely without
binding in the bore. Once the valve is correctly positioned,
fully tighten the screws and stake them over to lock them.
Support the spindle when staking the screws.

Persistent trouble can be caused by air leaks at the
manifold joints. Remove the carburetters and intake
manifolds. Use a steel straightedge to check that the
flanges are true and that they meet fully and squarely. A
fine file, scraper or oilstone can be used to remove minor
damage and nicks but more extensive damage can be
lapped down using fine-grade grinding paste spread
over a piece of plate glass. Make sure that all abrasive and
filings are cleaned away before installing the parts.

2:8 Carburetter adjustments

Fuel level:

Start the engine and run it briefly to allow the fuel level
to stabilize. Stop the engine and remove the carburetter
top cover, clamping the fuel hose to prevent fuel dribbling
into the float chamber. Remove the gasket and use a
depth gauge to measure the depth of the fuel from the top
of the carburetter float chamber, as shown in **FIG 2:8**.
The reading should be 12 to 14 mm (.47 to .55 inch). If
the level is incorrect, fit thicker or thinner washers under
the float chamber needle valve body to bring the level
within limits.

Accelerator pump:

If there are flat spots in acceleration, check the delivery
of the pump and the direction of its jet.

Remove the air cleaner duct. Back off the idling speed
adjustment screw so that the throttle valve is fully closed.
Insert a small graduated container (8 to 10 cc) into the
opening of the carburetter and smartly operate the
throttle linkage, catching the fuel from the pump discharge nozzle. Repeat the pumping a few times so that an
average reading can be obtained. The pump should

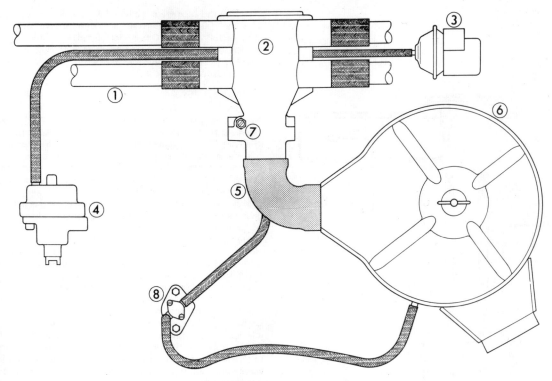

FIG 2:17   The air supply system

Key to Fig 2:17   1 Inlet manifolds   2 Air intake distributor   3 Pressure switch   4 Pressure sensor   5 Elbow   6 Air cleaner
7 Slow-running adjustment   8 Auxiliary air regulator

produce .7 to .9 cc per stroke. If the injection amount is incorrect vary the number of washers (.2 mm Part No. 111.905.231) on the operating rod to bring the amount within limits. Increase washers to increase fuel flow and decrease to decrease fuel. Only if the injection amount varies considerably from the correct amount should the operating rod be moved to another hole in the lever.

Check the depth from the end of the injection tube from the top face of the carburetter. This should be 12.5 mm. At the same time check that the direction of injection is correctly through the gap when the throttle is partially open. Carefully bend the tube to position if the injection is incorrect.

Choke adjustments:

The housing must be installed so that the marks shown in **FIG 2:7** are in alignment.

Further adjustment of the linkage can only be carried out with the carburetter removed and it will be necessary to reset the idle after the carburetter(s) have been installed.

With the carburetter removed, adjust the nuts on the rod **A**, shown in **FIG 2:9**, until the gap at the throttle valve is .8 mm (.030 inch) with the choke valve held closed. Install the carburetter and back out the idle speed adjustment screw until it is clear of lever, so that the throttle valve is fully closed. Turn in the adjusting screw until it just touches the throttle lever. Close the choke valve by briefly opening the throttle valve and pressing

the choke valve if necessary. Now measure the gap between the idling speed adjustment screw and the throttle lever, using feeler gauges or a suitable diameter rod. Use the adjusting nuts on the connecting rod to set the gap to 2.6 mm (.10 inch). Adjust the idle speed.

Throttle linkage:

The attachments are shown in **FIG 2:10**. Note the lefthand lever and lefthand pullrod are adjustable while the equivalent parts on the righthand side are not.

The complete throttle linkage assembly can be removed after disconnecting the accelerator cable and springs, disconnecting the crankcase breather hose, disconnecting the pullrods from the throttle levers, and taking out the bolts securing the brackets to the carburetters.

Before installing the linkage, check the parts for wear and lubricate bearing surfaces with molybdenum disulphide. Adjust the lefthand side pullrod to a length of 104 ± .5 mm and lock it at this length.

Fit the parts back into place and press down the levers at the end of the cross-shaft so that the throttle levers are in the idling positions. Push the shaft towards the left and press the lefthand side lever downwards to the right, then tighten the nut securing the lever. Push the cross-shaft to the right and slide the righthand lever towards the bracket until there is a clearance of 1.5 to 2.0 mm (.006 to .008 inch) between the lever and the bracket, as shown in **FIG 2:11**. Tighten the nut in this position.

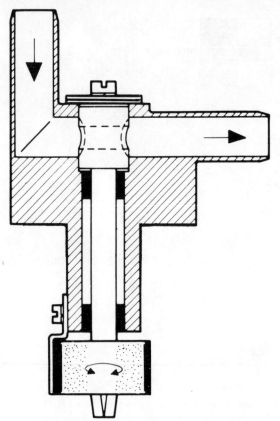

FIG 2:18 Sectioned view of the auxiliary air regulator valve

Attach the accelerator cable so that there is a distance of 1 mm (.04 inch) between the throttle lever and its stop at full throttle. On models fitted with automatic transmission make sure that there is sufficient further travel on the pedal to operate the kick-down switch when the throttle valves are fully open.

Idling adjustments:

The adjustment points are shown in **FIG 2:12**. It will be necessary to remove the air intake ducts. When installing these after adjustment there may be a drop in idle speed but no adjustments are required to cure this.

A balance meter should be used, though it is possible (but not recommended) to use a length of hose and listen to the hiss at the intakes so that they can be balanced by sound.

If the adjustments are totally lost they can be set to give safe running. The idle adjusting screw 1 should be set so that it is 1 turn in from the position where it just contacts the throttle lever when the throttle valve is closed. The volume control screw should be lightly seated, **do not seat it firmly as this causes wear to the tapered portion,** and then backed out by $1\frac{1}{2}$ turns.

Start the engine and run it until it has reached its normal operating temperature. Remove the air cleaner ducts, checking that both choke valves are fully open. Connect a tachometer into the ignition circuit. Use the idle speed adjustment screws to give an idle speed of 900 rev/min. Use the balance meter or some other method to check that the air flow through both carburetters is the same. Turn in the volume control screw 2 on both carburetters by equal amounts until the engine starts to run unevenly and then back them out by $\frac{1}{4}$ to $\frac{1}{2}$ turn each until the engine is running smoothly. Bring the idle speed back to 900 rev/min if necessary, using both idle speed screws 1.

Clip the throttle linkage open so that the engine is running at 1500 to 1800 rev/min. Check the balance of the carburetters using the balance meter and if necessary adjust the lefthand side pullrod to bring the carburetters into balance.

Remove the tachometer, clip on throttle linkage and install the air cleaner ducts.

2:9 Fault diagnosis

(a) Leakage or insufficient fuel delivered

1 Air vent in fuel tank blocked
2 Fuel pipes blocked
3 Air leaks at pipe connections
4 Pump filter blocked
5 Strainer on fuel tank sender unit blocked
6 Defective pump

(b) Excessive fuel consumption

1 Carburetters require adjustment
2 Dirty air cleaner
3 Sticking throttle linkage
4 Defective automatic choke
5 Jets loose or incorrect size fitted
6 Flooding or external leaks
7 Excessive engine temperature
8 Brakes binding
9 Tyres under-inflated
10 Car overloaded

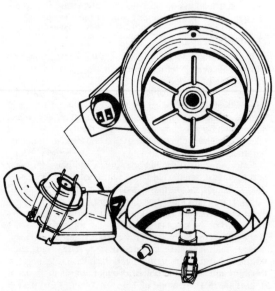

FIG 2:19 The air cleaner fitted with the fuel injection system

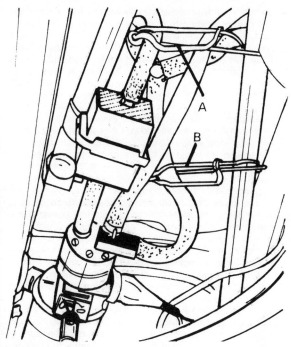

FIG 2:20 Changing the fuel filter on earlier models

(c) Engine will not start

1 Defective ignition
2 Fuel not reaching float chamber
3 Incorrect starting technique
4 Defective automatic choke cover assembly
5 Defective solenoid operated idling valve
6 Jets blocked

(d) Idling speed too high or erratic

1 Automatic choke not functioning
2 Accelerator linkage sticking
3 Incorrect slow-running adjustments
4 Defective volume control screws
5 Worn throttle valve assemblies

PART 2 THE FUEL INJECTION SYSTEM

2:10 Description

The components of a typical system are shown in **FIG 2:13** and the schematic layout of the system is shown in **FIG 2:14**. Two sensors are fitted, one measuring cylinder head temperature and the other crankcase temperature.

The fuel is drawn from the fuel tank through a renewable filter to the pump, which is electrically driven. A constant pressure is kept in the system by the action of the pressure regulator.

The electronic control unit is a cigar-box sized computer which takes in all the parameters and produces a series of pulses. These pulses, varying in duration, operate the injectors so that fuel is injected into the manifold at the correct moment. The longer the pulse, the longer will be the time that the injector is open and the more fuel will be injected.

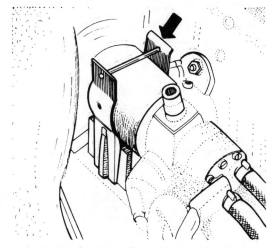

FIG 2:21 The fuel filter attachments on later models

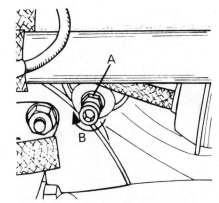

FIG 2:22 Adjusting the fuel pressure

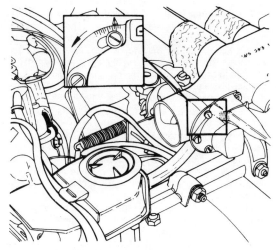

FIG 2:23 The throttle valve switch

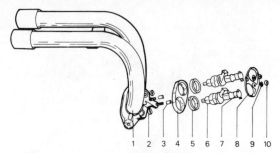

FIG 2:24 The injector and manifold components

Key to Fig 2:24   1 Suction tube with valve seat
2 Inner valve bearing   3 Sleeve   4 Injector valve plate
5 Outer injector valve bearing   6 Electromagnetic injector
valve   7 Hose connection with clamp   8 Injector valve
retainer   9 Spring washer   10 Nut

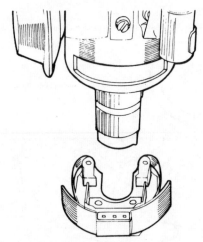

FIG 2:25 The trigger contacts of the distributor

The computer itself is far beyond the scope of this manual but it is a solid-state device using printed circuits. It can be considered as a highly sophisticated switch which turns the fuel on and off at the injectors. The computer has been found reliable in service but if it is thought to be defective, checks must be carried out using special test equipment. The owner should not attempt diagnosis or rectification.

The fuel circuit on its own is shown in **FIG 2:15**. The damper 8 is fitted to quieten the noise of the fuel through the lines. Return lines are fitted to lead back surplus fuel from the pressure regulator valve 4 and from the fuel pump 2. The pump is only operated when the engine is actually running but when the ignition is switched on the pump immediately runs for a short period to pressurize the system ready for starting.

The electrical circuit is shown in **FIG 2:16**. The throttle valve 6 is fitted to shut off the fuel completely on certain conditions of overrun so that the engine acts as a brake and since there is no combustion, emissions are reduced to the minimum. The relays 2 and 3 are fitted to allow

components to operate at a heavy current without the full current passing through the computer 4. The operation of the injectors 6 and fuel pump 1 have already been described. The temperature sensor 7 measures the cylinder head temperature and will therefore be quicker in its reactions than the sensor 8 which measures the crankcase temperature. The information from these sensors is fed to the computer so that the quantity of fuel injected can be increased when the engine is cold, making the mixture richer. The pressure sensor 5 is connected to the intake manifold and it measures the absolute pressure so that the computer will automatically compensate for changes in altitude or barometric pressure. The pressure switch 11 measures the difference between intake pressure and atmospheric pressure so that a signal proportional to throttle opening and engine load is sent to the computer. A set of non-adjustable contacts is fitted into the base of an otherwise conventional distributor. The distributor is synchronized with the engine so that the pulse from the contacts will trigger off injection at the correct moment. By integrating the pulses, the computer calculates the engine speed directly. From all these sensors the computer now has the information when to initiate fuel injection and the amount of fuel required.

The air system is shown in **FIG 2:17**. All the air for operation is drawn through the air cleaner 6. A standard throttle valve, operated by the accelerator linkage, is fitted in the air intake distributor 2 to control the air flow and engine speed. At idle, the throttle valve is fully closed and the air for idle passes through the bypass 7 which is used to set the idle speed. An auxiliary air regulator 8 is fitted to supply extra air when the engine is cold, so that the idle speed is increased. A sectioned view of the auxiliary air regulator is shown in **FIG 2:18**. The device is mounted in the crankcase and is purely mechanical in operation. When the engine is very cold, the bi-metallic spring fully opens the port so that maximum air flows through. As the spring warms up it closes the port, reducing the amount of air passing through. When the engine has been standing for some time it will be at ambient temperature and the auxiliary air regulator will then pass the amount of air required for starting at that temperature. When the engine starts and warms up, the bi-metallic spring will warm up with the engine until when the engine is hot the port is fully closed off and no auxiliary air passes through. The computer will have the equivalent information from the temperature sensors and will reduce the amount of fuel injected correspondingly.

2:11 Maintenance

Check that the accelerator linkage operates freely, lubricating the pivot points occasionally. Clean the air cleaner and renew the filter at the correct intervals.

Air cleaner:

An oil bath air cleaner is fitted, as for models with carburetters. The air cleaner must be cleaned out when there is a minimum of 4 to 5 mm (.16 to .2 inches) of oil left above the sludge. In extreme conditions, cleaning may be required daily but under normal conditions check at intervals of 1000 miles until the servicing period can be established which is correct for the use which the car is given.

Pull the crankcase breather hose off from the air cleaner. Disconnect the remainder of the hoses to the air cleaner. Slacken the wing screw and lift the complete air cleaner out, taking care to keep it horizontal.

Free the two clips and remove the upper portion of the air cleaner. **Do not lay this upper portion down on the bench so that the filter element is uppermost.**

Clean out the lower portion of the air cleaner, removing all sludge and old oil. If need be, scrape the upper portion with a piece of wood to clean the holes. Only if the air cleaner has been grossly neglected should it be necessary to swill the filter element portion in paraffin or diesel fuel to clean it.

Fill the lower portion to the mark with fresh oil (approximately .45 Litre .8 pint). Normally SAE.30 oil should be used but SAE.10 oil can be used in arctic conditions. Fit the top portion back into place so that the marks shown in **FIG 2:19** are again in alignment and install the air cleaner in the reverse order of removal.

Fuel filter:

The fuel filter on pre-1970 models should be renewed at intervals of 10,000 km (6000 miles) and on later models at intervals of 20,000 km (12,000 miles). **The filter cannot be cleaned and it must be renewed.**

The method of renewing the filter on earlier models is shown in **FIG 2:20**. Clamp the hoses to prevent fuel from draining out and disconnect them from the filter. Fit a new filter back into place, **making sure that the arrow points towards the pump.** Check for fuel leaks after removing the clamps.

The attachment of the later filters is shown in **FIG 2:21**. In both cases work will be easier if the front of the car is raised off the ground, as the filter is mounted at the front.

2:12 Adjustments

The adjustments that can be carried out by the owner are strictly limited in range. Special test equipment is made for diagnosing faults and making accurate adjustments so in case of difficulty the car should be taken to a suitable VW agent.

Fuel pressure:

An accurate gauge is required. Remove the air cleaner and take out the screw and washer from the righthand side distributor pipe between the righthand injectors. Install the gauge onto the pipe. Start the engine and allow it to run for a short while so that the pressure stabilizes. The correct pressure is 2.0 kg/sq cm (28 lb/sq inch). If the pressure is incorrect, adjust the pressure regulator below the righthand intake manifold. Slacken the locknut **A**, shown in **FIG 2:22**, and adjust the screw **B** to bring the pressure within limits. Tighten the locknut when the adjustment is correct.

Before making adjustments it is advisable to check that the fuel filter is clean and has not been left in for longer than its normal life. Check the fuel pump by connecting an ammeter in series with it and if it is satisfactory it will be taking a current of approximately 2.1-amps.

Idling speed:

A tachometer must be used when adjusting the idling speed as the ear alone is not sufficiently accurate. Connect the tachometer to the ignition circuit and start the engine. Run the engine until the temperatures have stabilized at normal. Adjust the idle speed to the slowest at which the engine continues to run and then increase the speed to 950 + 50 rev/min. If too fast an idle speed is set, slow down the engine to below the correct speed and then gradually adjust it back up until it is within limits.

Throttle valve switch:

The switch and its attachments are shown in **FIG 2:23**. Each graduation on the scale represents 2 deg.

Slacken the mounting screws and turn it in the opposite direction to the arrow. Slowly turn the switch back in the direction of the arrow until a click is heard; note the graduation mark at which this occurs and turn the switch a further graduation in the direction of the arrow. Tighten the screws to secure the switch in this position. Disconnect the return spring and check that the throttle linkage operates freely throughout its range of movement.

Note that on models fitted with automatic transmission a kick-down switch is also fitted.

2:13 Components

In 1970 the pressure switch was combined with the pressure sensor so it will only be found as a separate component on the earlier models.

Fuel injectors:

The injectors are operated in pairs and the pair at the rear are fitted with grey plugs while those at the front are fitted with black plugs. Each side of the engine will therefore have one grey plug and one black plug. The injectors are removed in pairs on the same side of the engine.

A brief test can be carried out on injector performance once they have been removed from the engine but left connected to their fuel lines and leads, with the earth lead grounded. Crank the engine on the starter motor and the injector should spray with a regular cone. The fuel system pressure is not high (as on diesels) but it is still not advisable to allow the spray to hit the skin. If there is no injection or if the spray comes out in a deformed cone, install a new injector.

To remove a pair of injectors from one side, disconnect the cable and earth plugs. Remove the two nuts and withdraw the complete assembly from the engine. **Take great care not to damage or knock the needles in the injectors.** The components are shown in **FIG 2:24**.

Install the injectors in the reverse order of removal, making sure that all seals are in position. Fit the washers and tighten the nuts to a torque of .6 kg m (4.3 lb ft). The grey lead must be connected to the rear injector and the black lead to the front one. Do not forget to connect the earth otherwise the injectors will fail to operate.

Fuel pump:

No repairs can be carried out to the unit if it is defective, and a new pump must be fitted in its place.

Clamp the hoses to prevent the fuel lines from emptying

and then cut the special crimped clips securing hoses in place. Remove the attachment bolts securing the pump and take out the pump.

Install the pump in the reverse order of removal, using worm-driven hose clips to secure the hoses. Remove the clamps and check for fuel leaks. Make sure that the electrical plug is correctly connected.

Distributor contacts:

These are secured in the base of the distributor by two screws, as shown in FIG 2:25. The contacts cannot be adjusted and if they are worn a new set must be fitted. Disconnect the plug, remove the two screws and withdraw the old contact set.

Refit the contacts in the reverse order of removal, after lightly greasing the pivot points and cam.

Pressure sensor:

On earlier models, slacken the front pair of screws (on the lefthand side of the engine compartment) but do not remove them. Disconnect the vacuum hose and blank both hose and adaptor on the sensor to prevent the entry of dirt. Disconnect the electrical plug. Remove the rear pair of screws, slide the unit rearwards to free it from the front screws and then remove it.

On the 1970 and onwards models, remove both attachment screws but still make sure that the vacuum hose and adaptor are blanked off.

Pressure switch (pre-1970 models only):

This is fitted under the righthand side manifold pipes and is secured to them by a nut and bolt. A narrow 10 mm socket spanner and extension will be required to remove the nut and bolt.

Take out the unit and disconnect the plug, after disconnecting the vacuum hose.

Connect the plug to the unit before fitting the unit. If the switch touches the manifold pipes after installation, fit a spacer washer to make sure that the unit is clear of the pipes. Reconnect the vacuum hose.

Temperature sensors:

The cylinder head sensor is fitted to the lefthand cylinder head. Disconnect the lead and then use an open-ended spanner to undo the nut. Withdraw the sensor when the nut is free. Do not overtighten the nut when installing the cylinder head sensor.

The crankcase sensor is attached to the auxiliary air regulator.

Detach the lead from the sensor and then unscrew the sensor from the auxiliary air valve. Disconnect the hoses to the auxiliary air regulator, after labelling them, and blank them off to prevent the entry of dirt. Take out the attachment and remove the air regulator, plugging the orifice to prevent the entry of dirt.

When installing the parts, tighten the attachment screw to a torque of 1.5 kg m (11 lb ft).

2:14 Fault diagnosis

(a) Engine will not start

1 Fuel pump not operating
2 Pressure sensor disconnected or defective (causes very rich mixture)
3 Temperature sensors disconnected or defective
4 Insufficient fuel pressure
5 Kinked or blocked fuel lines
6 Trigger contacts defective or disconnected
7 Defective lead between starter motor solenoid and computer

(b) Engine starts then stalls

1 Check 6 in (a)
2 Blocked fuel tank vent

(c) Misfiring (ignition satisfactory)

1 Dirty or defective trigger contacts*
2 Loose connections*
3 Defective injector (exhaust shows white smoke)
4 Poor injector earthing (usually cuts injectors in pairs)
*Engine may stop after a period of misfiring.

(d) Lack of power

1 Check 3 and 4 in (c)
2 Pressure switch disconnected or defective (combined unit on later models)

(e) High fuel consumption

1 Temperature sensors defective or loose connections to them
2 Mechanical faults on car (binding brakes, low tyre pressures, clutch slip)

(f) Engine hunts excessively while running in low range

1 Hose between auxiliary air regulator and air distributor disconnected

CHAPTER 3

THE IGNITION SYSTEM

3:1 Description
3:2 Maintenance
3:3 Ignition faults
3:4 Distributor removal and installation

3:5 Servicing the distributor
3:6 Setting the ignition timing
3:7 The sparking plugs
3:8 Fault diagnosis

3:1 Description

A schematic diagram of the ignition circuit is shown in **FIG 3:1**. The distributor is mounted on the engine and driven at half engine speed, and is synchronized with the engine. The distributor shaft carries a four-lobed cam which operates the contact points and the rotor arm is mounted on top of the distributor shaft.

When the contact points are closed, a low-voltage current flows through the primary circuit of the ignition, setting up a magnetic field around the primary windings in the ignition coil. When the contacts open, at the correct instant under the action of the cam on the shaft, the current is rapidly cut off (assisted by the action of the capacitor) and the magnetic field in the ignition coil collapses rapidly. The collapse of the magnetic field induces a very high voltage in the secondary windings of the ignition coil. This high voltage is led to the centre electrode of the distributor cap. A carbon brush leads the high-voltage from the centre electrode to the rotor arm. The rotor arm, being correctly set, guides the high-voltage to the correct side electrode in the cap from where it is led to the sparking plug of the correct cylinder. The voltage jumping across the electrodes of the sparking plug ignites the mixture in the cylinder.

The actual instant of firing is dependent on the engine speed and the mixture in the cylinder. Combustion is not instantaneous but spreads as a wave front through the mixture, and the rate of propagation of this wave front depends on the mixture strength. The ignition must be initiated at the correct instant to ensure that maximum pressure is being exerted on the pinion as it is travelling downwards.

The distributor shaft is fitted with two spring-loaded weights which move outwards under centrifugal force. As the engine speeds up, the weights move outwards and turn the cam portion of the shaft forward in relation to the remainder of the shaft, this action advancing the ignition point with increase in engine speed.

The suction in the inlet manifold is proportional to the throttle opening and load on the engine. A small bore vacuum tube connects the manifold to the vacuum unit of the distributor. A diaphragm is acted on by the vacuum and this diaphragm rotates the contact breaker plate in the distributor body to advance the ignition as required.

3:2 Maintenance

The HT leads, distributor cap and ignition coil top should be kept free of oil, dirt or moisture at all times. A

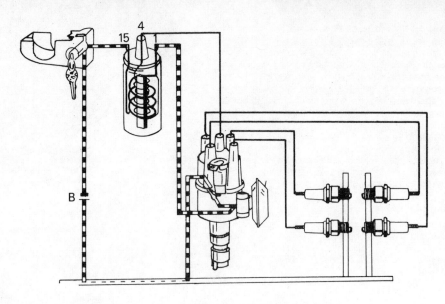

FIG 3:1   A schematic diagram of the ignition system

regular wiping over the outside of the parts with a soft clean cloth will keep them clean and ensure that no leakage paths can build up.

The sparking plugs should be cleaned at intervals of 8000 km (6000 miles) and renewed at intervals of 16,000 km (12,000 miles). The electrodes wear and deposits build up deep inside the plug which cannot be removed by cleaning and it is for this reason that the plugs should be renewed regularly. Some of these deposits only conduct when hot and therefore the effect will not show up when pressure-testing the plugs. Full details of sparking plug maintenance are given in **Section 3:7**.

Lubrication:

The distributor should be lightly lubricated at intervals of 6000 miles. Typical distributor components are shown in **FIG 3:2**. Free the clips 9 and lift off the distributor cap 2. Firmly but squarely pull off the rotor arm 3. A typical distributor will then appear as shown in **FIG 3:3**. Inject a few drops of oil through the hole arrowed and with a clean finger smear a little grease around the lobes of the cam. If a lubricator is fitted for the lower bush, add a few drops of oil through it. Pour a few drops of oil onto the felt pad exposed after the removal of the rotor arm. Check that the moving contact pivots freely about its pivot post and occasionally add a single drop of non-creeping oil to the pivot post (Ragosine Listate).

Take great care not to overlubricate or to allow any lubricant onto the contacts themselves. Wipe away all surplus lubricant. The aim is to lubricate lightly and regularly.

Distributor cap and rotor arm:

Wiping down all over with a clean soft cloth is usually sufficient cleansing, but if there is excessive oil or dirt use a small stiff brush and chloroform or methylated spirits (denatured alchohol). Check the parts for cracks or signs of 'tracking' in the cap. Tracking shows up as thin black lines between electrodes or an electrode and the edge of the cap. If a defect is found, the part must be renewed otherwise it can be a cause of persistent misfiring.

Cleaning contact points:

In normal use metal will be transferred from one contact to the other, forming a crater on one and a pit in the other. This build-up of metal will not affect performance until it has reached the normal gap of the contacts and the contacts should then be renewed. In an emergency they can be cleaned by grinding or using a special file.

Normally the contacts should only require cleaning if they are contaminated with oil or grease. The contacts should have a slate-grey frosted appearance for optimum efficiency but lubricant will blacken them. Contamination will also show up as a smudgy line of black on the base-plate under the contacts. Clean using a small stiff brush with chloroform or methylated spirits as a solvent.

Renewing contact points:

The points must be renewed when the build-up of metal exceeds the correct gap, also if they are excessively burnt or it is no longer possible to set the correct dwell and gap.

Remove the distributor cap and rotor arm. There are slight differences in the construction of various distributors but these general instructions will cope with all types. **Check the position of all insulating washers as parts are removed and make sure that they are correctly refitted.** Free the spring end of the moving contact from its terminal, noting that if the spring is secured to the terminal on the side of the distributor body the spring will be slotted so that it can be pulled out after slackening the attachment. If necessary, remove the spring clip securing the contact to the pivot post and slide the moving contact up and off. Remove the securing screw for the fixed contact and take out the contact, noting the positions of insulating washers.

New contacts are installed in the reverse order of removal, after washing them in methylated spirits to remove any protective. Adjust the gap after the contacts are fitted.

Check that the moving contact pivots freely about its post and that the spring has not weakened with use. If the contact sticks, remove it and lightly polish the post with fine emerycloth, lubricating it with a single drop of oil before installing the moving contact.

Adjusting the points:

The most satisfactory method is to use a dwell meter but this should be left to an agent as a special meter is required.

The gap can also be set using feeler gauges, though if this is done on used points care must be taken to insert the feeler gauge only between the unworn portions of the contacts.

Remove the distributor cap and rotor arm. Crank the engine by hand until the foot of the moving contact is on the lobe of the cam and the points are at their widest gap. Three differing types of adjustment are shown in **FIG 3:4**. Slacken the fixed contact hold-down screw **A** slightly so that the fixed contact can be moved but does not move under its own weight. Fit the blade of a screwdriver to **B** and by turning the screwdriver alter the contact gap. Slide a clean feeler gauge between the unworn portions of the contacts and adjust the gap until slight drag is felt on the feeler gauge. Tighten the securing screw and check that the gap has not altered. Crank the engine over and check the gap at the other three lobes of the cam. The correct gap is .4 mm (.016 inch).

Install the rotor arm and distributor cap.

3:3 Ignition faults

Before carrying out checks on the ignition system make sure that the symptoms are not caused by a defective fuel system. Check the points in the distributor and make sure that they are clean and correctly set. It is also worthwhile to check that the ignition timing is correct. Note that a persistent misfire can be caused by an engine defect, such as a sticking valve.

If the engine has a persistent misfire and the fault is traced to the ignition circuit, start the engine and run it until it has reached its normal operating temperature. Clip the throttle open to give a fast-idle speed. Disconnect each HT lead from its sparking plug in turn. **Do not use the bare hands in case the lead is defective but use rags or a thick glove as insulation.** If the rough running or misfire becomes more pronounced when an HT lead is disconnected then that cylinder is satisfactory. If there is no difference in the running of the engine when a lead is disconnected then that cylinder is not firing for some reason.

Having identified the faulty cylinder, stop the engine and fit an old sparking plug or piece of rod into the moulded HT lead connector. Start the engine and hold the lead so that the end is approximately 5 mm ($\frac{3}{16}$ inch) away from a grounded metal part of the engine or car.

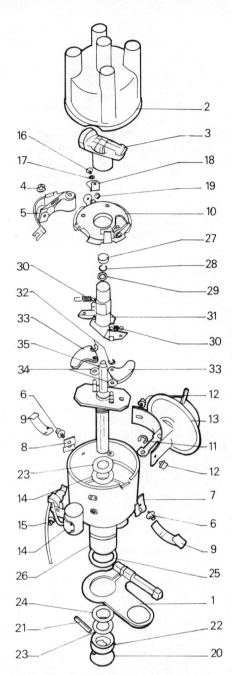

FIG 3:2   Typical distributor components

Key to Fig 3:2   1 Distributor clamp bracket
2 Distributor cap   3 Distributor rotor   4 Contact securing screw   5 Contact breakers   6 Screw   7 Securing tab   8 Securing tab   9 Retaining clip   10 Breaker plate   11 Pullrod securing clip   12 Screw   13 Vacuum unit   14 Condenser   15 Screw   16 Screw   17 Spring washer   18 Ball retaining spring 19 Ball 20 Circlip 21 Securing pin   22 Driving dog   23 Shim   24 Fibre washer   25 Rubber sealing ring   26 Distributor body   27 Felt washer   28 Circlip   29 Thrust ring   30 Return spring   31 Distributor cam   32 Circlip   33 Flyweight   34 Washer   35 Drive shaft

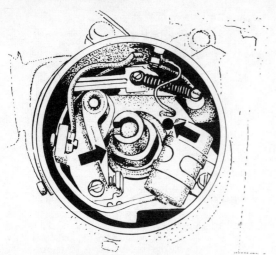

FIG 3:3 Lubricating the distributor

Do not hold the lead near the fuel system because of the danger of fire. If the ignition system is satisfactory there will be a series of fat blue sparks jumping across. If the sparks are satisfactory, remove the sparking plug and either have it cleaned and tested or install a new one in its place. If the fault persists then the defect lies in the engine.

If the sparks are weak, irregular, and reddish in colour check the HT lead for signs of perishing, burn marks, or other defect. If the lead appears at all defective, renew it and repeat the test. If renewal of the lead fails to bring any improvement, check the distributor cap and rotor arm for cracks, dirt, or tracking, as well as making sure that the carbon brush in the cap is satisfactory.

If all leads give poor sparks, disconnect the main HT lead between the ignition coil and distributor, crank the engine over on the starter motor and check that there is a regular fast stream of good sparks between the end of the lead and a good ground. If the sparks are weak or irregular, the ignition coil or its HT lead is defective.

Testing the low-tension circuit:

As a quick check, remove the distributor cap and crank the engine until the contact points are closed. Switch on the ignition and flick the contact points apart with a fingernail. If current is flowing there will be a small low-voltage spark across the contacts. If the central HT lead is held 5 mm from a grounded metal part there should be a good spark every time that the contacts are flicked apart.

A better test is to disconnect the low-tension lead between the distributor and ignition coil and then reconnect it with a test lamp in series. Slowly crank the engine over while watching the test lamp. Preferably remove the distributor cap so that the action of the points can be observed and there is no danger of the engine actually starting. When the points are closed the lamp should be lit and the lamp should go out as the points open.

If the lamp stays on continuously, there is a shortcircuit in the distributor. Check for correct assembly of all insulating washers and check that the leads are correctly connected and that their insulation is not frayed or damaged. If the distributor is satisfactory, repeat the test with the capacitor disconnected.

If the lamp does not light at all, check that the points are closing and that they are not excessively dirty. Use the test lamp to trace back through the wiring until the fault is found and can be rectified.

Capacitor:

On some models the capacitor is mounted externally on the distributor but on others it is mounted internally.

Shortcircuits in the distributor are usually self-healing, as the spark erodes away the metal foil in the area of the short. A shortcircuit is easily found using a test lamp as described just previously.

An open-circuit failure is more difficult to detect without special test equipment but it should be suspected if starting is difficult and the points are excessively blued or burnt. Note that capacitor failure is fairly rare so check for other faults before renewing the capacitor.

3:4 Distributor removal and installation

Distributor:

The cylinder numbering sequence, firing order, and correct position of the lead to No. 1 electrode on the cap are shown in **FIG 3:5**.

Remove the distributor cap and note the position of the rotor arm in the distributor. Free the attachments securing the clamp plate to the engine and withdraw the distributor after disconnecting the vacuum line and primary lead.

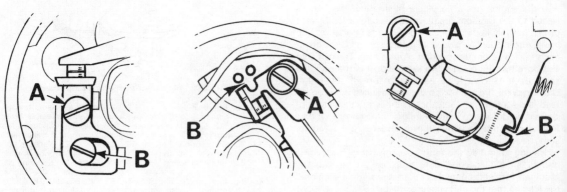

FIG 3:4 Various methods of adjusting the contact gap

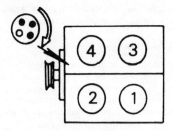

1-4-3-2

FIG 3:5 The cylinder numbering sequence and firing order

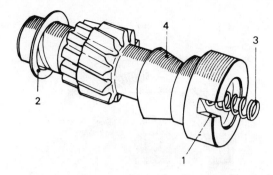

FIG 3:7 The distributor drive shaft in the engine

Do not slacken the pinch bolt securing the clamp plate to the distributor. Provided that the engine is not cranked while the distributor is out, the distributor can be installed in the reverse order of removal without losing the timing. Note that the drive dog on the end of the distributor shaft has an offset on it so that it will only fit in one position.

If the engine is to be cranked or otherwise worked on, set it to TDC on No. 1 cylinder before removing the distributor. The TDC point is found from the timing marks on the cooling fan and the firing position is found by observing the valves (with the rocker cover off) or blocking the spark plug hole with a finger. Both valves will be fully closed at the firing TDC or a pressure rise will be felt in the cylinder as the engine is cranked while the piston rises on the compression stroke. Some distributors will have a dot or mark on the body, as shown in **FIG 3:6**, indicating the position of the rotor arm at the firing point of No. 1 cylinder. After the engine has been cranked, return it to the correct position and then install the distributor in the reverse order of removal.

Distributor drive:

Remove the distributor as described earlier. Lift out the spacer spring from the shaft. A typical shaft is shown in **FIG 3:7**. The shaft can now be withdrawn from the engine. Preferably use the special tool VW.228B inserted into the top of the shaft, but a piece of wood, sharpened

to a suitable taper and pressed firmly in, can be used instead. The shaft will rotate slightly as it is withdrawn. The thrust washer will most probably remain in the crankcase. Withdraw the thrust washers preferably using a magnetized rod but a wire hook can be used. **Take great care not to allow the thrust washer to drop down into the engine.**

Clean the parts and check for wear or damage. Pay particular attention to the condition of the thrust washers and the gear teeth. If the gear on the drive shaft is worn it is likely that the mating gear in the engine is also worn.

Refit the thrust washer, taking great care not to drop it (or them) into the crankcase. Slide them down into place using a suitable piece of rod and make sure that they stay in place by smearing them with thick grease.

Set No. 1 cylinder to the firing position. Hold the drive shaft above the engine so that the slot is positioned as shown in **FIG 3:8**, with the smaller segment outwards. Rotate the shaft to allow for the meshing and lower it down into position so that it ends up as shown in the figure. Install the spacer spring and refit the distributor.

3:5 Servicing the distributor

Typical distributor components are shown in **FIG 3:2**. It should be noted that VW run an excellent exchange scheme and if the distributor is excessively worn it will be far more satisfactory to exchange it rather than to try

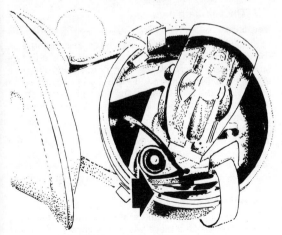

FIG 3:6 Timing mark on distributor case

FIG 3:8 The distributor drive shaft correctly installed

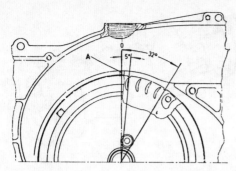

FIG 3:9 Typical ignition timing marks

to repair. Difficulty may also be found in obtaining items such as shafts, bushes etc.

The models fitted to cars with fuel injection systems have trigger contacts installed in the base. These contacts are non-adjustable and must be renewed when defective (see **Chapter 2, Part 2**).

The adjustment and renewal of the contact points is dealt with in **Section 3:2** and the capacitor in **Section 3:3**.

Vacuum unit:

This is a sealed unit and must be renewed if it is defective. Disconnect the link of the unit from the base-plate and also disconnect the vacuum line. Remove the screw securing the unit to the side of the case and with-draw it from the distributor. Refit in the reverse order of removal.

The vacuum unit can be checked by pressing in the link and blocking the vacuum connection with a finger. Release the link and suction should be felt. If there is no suction, or it drops rapidly, the diaphragm is punctured and the vacuum unit must be renewed.

Baseplate:

Remove the contact points and capacitor. Take out the screws that secure the baseplate assembly and lift it out of the distributor. On some models, the screws securing the baseplate will also secure the clips that hold on the distributor cap.

Cam and weights:

Remove the baseplate assembly. Carefully free the return springs from between the weights and cam. **Take great care not to distort or stretch these springs as they control the amount of advance.** One spring may be longer than the other but it has been designed so and is not necessarily defective. Note the relation of the slot for the rotor arm in relation to the offset of the drive dog, as this must be correct on reassembly. Free the clips so that the cam and weights can be removed.

Lubricate the parts lightly with oil after cleaning them and reassemble them in the reverse order of dismantling. The indented faces on the weights are fitted uppermost.

Shaft assembly:

If there is excessive wear, install a new or reconditioned distributor as it will be difficult to obtain spares. The shaft can be removed, after taking off the cam assembly, by driving out the pin and removing the drive dog.

3:6 Setting the ignition timing

The timing should be set statically first and then checked with the engine running, using a stroboscopic light. On models fitted with carburetters, the static setting is sufficiently accurate but on models fitted with fuel injection a stroboscopic light must be used afterwards.

Typical timing marks are shown in **FIG 3:9**. Note that there may be variations.

Crank the engine until No. 1 piston is at TDC on the firing stroke, using the alternator belt. Set the engine so that the black mark on the fan is in line with the notch on the fan housing. Disconnect the primary lead from between the distributor and ignition coil and reconnect it with a test lamp in series. Slacken the pinch bolt securing the distributor in the clamp. Switch on the ignition and gently turn the distributor body in either direction until the point is found where the test lamp just goes out, indicating that the contacts have just opened. Tighten the pinch bolt without allowing the distributor body to rotate.

Crank the engine over for two full revolutions, slowing down the rate of turning towards the end of the second revolution. Stop turning the instant that the test lamp goes out. If the timing is correct, the timing marks will again be in alignment.

Stroboscopic method:

Set the static ignition timing. Start the engine and run it until it has reached its normal operating temperature. Stop the engine and connect the stroboscopic lamp as instructed by the makers of the instrument. Set the lamp so that it will shine down onto the timing marks. Slacken the pinch bolt on the distributor slightly and disconnect the vacuum line from the distributor.

Start the engine and clip open the throttle so that the engine is running at a speed of 3500 rev/min. Rotate the distributor body until the red timing mark (32 deg. BTDC) appears in line with the notch in the fan housing. Tighten the distributor pinch bolt and check that the timing has not altered.

3:7 The sparking plugs
Removal:

Slacken the sparking plug using a well fitting box spanner or suitable plug spanner. Use an air line or tyre pump to blow away all loose dirt from around the base of the plug. Fully unscrew the plug, without the aid of leverage on the box spanner. Once the plugs have been removed, store them in order for later examination of the firing ends.

If the plug is stiff, work it in and out as far as possible, gradually unscrewing it further as the threads free. If the plug is very stiff, wrap a piece of rag around the base and soak it with penetrating oil, paraffin, or suitable solvent and leave it overnight before attempting to remove it.

Examination:

The colour and condition of the deposits on the firing ends of the sparking plugs will give a good guide to the conditions inside the combustion chambers. After examining the plugs, throw away any that have badly burnt electrodes or cracked insulators without bothering to have them cleaned or checked.

A light powdery deposit ranging in colour from brown to greyish tan, coupled with light wear on the electrodes, indicates that the conditions are normal. Much city or constant-speed driving will leave the deposits white or yellowish but again this is satisfactory. Such plugs need only cleaning and testing.

If the deposits are wet and black, they are caused by excessive oil entering the combustion chamber (either past worn valve guides and stems or past worn piston rings and bores). Fitting a hotter-running grade of plug may help to alleviate the problem but the only cure is an engine overhaul.

If the deposits are black but dry and fluffy they are caused by incomplete combustion. Excessive idling or incorrectly adjusted fuel system will cause all the plugs to have such deposits. Individual plugs may be defective or there may be a fault in the ignition.

Overheated sparking plugs have a white blistered look about the central insulator and the electrodes will be excessively burnt. If lead-based fuels are used, glints of metal may be seen on the central insulator and electrode. Some possible causes are engine overheating, very weak mixture, incorrectly set ignition timing (or using a very low grade fuel), incorrect grade of plug, or running at high speeds with the car overloaded.

Cleaning, adjusting and testing:

Wash oily sparking plugs in fuel or methylated spirits as oil will cause the abrasive to stick and prevent cleaning. Have the sparking plugs cleaned on an abrasive-blasting machine and then tested under pressure after attention to the electrodes.

Trim the electrodes square with a fine file and adjust them to the correct gap of .7 mm (.028 inch) by bending the side electrode. **Do not bend the central electrode otherwise the insulator will crack.**

In an emergency, the plugs can be cleaned by scrubbing them with a steel-wire brush, though this method is not so effective.

Clean the external portion of the insulator using some suitable harsh solvent. If the threads have not been effectively cleaned by the abrasive-blaster, scrub them with a wire brush so that there are no carbon deposits left.

Installation:

If the threads in the cylinder head are dirty, clean them using a well greased tap. Failing a tap of the correct size, use an old sparking plug with crosscuts down the threads.

Use only graphite grease on the sparking plug threads as any other grease will bake hard with use and lock the plug in place.

Check the sealing gaskets and renew them if they are compressed to less than half their original thickness. Screw the plugs in by hand until they bottom and then tighten them with a torque spanner to a load of 3 to 3.5 kg m (21 to 25 lb ft). If a torque spanner is not available, tighten them by a maximum of half-a-turn from the hand tight position. Great care must be taken not to strip the threads or cross-thread the plug as it is installed, so any stiffness must be investigated immediately. If the threads are stripped, the cylinder head must be removed and Heli-Coil inserts fitted.

3:8 Fault diagnosis

(a) Engine will not start

1 Battery low or discharged, dirty or loose connectors
2 Distributor points dirty or out of adjustment
3 Distributor cap dirty, wet, cracked, or tracking
4 Carbon brush in distributor cap defective
5 Defective low-tension circuit
6 Rotor arm cracked
7 Broken contact breaker spring
8 Contacts stuck open
9 Water on HT leads
10 Defective ignition coil
11 Defective capacitor
12 Rotor arm omitted on reassembly

(b) Engine misfires

1 Check 2, 3, 5 and 10 in (a)
2 Weak contact breaker spring
3 Defective HT lead
4 Sparking plug defective, fouled, loose, or incorrectly set
5 Ignition too far advanced

CHAPTER 4

THE COOLING SYSTEM

4:1 Description

4:2 Heater

4:3 Winter precautions

4:4 Alternator belt tension

4:5 Thermostatic control

4:6 Fault diagnosis

4:1 Description

The engine is aircooled and therefore many of the parts required for a watercooled engine are not required. This not only simplifies the system but reduces cold weather precautions to a minimum. The car can be left out in the coldest weather without any danger of coolant freezing and damaging the engine. There is the disadvantage that the thickness of material around the cylinders is reduced and therefore the engine will sound noisier than a conventional one.

The components of the cooling system are shown in **FIG 4:1**. The cooling fan 11 is mounted on the engine crankshaft and draws cold air in from outside the car. The action of the fan blows air outwards and the fan housing ducts the air so that it blows over the cylinders and cylinder heads. Baffles are fitted to ensure that all four cylinders are evenly cooled.

The two outlets of the fan front housing are fitted with thermostatically controlled flap valves. The thermostat 55 senses the temperature of the air coming from the engine and controls the flaps. This ensures that when the engine is cold, the flaps are closed and the cooling air flow is restricted. The engine warms up rapidly with the flaps opening progressively to ensure that the engine does not overheat. The thermostat is designed to 'fail-safe' so that if it is defective the flaps will be left open continuously. This ensures that the engine will not overheat but it does mean that the engine will take a long time to reach its normal operating temperature.

The heating system is shown in **FIG 4:2**. Air is blown through the heat exchangers on the engine exhaust pipes and it then passes through a fuel-fired heater before entering the car. An optional time switch can be fitted which switches on the fuel-fired heater and runs it for 10 minutes at a pre-set time. This gasoline-fired heater can be used at any time, even with the engine not running, but because of the drain on the battery running time is limited to 10 minutes.

One drive belt is fitted and this drives the alternator only, as there is no water pump and the fan is attached to the crankshaft.

4:2 Heater

If there are faults in the fuel-fired heater the owner should not attempt to service or repair the unit but should take the car to a VW agent. A safety switch, shown in **FIG 4:3**, is mounted in the engine compartment. If the heater fails, leave it for three minutes and then pull the lever

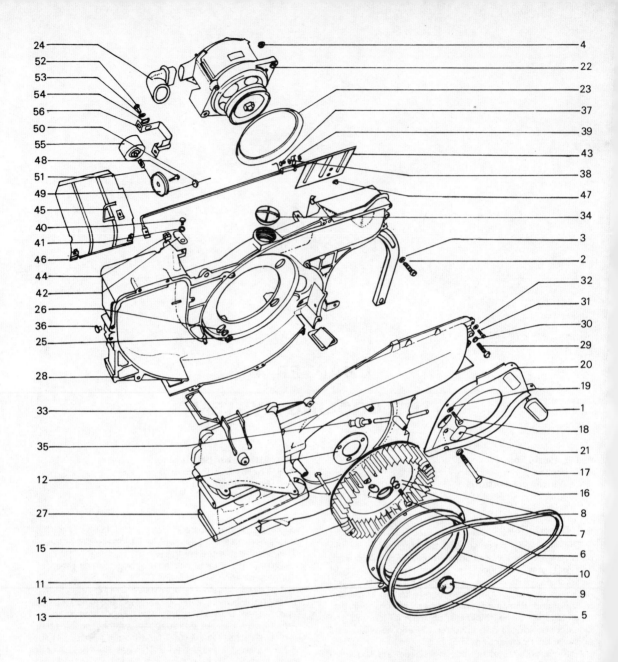

FIG 4:1 The components of the engine cooling system

Key to Fig 4:1 1 Coverplate insert 2 Socket head screw 3 Spring washer 4 Hexagon nut 5 Belt 6 Socket head screw 7 Spring washer 8 Flat washer 9 Cap 10 Crankshaft pulley 11 Fan 12 Spacer 13 Square nut 14 Spring washer 15 Socket head screw 16 Hexagon head bolt 17 Spring washer 18 Cheese head screw 19 Spring washer 20 Coverplate 21 Dipstick grommet 22 Alternator 23 Sealing ring 24 Elbow 25 Nut 26 Spring washer 27 Rear half of fan housing 28 Front half of fan housing 29 Bolt 30 Spring washer 31 Cheese head screw 32 Spring washer 3 Air non-return flap 34 Inspection hole cover 35 Boot for dipstick 36 Plug 37 Bolt 38 Washer 39 Square nut 40 Cheese head screw 41 Spring washer 42 Shaft retaining spring 43 Righthand flap with shaft 44 Bearing 45 Flap link 46 Lefthand flap 47 Plug 48 Hexagon head bolt 49 Roller for cooling air cable 50 Sealing washer 51 Cooling air control cable 52 Hexagon head bolt 53 Washer 54 Washer for thermostat 55 Thermostat 56 Thermostat bracket

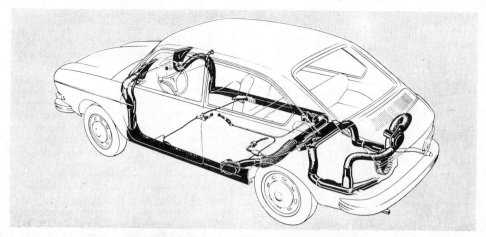

FIG 4:2   The layout of the interior heating system

arrowed to the rear and release it again. If the heater still fails to operate or if it cuts out again within a short period there is a defect and the car should be taken to a VW agent.

Levers on the floor between the front seats control the distribution of the air between footwells and car and further levers on the facia control the air distribution between vents and windscreen.

A rotary knob controls the operation of the fuel-fired heater. Turning the knob to the right turns on the heater and further movement progressively controls the amount of heat produced. The warning lamp which lights when the heater is actually operating is connected into the circuit so that it dims when the parking lights or headlamps are on. It should be noted that when the heater is switched off the lamp will go out but the fan will continue to run for a short period to cool the heater.

The heater may be used without running the engine, but an internal clockwork timer will shut it off after approximately 10 minutes running, to avoid undue drain on the battery.

In summer or warm climates, the heater should be run for at least 10 minutes every 2 months. This ensures that the unit is purged so that there is no build-up of gum.

When refuelling the car, switch off the heater. There is no need to wait until the fan run-down has ceased but the operating light must be off.

4:3 Winter precautions

No special precautions are needed on the cooling system itself, apart from checking that the thermostatically controlled flaps are operating correctly. However this does not mean that antifreeze can be forgotten utterly.

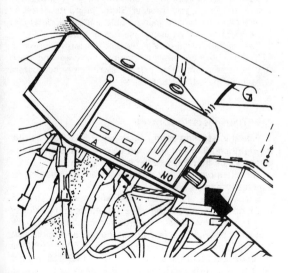

FIG 4:3   The safety switch for the fuel fired heater unit

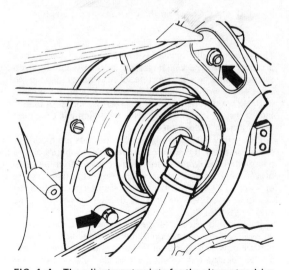

FIG 4:4   The adjustment points for the alternator drive belt

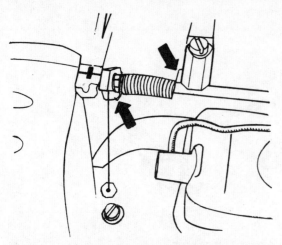

FIG 4:5 The correct installation of the thermostatically controlled linkage retaining spring

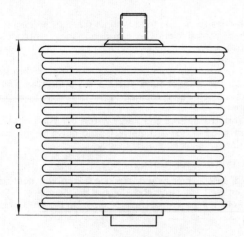

FIG 4:6 Checking the thermostat expansion

The screen washer is filled with water and if precautions are not taken this will freeze up in cold weather. Even worse, it may be just cold enough for the windscreen to be ice cold without the washer water having frozen and in these conditions, use of the screen washer produces a film of instant ice on the windscreen which will only melt when the car has warmed up.

Proprietary special antifreeze compounds are made for screen washers. If these are not available, a mixture of one part methylated spirits (denatured alchohol) to three parts of water will protect against freezing down to a temperature of —12°C (+10°F). Do not use antifreeze which is for use in watercooled engines, as this will leave the glass very smeared.

If the car is used after heavy snow falls, clear away snow from the air intake grilles below the windscreen and rear window so that the ventilation system and air cooling are not obstructed. While clearing the snow, also clear the grilles at the rear end of the body sides as these allow stale air to pass out from the car.

Additional precautions:

These are not connected with the cooling system but it is convenient to list them all under one heading.

For cold weather it is advisable to use a thinner grade oil in the engine so that it starts more easily. The various grades recommended are in **Chapter 1, Section 1:3**. In arctic climates the transmission oil may be changed from SAE.90 to SAE.80, to reduce the drag in the transmission, but this only applies to arctic conditions and need not be carried out normally.

Winter tyres may be used in conditions of ice and snow and the fitting of studded tyres will ensure grip under practically all conditions. If chains are fitted, make sure that they do not stand proud of the tyre wall by more than .6 inch (15 mm) at any point. If chains are fitted to the front wheels as well, though this should very rarely be needed, do not turn the steering to full lock in case the chains foul on the chassis.

The only other point to remember is the battery, which loses efficiency when cold and at the same time has greater demands made on it. A monthly boost on a trickle charger will ensure that it is at full capacity. The battery is inside the car and therefore partially protected from extremes of temperature but in extremely cold climates it will be found that starting is easier if the battery is removed and stored in a warm room overnight.

When the engine has started, drive off. Do not try to warm the engine by running it at idle. While the engine is cold do not race it but otherwise drive the car normally for the least wear and most rapid warm-up.

4:4 Alternator belt tension

The belt tension is correct when it can be depressed by approximately .6 inch (15 mm) at the centre of its run when firm thumb pressure is applied.

If the belt is too tight it will cause damage to the alternator bearings and if it is too slack it will allow the alternator to slip and not produce its full output. At the same time as checking the tension, make sure that the belt is not fraying or greasy. Slight amounts of oil or grease can be removed using a mild and weak detergent but under no circumstances use fuel or paraffin.

The method of adjusting the belt tension is shown in **FIG 4:4**. Slacken the attachments arrowed and push the generator until the belt tension is correct before tightening the attachments.

4:5 Thermostatic control

Free the retaining spring, arrowed in **FIG 4:5**, so that the righthand flap and shaft can be removed. Unhook the lefthand side flap and free the control cable.

The thermostat itself can be removed after freeing its attachments to its bracket.

Suspend the thermostat in a container of water, so that it does not contact the sides or bottom, and gradually heat the water while stirring with a thermometer. Check that air bubbles do not leak out of the unit and check that it expands as it heats. At a temperature of 60 to 70°C the minimum length of the thermostat, 'a' in **FIG 4:6**, should be 1.8 inch (46 mm). Renew the thermostat if it is defective.

Lubricate all pivot points with molybdenum disulphide paste and install the parts in the reverse order of removal. Make sure that the return spring is correctly fitted as shown in **FIG 4 : 5**. Clamp the cable so that the valves are shut when the thermostat is cold.

4 : 6 Fault diagnosis

(a) Engine runs cool, warms up slowly

1 Cooling thermostat defective
2 Linkage sticking or flaps jammed in open position

(b) Engine overheats

1 Air leakage past dipstick or sparking plug seals
2 Air leakage past defective joints
3 Excessive dirt or oil on cooling fins

4 Low engine oil level
5 Mixture too weak
6 Retarded ignition
7 Choked exhaust
8 Binding brakes
9 Slipping clutch
10 Tight engine

(c) Heater ineffective

Determine which portion of the heating system is not operating. If the fuel-fired heater is not operating, take the car to a VW agent.

1 Check (a)
2 Control cables incorrectly set or broken
3 Ducts and pipes disconnected or leaking

CHAPTER 5

THE CLUTCH

5:1 Description
5:2 Maintenance
5:3 Adjustments
5:4 The slave cylinder
5:5 The master cylinder

5:6 Bleeding the hydraulic system
5:7 Release mechanism
5:8 The clutch
5:9 Fault diagnosis

5:1 Description

All the models covered by this manual are fitted with a single dry-plate hydraulically-operated clutch.

A sectioned view through the clutch is shown in **FIG 5:1**. The clutch cover assembly 4 is bolted to the engine flywheel and therefore rotates with it. The driven plate of the clutch has an internally splined hub which fits onto the splines of the transmission input shaft so that they revolve together.

When the clutch is engaged, the diaphragm spring in the cover assembly forces the pressure plate forwards so that it grips the driven plate, by its friction linings, between the face of the pressure plate and the face of the engine flywheel. The driven plate then revolves with the cover and flywheel, transmitting drive to the transmission.

When the clutch pedal is pressed, hydraulic pressure is generated by the master cylinder and this pressure is led by a system of pipes to the slave cylinder mounted on the flywheel housing. The pressure forces out the piston and pushrod of the slave cylinder. The pushrod acts on the withdrawal lever 2 and this in turn presses the release bearing 3 forwards. The release bearing acts on the fingers of the diaphragm spring so that the spring pivots about rings in the cover and the outside of the

diaphragm spring releases the pressure on the pressure plate. The driven plate and transmission input shaft are then free to rotate independently, or even come to a stop with the engine still running.

When the clutch pedal is released, there is a progressive increase of pressure on the driven plate. At first there is slip but then the driven plate revolves at the same speed as the engine, ensuring a smooth take-up of drive.

5:2 Maintenance

Regular adjustments are not required but the fluid level in the master cylinder reservoir should be checked. A typical reservoir for a standard model is shown in **FIG 5:2**.

This type of reservoir is divided into three compartments so that filling it up to the level shown ensures that the braking system, as well as the clutch, has the correct amount of fluid. **Do not fill the reservoir higher than the level shown.**

As the reservoir is translucent there is no need to remove the filler cap for checking. If the level is low, **clean the filler cap and top before removing the cap.** If there is a regular or excessive drop in fluid level, check the system carefully for leaks.

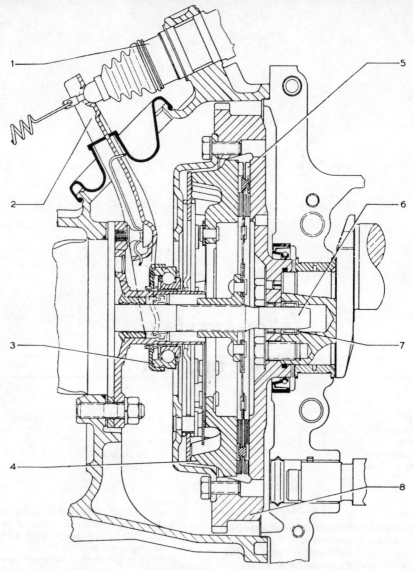

FIG 5:1 Sectioned view of the clutch assembly

Key to Fig 5:1   1 Clutch slave cylinder   2 Clutch withdrawal lever   3 Clutch release bearing   4 Diaphragm spring clutch
5 Clutch pressure plate   6 Main drive shaft   7 Needle roller bearing   8 Flywheel

On models fitted with a brake booster unit, the reservoir for the clutch is mounted separately and slightly higher up.

5:3 Adjustments

For satisfactory operation it is essential that the correct pedal and master cylinder clearances are set.

There should be a total pedal travel of 7.1 inch (180 mm). The setting of the stop for the clutch pedal is shown in **FIG 5:3**. Remove the rubber stop on the bolt and pull back the rubber bellows from around the master cylinder, also shown in the figure. Slacken the locknuts on the pushrod, shown in **FIG 5:4**, and adjust the pushrod to

approximately $3\frac{3}{4}$ inch (95 mm), ensuring that there is a large clearance **S**. If need be, slacken the master cylinder mounting bolts, push the master cylinder firmly towards the pushrod and tighten the attachments to a torque of 58 to 65 lb ft (8 to 9 kg m).

Adjust the length of the stop bolt for the pedal so that the dimension **S2** is correct at .9 inch (22.5 mm), and refit the rubber cap. Adjust the length of the pushrod in the master cylinder so that the gap **S** is correct at .04 inch (1 mm). The gap itself cannot be measured but will be correct when the pedal free play, felt by hand, is $\frac{1}{4}$ inch (6 to 7 mm). The length of the pushrod assembly will then be close to the standard dimension of 3.98 inch (101 mm). Tighten the locknuts and refit the rubber bellows.

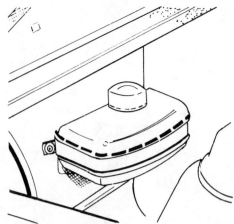

FIG 5:2 Typical hydraulic reservoir, showing the maximum level mark

5:4 The slave cylinder

Removal:

Syphon out the fluid from the reservoir and open the bleed screw on the slave cylinder. Attach a length of rubber tubing to the bleed screw, open the bleed screw and pump the clutch pedal until the system is empty.

Disconnect the hydraulic line from the slave cylinder. The attachments of the unit are shown in **FIG 5:5**. Free the retaining ring 2 and disconnect the return spring 1. Pull back the rubber bellows 5 and remove the circlip 3. The slave cylinder can now be removed from the flywheel housing.

Install the unit in the reverse order of removal, but once it is fitted bleed the hydraulic system as described in **Section 5:6**.

Servicing:

The components of the slave cylinder are shown in **FIG 5:6**. Remove the rubber bellows. Pull out the internal parts of the unit from the bore of the cylinder. Pull the pushrod out of the piston, overcoming the pressure of the spring ring 5, and remove the old seals 7 from the piston 6.

Service kits of parts are available, and the old parts should be discarded. Any suitable solvent may be used to wash the metal parts but great care must be taken to ensure that they are free of all traces of solvent before reassembling the parts. If fuel or paraffin are used for cleaning, or similar slow-evaporating or trace-leaving solvents is used, swill the parts in methylated spirits as this is the only solvent that will not contaminate rubber and seals.

Check the bore of the cylinder for wear, corrosion or scores. Renew the unit complete if the bore is found to be defective.

Wet the new seals with hydraulic fluid (ATE Blau) and fit them back onto the piston. Use no other tools than the fingers and rotate the seals so that they are fully and squarely seated. Make sure that the lips of the seals face in the correct directions.

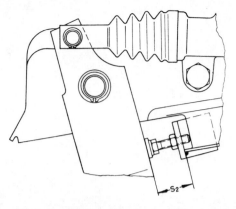

FIG 5:3 Adjusting the clutch pedal stop bolt

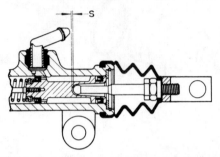

FIG 5:4 Adjusting the master cylinder pushrod

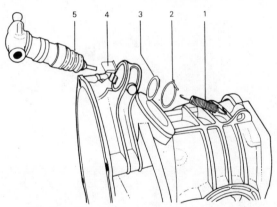

FIG 5:5 The attachments of the slave cylinder

Key to Fig 5:5 1 Return spring 2 Retaining ring 3 Circlip 4 Spring clip 5 Slave cylinder

Wet the internal parts in clean hydraulic fluid and press the pushrod back into the piston. Carefully enter the internal parts back into the bore, taking especial care not to bend back or damage the lips of the seals.

5:5 The master cylinder

The components of the master cylinder are shown in **FIG 5:7**. Before removing the master cylinder, empty the system by syphoning out the reservoir and pumping the fluid out through the bleed screw on the slave cylinder.

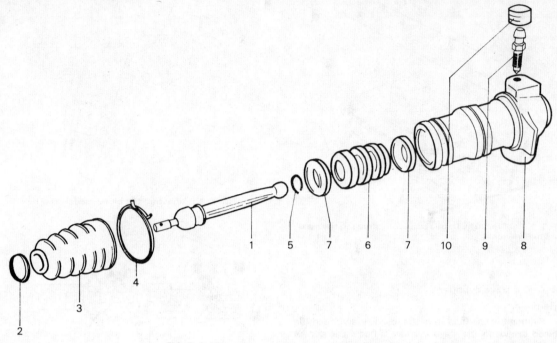

FIG 5:6 The components of the slave cylinder

Key to Fig 5:6 1 Pushrod 2 Retaining ring 3 Rubber bellows 4 Retaining ring 5 Spring ring 6 Piston 7 Cup seal
8 Cylinder 9 Bleed screw 10 Dust cap

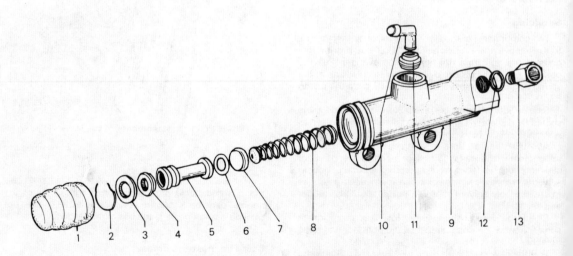

FIG 5:7 The components of the master cylinder

Key to Fig 5:7 1 Rubber boot 2 Spring ring 3 Stop ring 4 Secondary cup 5 Piston 6 Cup washer 7 Primary cup
8 Spring and spring retainer 9 Cylinder body 10 Connection elbow 11 Sealing plug 12 Seal 13 Residual pressure valve

Disconnect the hose between unit and reservoir and undo the hydraulic line. **Take care to catch any fluid spillage with rags, as it rapidly softens and removes paint.** Pull back the rubber bellows, remove the attachment bolts and remove the master cylinder from the car.

The internal parts of the master cylinder can be removed after taking out the spring ring 2 and removing the stop washer 3. The servicing instructions for the slave cylinder apply equally to the master cylinder (see previous section).

When installing the master cylinder, slacken the locknuts on the pushrod assembly and shorten it to ensure adequate clearance. Check the pedal stop adjustment and set the pushrod clearance. Once the master cylinder is fully in place, bleed the hydraulic system as described in the next section.

5:6 Bleeding the hydraulic system

This is required when air has entered the system, either by accident or when the system has been dismantled.

Use only fresh fluid for bleeding the system (ATE Blau or one meeting specifications SAE.70.R3) and discard fluid that has been bled through the system.

Fill the reservoir as full as it will go without spillage at the beginning of the operation and then top up when the level drops to ensure that air is not again drawn into the master cylinder.

Attach a length of rubber or plastic tube to the bleed screw and dip the free end of the tube into a little clean fluid in a glass container.

An assistant is now required. Open the bleed screw by about a ½ turn and have the assistant pump the clutch pedal with full strokes. At first air will come out but as bleeding progresses there will be less and less air. When there is no air coming out of the bleeder tube and the fluid comes out in an unbroken stream with no bubbles in it, close the bleed screw on a downstroke of the pedal. Remove the bleeder tube and have the assistant operate the pedal once more, holding it down at the bottom of the stroke. Check that there are no leaks. Top up the reservoir to the correct level.

5:7 Release mechanism

This can only be examined or removed after the engine has been removed from the car (see **Section 1:2** in **Chapter 1**) or if the transmission has been removed.

Remove the slave cylinder and take off the rubber boot around the withdrawal lever. Refer to **FIG 5:1**, and free the release bearing 3. Pull the withdrawal fork 2 off from the ball-headed pin.

The release bearing is sealed and must not be washed in any solvent. Check the bearing for noisy or rough operation and examine the thrust face for undue wear. Renew the bearing complete if any defect is found.

Check the withdrawal lever for wear, distortion or cracking (renewing it if defective). The ball-head of the pin is protected by the lever but still check the spherical surface for scores or wear.

The parts are installed in the reverse order of removal. Bearing and pivot surfaces should be lightly lubricated with zinc-oxide grease or molybdenum disulphide paste.

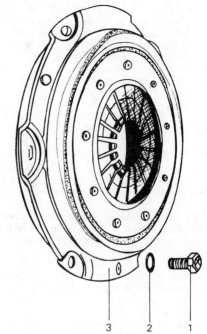

FIG 5:8 The clutch cover assembly

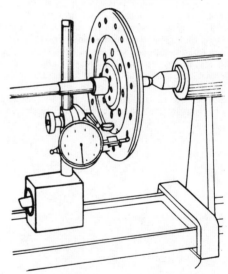

FIG 5:9 Checking the runout of the driven plate

5:8 The clutch

The removal and installation of the clutch is dealt with in **Chapter 1, Section 1:9**.

Cover assembly:

A typical cover asssmbly and its attachment bolts are shown in **FIG 5:8**. If there is any defect, the unit cannot be dismantled and it must be renewed.

Check the cover for cracks or distortion, paying particular attention to the areas around rivets and attachment holes. Use an air line and brush to remove dirt. If there is oil on the unit, do not soak it in solvent but wipe off the oil with a cloth moistened with solvent.

Check the face of the pressure plate for burn marks or scores. Very minor damage should be smoothed down with a fine grade of emerycloth.

Check the assembly for general wear. If the rings in which the diaphragm spring pivots are worn, renew the assembly.

Driven plate:

Check the linings for excessive wear or contamination and check the unit for wear or mechanical faults, renewing it if any defect is found. Riveting on new linings is not recommended.

The linings must be standing well clear of the rivets and the rivets must be securely holding the linings in place. Check the hub for wear on the splines or breakage of its attachments.

For maximum efficiency the linings should have a polished surface through which the grain of the friction material is clearly visible. Oil, grease or paint on the clutch linings will cause poor operation. Small amounts of oil will burn off to leave dark coloured smears, while larger amounts will give a dark glaze to the surface. Excessive oil leaks will be obvious from the soaked appearance of the linings and the free oil in the housing. The driven plate can be used again provided that the grain of the friction material can be seen. If the grain is hidden by a dark glaze then a new driven plate must be fitted. Do not attempt to remove oil or contamination from linings as any treatment sufficiently drastic to be effective will also be drastic enough to ruin the linings.

Before installing the driven plate, mount it on an arbor between centres and use a DTI (Dial Test Indicator gauge) to measure the runout on the disc, as shown in

FIG 5:9. The runout should not exceed .020 inch (.5 mm). If the runout is slightly too much, try straightening the disc using a piece of wood with a slot cut in it which fits over the linings.

5:9 Fault diagnosis

(a) Drag or spin

1 Oil or grease on the friction linings
2 Incorrectly adjusted pedal clearance
3 Misalignment between engine and transmission input shaft
4 Leaking slave cylinder, master cylinder, or hydraulic line
5 Binding spigot bearing in crankshaft
6 Distorted driven plate
7 Warped or damaged pressure plate
8 Broken driven plate linings
9 Dirt or foreign matter in clutch
10 Air in the hydraulic system

(b) Fierceness or snatch

1 Check 1, 2, 3 and 4 in (a)
2 Excessively worn clutch linings
3 Worn or loose driven plate hub

(c) Slip

1 Check 1 and 2 in (a) and 2 in (b)
2 Weak diaphragm spring
3 Seized piston in slave cylinder

(d) Judder

1 Check 1, 2 and 3 in (a)
2 Pressure plate not parallel with flywheel
3 Buckled driven plate
4 Faulty or loose power unit mountings
5 Defective suspension

CHAPTER 6

THE GEARBOX AND DIFFERENTIAL

6:1 Description
6:2 Maintenance
6:3 Removing the transmission
6:4 Dismantling the gearbox

6:5 Reassembling the gearbox
6:6 The final drive unit
6:7 Fault diagnosis

6:1 Description

The complete engine, transmission and rear suspension is shown in **FIG 6:1**. A sectioned view of the transmission is shown in **FIG 6:2**. The final drive unit is bolted directly in front of the engine and the gearbox is then bolted directly in front of the final drive unit.

The transmission is a fourspeed unit with synchromesh engagement on all four forward speeds. Synchromesh units with baulk rings are used for synchronizing the drive. Reverse is engaged by sliding an idler gear into mesh.

The final drive unit is of conventional construction using hypoid bevel gears. Drive shafts then transmit the drive from the final drive unit to the road wheels.

Special tools and a press are required for many dismantling and reassembling operations. The correct clearances must be set on reassembly otherwise the unit will not function correctly or quietly. This is particularly applicable to the final drive unit and the owner is strongly advised not to carry out any work on this but to take it to a VW agent who will have the necessary tools and experience.

6:2 Maintenance

The final drive unit and gearbox share the same oil supply. Seasonal or regular changes of oil are not required.

The only time an oil change is required is after running in a new part. During the running-in period the trans-

mission should be filled with special lubricant VW Part No. 004.598.99. This special lubricant is drained out after the first 500 to 750 miles (800 to 1200 kilometres)—preferably at 600 miles (1000 kilometres)—and the transmission then filled with SAE.90.EP oil (meeting specification MIL.L.2105.B). In arctic climates SAE.80.EP oil should be used, meeting the same specification.

The oil level should be checked at intervals of 6000 miles (1000 kilometres). The combined filler and level plug is shown at **B** in **FIG 6:3** (the plug **A** being the drain plug). Wipe the area clean and remove the filler plug. With the car standing on level ground the oil should just come up to the bottom of the filler hole. Top up as required and allow any surplus to drain out before refitting the filler plug. Be sure to use the same brand of oil, as not all brands, though individually suitable, are compatible when mixed.

If the transmission has been drained, fill slowly. The oil is very thick and if the unit is filled rapidly the level will not have time to settle, so that oil will overflow from the filler plug before the unit is actually full.

6:3 Removing the transmission

The complete power unit is removed from the car and the transmission is then separated from the engine. Before starting work, disconnect the battery.

From inside the engine compartment, remove the cooling air intake duct, cooling air intakes and air cleaner.

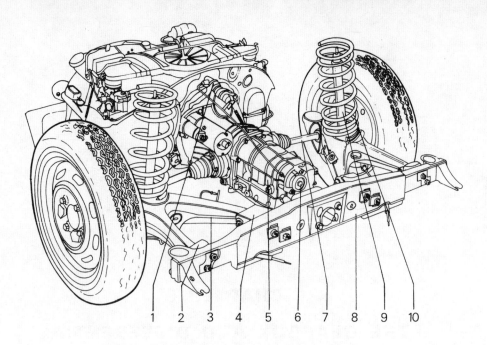

FIG 6:1 The power unit and rear transmission

Key to Fig 6:1 1 Clutch slave cylinder 2 Suspension arm bracket (outer) 3 Suspension arm 4 Suspension arm bracket (inner) 5 Gearbox (transmission) 6 Coverplate 7 Drive shaft 8 Rear axle carrier 9 Shock absorber 10 Coil spring

Disconnect the electrical leads to the starter motor, the low-tension terminal of the ignition coil, and the oil pressure switch. Disconnect and free the accelerator cable. Disconnect the fuel line from the pump, plugging it with a suitable bolt to prevent fuel from syphoning through. Remove the engine compartment seal.

Jack up the rear of the car and support it securely on chassis stands. Remove the control boxes of the interior heating system, from the heat exchangers. Remove the exhaust heat shield. Remove both drive shafts (see **Chapter 8, Section 8:3**). Note that when the drive shafts have been removed, blanking plates must be fitted to prevent dirt entering.

Pull back the rubber bellows and remove the square-headed bolt securing the gearshift mechanism, shown in **FIG 6:4**. A special T-headed spanner, VW.114 is made for the purpose. Leave the front transmission bolts, also arrowed in the figure, for the moment.

Disconnect the fluid line for the clutch slave cylinder, after emptying the system, and blank off the lines to prevent dirt from entering them. Disconnect the reverse light cables and engine earthing strap from the transmission.

Support the power unit on a trolley jack, using a pad of wood to prevent damage. Remove the front transmission mounting bolts arrowed in **FIG 6:4**, and free the engine mountings. Lower the complete unit and withdraw the power unit from under the car.

Remove the starter motor. Take out the bolts securing the transmission to the engine and draw the transmission off from the engine.

Installation:

This is the reversal of the removal procedure.

Before fitting the transmission back onto the engine, check the clutch, clutch release mechanism and spigot bearing in the crankshaft. Lubricate the splines on the input shaft and the release mechanism with a light coating of molybdenum disulphide grease and lubricate the bush for the starter motor with lithium-based grease. Note that the starter motor bush should be renewed if it is defective.

Fit the transmission back to the engine. Support the weight of the transmission while guiding the input shaft back into place, as damage will be caused if the weight of the transmission hangs up by the shaft in the clutch. If the splines do not align, crank the engine until the shaft enters easily. Tighten the transmission to engine attachments to a torque load of 18 lb ft (2.5 kg m).

Install the power unit in the reverse order of removal. Raise the unit into position and alternatively tighten the attachments to a torque of 18 lb ft (2.5 kg m).

Bleed the clutch hydraulic system after the power unit is fully installed (see **Chapter 5, Section 5:6**).

6:4 Dismantling the gearbox

Drain out the oil and loosely refit the drain plug. Remove the clutch release bearing and withdrawal lever. Wash down the outside of the gearbox and final drive unit to remove road dirt.

The components of the gearbox are shown in **FIG 6:5**. Take out the screws 37 and remove the oil sump plate 35 with its gasket 36. Remove the nuts securing the selector

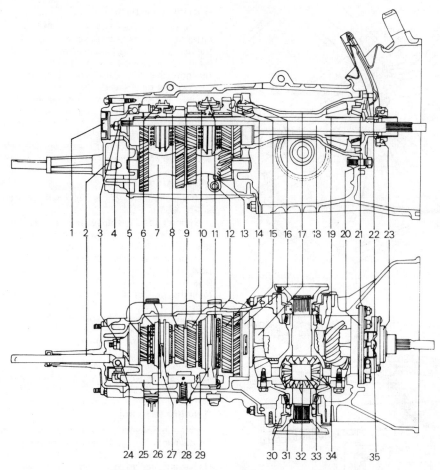

FIG 6:2   Sectioned view of the transmission unit

Key to Fig 6:2   1 Coverplate for selector housing   2 Inner shift lever   3 Drive shaft nut   4 Washer   5 Countershaft drive gear   6 3rd/4th-speed synchronizer hub   7 Countershaft gear cluster   8 3rd-speed gearwheel   9 Spacer   10 2nd-speed gearwheel   11 1st/2nd-speed synchronizer   12 Reverse gear selector shaft   13 Reverse idler gear   14 1st-speed gearwheel   15 Reverse gear   16 Centring ring   17 Mainshaft carrier   18 Drive shaft   19 Mainshaft and drive pinion   20 Pinion shim   21 Mainshaft carrier cover   22 Clutch release lever   23 Clutch release bearing   24 Relay lever   25 3rd/4th-speed selector shaft   26 Oil filler plug   27 3rd/4th-speed selector fork   28 1st/2nd-speed selector shaft   29 1st/2nd speed selector fork   30 Adjusting ring   31 Flange   32 Differential side gear   33 Spacer sleeve   34 Differential pinion   35 Release lever pivot pin

housing 42. Select reverse gear and draw the selector housing off its studs as far as it will go. Tilt the housing upwards allowing the relay lever to clear the first and second-speed selector rod, and the selector housing can be removed. The relay lever and gasket can then be removed from the housing.

Take out the bearing pins 29 and their washers 30 and pull the reverse sliding gear fully forwards so that the selector shaft and gearchange segment can be removed.

Engage reverse gear and a forward gear, by hand, so that the gearbox is locked and the parts cannot rotate. Unscrew the self-locking nut 38 from the end of the drive shaft 40. Use a rubber or plastic mallet to tap lightly on the end of the drive shaft so that the lockwasher 39 slips over the taper. Withdraw the drive shaft from the rear. The drive shaft acts as a torsion rod and is finished with a special

protective paint. **Great care must be taken not to damage the surface of the drive shaft, or break the paint film, otherwise corrosion or weak points may form (which will cause the drive shaft to break in service).**

A threaded piece of rod, spacer tube, washer and nut are now required. Screw the rod, which should have a thread of 10 mm diameter and be of approximately $3\frac{1}{2}$ inch (90 mm) long, into the end of the countershaft. Fit a suitable piece of tube over the threaded rod and then fit the washer. Screw on a nut and by tightening the nut down onto the washer and spacer tube the countershaft will be withdrawn. Allow the countershaft gear cluster and thrust washers to slide out of position.

Ease out the screws 19 securing the coverplate 18 and its gasket 17. **Take care as the springs 16 are under**

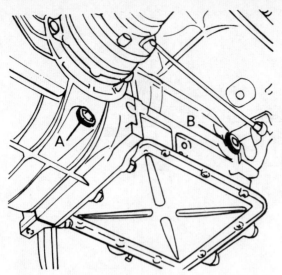

FIG 6:3 The transmission unit drain and filler plugs

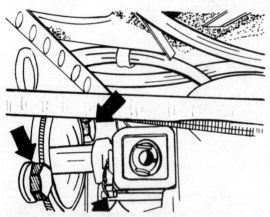

FIG 6:4 The gearshift rod attachment, note wire locking. Also shown are the transmission front attachments

pressure and may fly out. Once the cover is off, remove the springs 16 and withdraw the detent plungers 15. Pull out the reverse lever, turn it through 90 deg. and remove the rocker lever 31.

Slacken the square-headed bolts 10 securing the selector forks 9 and 7 to the selector shafts 6 and 8. Withdraw all three selector shafts from the gearbox, taking care to collect the interlock pin and plunger 11 and 12.

Remove the nuts securing the gearbox to the final drive unit. Make up some form of plate as shown in **FIG 6:5** and mount it onto the studs of the gearbox casing. Use a slide hammer attached to the plate to carefully draw off the gearbox casing from the final drive unit. Check at frequent intervals that the gearwheels on the mainshaft assembly are not catching on the casing and that they have adequate clearance.

Gearbox case parts:

The gearbox case is shown in **FIG 6:7**. Remove the circlip 3 and drive out the countershaft drive gear 2 with the aid of a suitable drift. The bearing itself can be removed from the gear with the aid of a suitable extractor, but note that the sealed side of the bearing must face towards the gearwheel on reassembly.

Use a M8 x 150 mm stud, tube spacer, washer, and nut to draw out the reverse idler gearshaft 5. Note that the longest screw securing the sump cover in place also locates the reverse idler shaft.

The filler plug and the reverse light switch 7 should also be removed from the casing.

Mainshaft assembly:

The components of the mainshaft assembly are shown in **FIG 6:8**.

Support the final drive unit so that the mainshaft is vertical. Use a screwdriver to remove the retainer 14 and then use circlip pliers to remove the circlip 13.

A suitable extractor, thrust piece and circlip pliers are now required, as shown in **FIG 6:9**. The hooks of the legs must engage under the centring ring. Spread the retaining ring of the centring ring with external circlip pliers, as arrowed in the figure, and then start to pull off the mainshaft gears. Keep pulling until the reverse gear contacts the splines, then release the pressure and turn the reverse gear until it is aligned with the splines and can be pulled off.

When removing the synchromesh units, keep them in one piece and make sure that the baulk rings are correctly identified for position.

Synchromesh units:

The components of the units are shown in **FIG 6:10**. To dismantle the unit, remove the springs and pull the sleeve of the hub (collecting the keys). The hub and sleeve are marked with etched lines which, when they index, show the position of optimum fit and minimum backlash. **Take care not to interchange the sleeves between the two units.**

Selector housing:

The components of the selector housing are shown in **FIG 6:11**. The method of removing the relay shaft, after taking out the screw 8, is shown in **FIG 6:12**. The bushes 5 and 6 can then be removed using a screwdriver on bush 5 and a pair of pliers on bush 6, if they are worn or damaged.

6:5 Reassembling the gearbox

Selector housing:

Refer to **FIG 6:11**. Special tools are required for pressing a new split bush back into position, but if care is taken a suitably sized piece of rod and press may be used. Check the fit of the inner shift lever in the split bush and only if the lever is stiff to rotate should the bush be reamed. Ream to a diameter of .5917 to .5925 inch (15.03 to 15.05 mm) only if necessary.

The remainder of the parts are installed in the reverse order of removal but metal should be peened into the slot of the screw 8 to lock it in position.

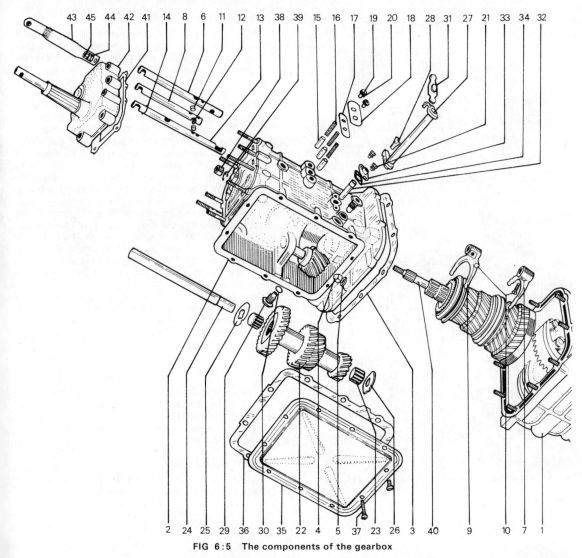

FIG 6:5   The components of the gearbox

Key to Fig 6:5   1 Final drive case   2 Gearbox (transmission case)   3 Gearbox case gasket   4 Dome nut   5 Washer   6 1st/2nd-speed selector shaft   7 1st/2nd-speed selector fork   8 3rd/4th-speed selector shaft   9 3rd/4th-speed selector shaft   10 Square-headed bolt   11 Interlock pin   12 Interlock plunger   13 Reverse speed selector shaft   14 Circlip   15 Gear detent plunger   16 Gear detent spring   17 Coverplate gasket   18 Coverplate   19 Screw   20 Lockwasher   21 Screw   22 Counter-shaft gear cluster   23 Needle roller bearing   24 Countershaft   25 Thrust washer   26 Thrust washer   27 Reverse speed shift rod   28 Reverse change segment   29 Bearing pin   30 Washer   31 Rocker lever   32 Eccentric pin   33 Knurled cap   34 Gasket   35 Oil sump   36 Oil sump gasket   37 Lock screw   38 Locknut   39 Lockwasher   40 Drive shaft   41 Selector housing gasket   42 Selector housing   43 Earth strap   44 Spring washer   45 Nut

Synchromesh units:

Wash the parts in clean solvent and check them for wear or damage. Slide the sleeve back onto the hub, so that the alignment marks are in line, and check that the sleeve slides freely without excessive rotational play.

Check the play of the selector fork in the annular groove of the sleeve. The clearance should be .027 to .039 inch (.69 to .99 mm) but no action need be taken provided that the wear limit of .047 inch (1.2 mm) is not exceeded.

Fit the baulk rings back into their original positions and measure the clearance 'a' shown in **FIG 6:13**. The tolerance for first/second gear is .040 to .069 inch (1.0 to 1.75 mm) and that for the third/fourth synchronizer is .047 to .077 inch (1.2 to 1.95 mm). If the wear is such that the clearance is less than .020 inch (.5 mm) in either case then parts must be renewed.

The units are reassembled in the reverse order of dismantling, making sure that the marks on the faces align, and the springs are offset so that their gaps are not in line.

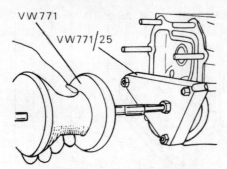

FIG 6:6 Withdrawing the gearbox casing

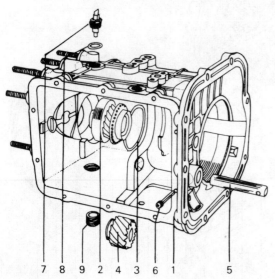

FIG 6:7 The components of the gearbox casing

Key to Fig 6:7

		1	Gearbox case
2	Countershaft drive gear	3 Circlip	4 Reverse idler gear
5	Reverse idler gear shaft		6 Shaft locating screw
7	Reversing light switch	8 Washer	9 Oil filler plug

Mainshaft assembly:

Check all the gears for worn or damaged teeth. Check the bushes for wear or fret marks and also check the shaft at the same time. While checking the mainshaft gears, also check all the other gears.

Heat the centring ring to a temperature of 100°C (in boiling water). Fit the centring ring back onto the mainshaft so that the two lugs engage in the carrier and at the same time spread the circlip, as shown in **FIG 6:14**.

Heat the reverse gear 2 (see **FIG 6:8**) in boiling water and when it is hot fit it back into place with the narrow shoulder downwards. Drive the gear fully into place with the aid of a suitable piece of tube.

If new parts are being fitted, the assembly should be taken to a VW agent so that the end float of the gears can be accurately set, by selectively fitting the spacer ring 9. A special tool, VW.390, is required for setting the end float and it is unlikely that the average owner will have access to this tool. The tool is fitted as shown in **FIG 6:15**. The DTI (Dial Test Indicator) is zeroed to a preload of 1 mm and is then used to check the clearance **A** shown in **FIG 6:16**. The correct size and part number spacer washer is then selected.

Once the correct spacer washer has been selected, the remainder of the parts are installed in the reverse order of removal. The first/second-speed synchromesh unit must be fitted so that the annular groove is pointing towards the second-speed gearwheel (upwards when the shaft is vertical). The bush 10 for the third-speed gearwheel must be heated in boiling water before it can be fitted. The annular groove of the third/fourth synchromesh unit must be towards the four-speed gearwheel. Note that the circlip must be fitted so that its gap is by the recess for the key, as shown in **FIG 6:17**. When all the parts are on place, fit a new gasket to the final drive ready for installing the gearbox casing.

Gearbox case parts:

The parts are shown in **FIG 6:7**. Check the bearing of the countershaft drive gear for wear or noisy operation. The bearing should be washed by rotating it in a bath of clean solvent and then dried with an air line, holding the bearing so that it cannot spin in the airblast. If the bearing

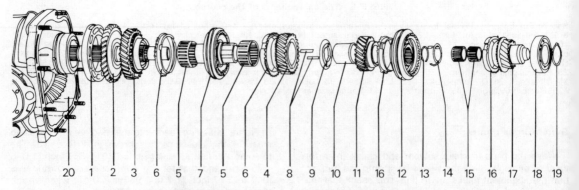

FIG 6:8 The gearbox mainshaft components

Key to Fig 6:8 1 Centring ring 2 Mainshaft reverse gear 3 1st-speed gearwheel 4 2nd-speed gearwheel 5 Needle roller bearing 6 1st/2nd-speed baulk rings 7 1st/2nd-speed synchronizer unit 8 Spacer ring plate 9 Spacer ring 10 3rd-speed gearwheel bush 11 3rd-speed gearwheel 12 3rd/4th-speed synchronizer unit 13 Circlip 14 Retainer for circlip 15 Needle bearing 16 3rd/4th-speed baulk rings 17 Countershaft drive gear 18 Drive gear ballbearing 19 Lockring 20 Final drive case has been removed, press it back onto the gear so that the sealed end faces the gearwheel. Install the drive gear assembly back into the casing and secure it with the circlip.

Drive the reverse idler gearshaft 5 back into place, fitting the reverse idler gearwheel onto it. The groove for the selector in the reverse idler must be on the front of the gear. Remember that the shaft is held in place by the long stop bolt which also secures the sump plate, so make sure that the hole in the shaft aligns with the hole in the casing.

The reverse light switch is fitted, using a new sealing washer, and should be tightened to a torque of 14 lb ft (2 kg m). Temporarily refit the filler and drain plugs, after wiping the magnetic drain plug clean, noting that the drain plug is the final drive unit.

Drive the casing back into place on the final drive unit. Use a rubber mallet and make sure that parts do not 'hang-up'. Fit the washers and dome nuts, tightening the dome nuts to a torque of 14 lb ft (2 kg m). Make sure that a new gasket is fitted between the two housings.

Turn the transmission over and insert back into place the selector shafts, interlocks and forks. Start with the selector shaft 6, and pick up the selector fork 7 on the shaft positioning the fork so that it fits into the groove of the first/second-speed synchromesh unit. Secure the fork to the shaft by tightening the square-headed bolt to a torque of 14 lb ft (2 kg m). Fit the interlock pin 11 back into place before fitting the next shaft. Install the third/fourth selector parts in a similar manner. Install the interlock plunger 12 and remaining pin 11, pushing them fully into place. Set both the fitted selector shafts into their neutral positions and install the reverse selector shaft and the rocker lever 31. The rocker lever must be installed with the longer end towards the opening in the casing and the crank towards the side, as shown in **FIG 6:18**.

Hold the countershaft gear cluster thrust washers 24 and 25 in position in the casing using thick grease. Check the needle roller bearings in the cluster for wear, renewing them if required. Ease the gear cluster into position between the thrust washers, make sure that it and the thrust washers are aligned, and slide the countershaft 24 back into position to secure the parts. Check the meshing of

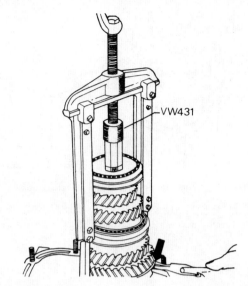

FIG 6:9 Removing the mainshaft gears. Note the method of opening the circlip

the gear on the countershaft cluster with that of the second-speed gearwheel on the mainshaft. The gears must align centrally as shown in **FIG 6:19**. If new parts have been fitted the gears may align as shown on either side of the figure. Fit the thrust washers so that the gears mesh correctly as in the central illustration. Two thicknesses of thrust washer are available and a thick one should be fitted on one side with a thin one on the other, so that a pair of thrust washers of equal thickness is never used.

Fit the detent plungers 15, springs 16 and secure them in place using a new gasket 17 and the coverplate 18. A sectioned view of the detent assembly and interlock parts is shown in **FIG 6:20**. Use a spring balance to check the pull required to move each rod in turn from its neutral position. The maximum pull required should be 14 lb

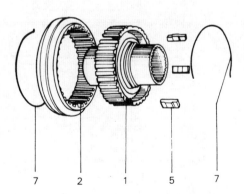

FIG 6:10   The components of the synchromesh units

Key to Fig 6:10 synchromesh hub   1 First/second-speed synchromesh hub   2 First/second-speed operating sleeve   3 Third/fourth-speed
4 Third/fourth-speed operating sleeve   5 Keys   6/7 Springs

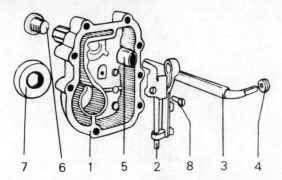

FIG 6:11   The components of the selector housing

Key to Fig 6:11
2 Relay lever and shaft   1 Selector housing
4 Ball joint/relay lever   5 Guide bush   3 Inner shift lever
7 Coverplate   8 Screw   6 Bush with oil seal

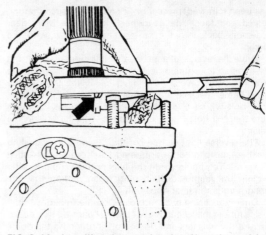

FIG 6:14   Installing the centring ring. Note the position of the lugs which must engage in the carrier

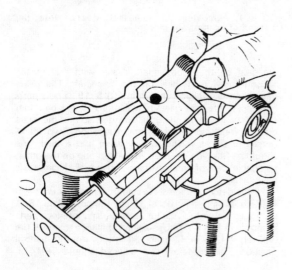

FIG 6:12   Removing the relay shaft from the selector housing

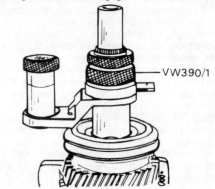

VW390/1

FIG 6:15   The tool for checking the mainshaft gear float

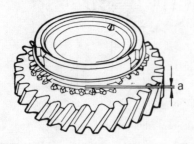

FIG 6:13   Checking the wear on the baulk rings

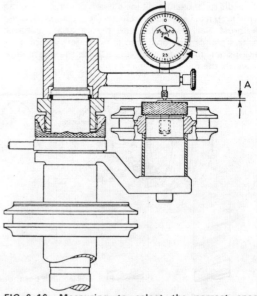

FIG 6:16   Measuring to select the correct spacer washer

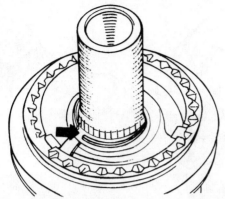

FIG 6:17 The correct positioning of the gap in the circlip

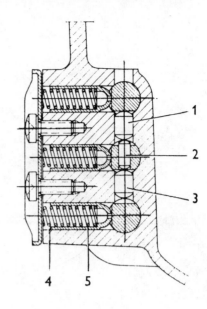

FIG 6:20 Sectioned view through the detent and interlock mechanism

Key to Fig 6:20   1 Upper interlock pin   2 Plunger
3 Lower interlock pin   4 Spring   5 Detent plunger

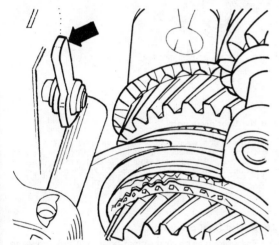

FIG 6:18 Installing the rocker lever with the longer end towards the opening in the casing

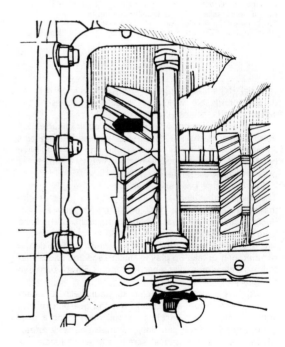

FIG 6:19 The second-speed gears must be adjusted to mesh as shown in the central diagram

FIG 6:21 Adjusting the eccentric pin to set the correct mesh of the reverse idler gear

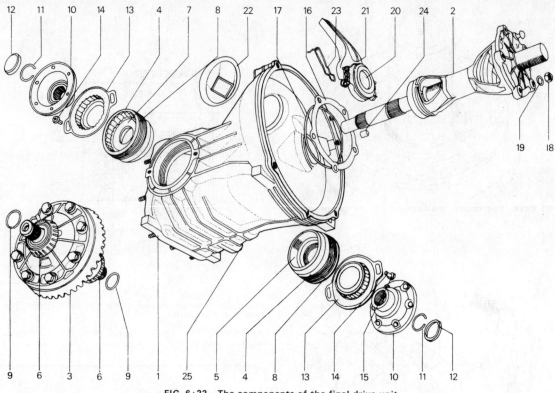

FIG 6:22 The components of the final drive unit

Key to Fig 6:22 1 Final drive case   2 Mainshaft carrier   3 Crownwheel and differential   4 Adjusting ring   5 Taper roller bearing outer race   6 Taper roller bearing inner race   7 Oil seal   8 O-ring   9 Spacer   10 Flange   11 Circlip   12 Cap   13 Lockplate   14 Screw   15 Lockwasher   16 Shim   17 O-ring   18 Nut   19 Spring washer   20 Clutch release bearing   21 Clutch withdrawal lever   22 Bolt   23 Clutch withdrawal lever spring   24 Starter motor bush   25 Oil drain plug

(6.5 kg). If the load required is very low, it is likely that the detent springs are weak or the detent grooves in the selector shafts excessively worn.

Assemble the parts of the reverse selector linkage. Use new sealing washers 30 and note that the bearing pins 31 are only locked when the sump plate and its gasket have been fitted. The sump plate has a notch in it which fits over one apex of the hexagon head.

Select reverse gear and check the mesh of the gears. The reverse idler should be flush with the gear on the mainshaft, as shown in **FIG 6:21**. If the gears are not flush, because of renewal of parts, remove the knurled cap from the eccentric pin and adjust until the correct mesh is set. Move the gear out of mesh and press it towards the centring ring to take up play in the linkage and check that there is a clearance of at least .020 inch (.5 mm) between the gears.

With the transmission inverted, pour fresh lubricant over the gear trains and check that the gearbox rotates and operates freely. Install the sump plate using a new gasket, noting that it can only be fitted one way round. Make sure that the longest screw is fitted to locate the reverse idler shaft and smear the threads of this bolt with jointing compound. Fill the unit once it is fitted to the car.

6:6 The final drive unit

The components of the final drive unit are shown in **FIG 6:22**. The unit can be dismantled and reassembled, provided that all shims are installed back into their original positions, the outer races of the bearing are not interchanged, and the bearing retainers are tightened to exactly their original positions (using index marks and a depth gauge). Even then special tools will be required to remove the mainshaft assembly.

If new parts are fitted it is essential that the correct clearances and tolerances are set. If there is a fault in the final drive unit, the owner should make an arrangement with the local VW agent and take the final drive unit in for repairs and adjustments. Because of the special tools required, it is best to take the complete transmission in, saving money on the removal and installation of the unit and external cleaning operations.

6:7 Fault diagnosis

(a) Noisy operation

1 Incorrect lubricant used
2 Low lubricant level
3 Worn bearings and bushes

4 Incorrect mainshaft gear float
5 Gears not set to mesh correctly
6 Worn or damaged gears

(b) Jumping out of gear

1 Broken or weak spring on selector detent
2 Detent notches in selector shafts excessively worn
3 Worn gears
4 Worn baulk rings
5 Loose fork to shaft attachment bolts
6 Excessive end floats
7 Worn or defective synchromesh units
8 Excessive clearance of selector fork in synchromesh groove

(c) Difficulty in changing gear

1 Defective or excessively worn clutch
2 Defective spigot bearing in crankshaft
3 Defective clutch hydraulic system
4 Defective, worn, or incorrectly assembled synchromesh unit
5 Worn baulk rings
6 Worn or loose selector forks
7 Stiff gearshift mechanism
8 Bent selector shafts
9 Too thick a grade of transmission oil

(d) Oil leaks

1 Unit overfilled
2 Defective gaskets or oil seals
3 Damaged joint faces on castings
4 Attachments not correctly torqued or threads stripped

CHAPTER 7

AUTOMATIC TRANSMISSION

7:1 Description
7:2 Maintenance
7:3 Operation

7:4 Removal and servicing
7:5 Fault diagnosis

7:1 Description

An automatic transmission unit can be fitted in place of the manually operated fourspeed transmission described in the previous chapter. The automatic gives three forward speeds and one reverse with automatic selection of the forward speeds. A selector is fitted in place of the gearlever to select the direction of drive, or neutral, as well as giving some degree of override on the action of the automatic gearbox.

The differential unit is virtually similar to the one fitted with manual transmission, though it has its own separate supply of lubricant. The drive shafts are all of the double-jointed type, as fitted to the later models with manual transmission.

The mechanical clutch is completely dispensed with and a hydraulic torque converter is fitted in its place. The three main components of a torque converter are shown in **FIG 7:1**. In practice the unit is sealed together on manufacture and filled with automatic transmission fluid. Fluid is pumped through the torque converter from the gearbox, and then returns to the gearbox, to ensure that the unit is kept filled at all times. The impeller is integral with the outer casing and as the casing is bolted to the crankshaft the impeller rotates at the same speed as the engine. The stator can revolve freely in one direction but is prevented from rotating in the other direction by a one-directional clutch. On start up or acceleration the impeller is rotating faster than the turbine and a spiral flow of fluid is set up between them. The oil flow follows the path of an imaginary coil spring laid into the annular space between the turbine and impeller, where the blades are actually fitted. The stator locks to the impeller and the resultant flow of oil produces a greater torque on the turbine than is put onto the impeller. This torque then causes the impeller to speed up and the slip between impeller and turbine rapidly decreases. At the same time as the slip decreases so does the torque multiplication factor until there is no torque multiplication and the turbine is running nearly at the same speed as the impeller. There will always be a small speed difference, even in steady running conditions, as some energy is wasted as friction and heat losses. At minimum slip the stator spins freely and the torque converter acts as a fluid flywheel with the spiral oil flow transmitting drive between the impeller and the turbine. From this it can be seen that the torque converter multiplies the torque at high slip (such as when the car is stationary) and then produces a gradually decreasing torque multiplication as the slip decreases (as when the car pulls away) and therefore it acts as a constantly variable ratio gearbox for acceleration or pulling away from rest.

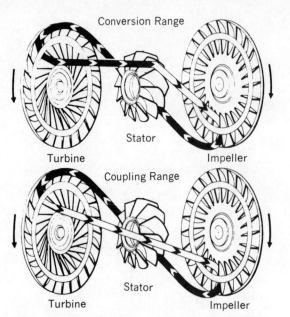

FIG 7:1 The torque converter showing the fluid flow in the two different stages

Slip causes churning and overheating of the oil and therefore the car must not be held stationary on the brakes with drive selected and the throttle open.

The gearbox is fitted with epicyclic gear trains. An epicyclic train consists of a sun gear, planet gears and carrier as well as an outer gear. The outer gear has its teeth on its inside circumference and it is fitted concentrically with the central sun gear. The planet gears are fitted between the teeth of the outer and sun gears so that they are individually free to revolve but rotation between the sun and outer gears draws the planet carrier with them. By holding the different parts stationary a variety of ratios, and even reverse drive, can be obtained. FIG 7:2 shows the difference in speeds between the planet carrier and sun gear if the outer gear is held stationary, while FIG 7:3 shows the method of obtaining a reverse drive of different ratio by holding the planet carrier stationary. If two elements are locked together then the complete unit will lock and it can be used as a direct drive. On the actual gearbox a series of clutches and brake bands lock or release the appropriate elements as required. The brake bands and clutches are applied by hydraulic pressure generated by a pump in the unit. A schematic sectioned view of the gearbox is shown in FIG 7:4.

An extremely complex hydraulic valve system is fitted to control the operation of the brake bands and clutches. The system uses a centrifugal governor to measure the road speed of the car and a vacuum line to the inlet manifold of the engine to sense the position of the throttle and load on the engine. The gear selector can partially override the action of the controls and a kick-down switch is fitted to the throttle linkage to ensure that the maximum speed in each gear is reached when the accelerator pedal is floored.

Dismantling the transmission or carrying out repairs is well beyond the capacity of the owner, and it is also well beyond the capacity of many garages. Special test equipment is essential for checking that the correct pressures in the systems are produced at the correct instant, so even fault diagnosis is fraught with difficulty. If there are difficulties with the unit it is most advisable to take the car to an authorized agent. Volkswagen run a very strict system of franchises and dealers, as well as giving accurate times and costing for most work, so the opinion and word of the agent can safely be accepted.

FIG 7:2 The rotation of an epicyclic gear with the outer gear held stationary

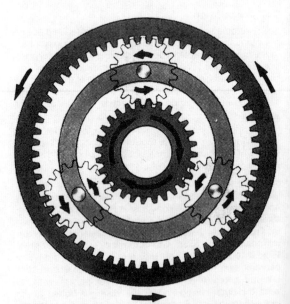

FIG 7:3 An epicyclic gear reversing the direction of rotation by holding the planet carrier stationary

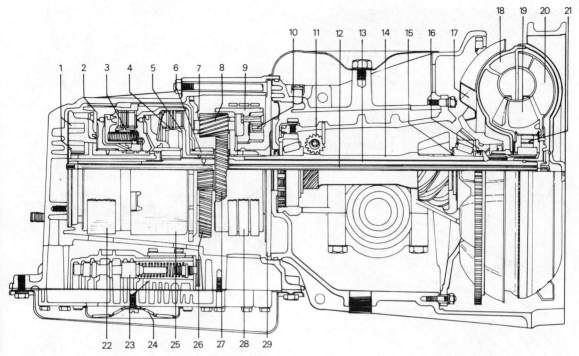

FIG 7:4   A schematic sectioned view of the gearbox, without the control system

Key to Fig 7:4   1 Oil pump   2 Clutch drum   3 Direct and reverse clutch   4 Forward clutch   5 Forward clutch hub   6 Small sun gear   7 Planetary gear carrier   8 Small planet pinion   9 Annulus gear   10 1st gear one-way clutch   11 Governor drive   12 Oil pump drive shaft   13 Turbine shaft   14 Pinion   15 Adjusting shim for pinion   16 One-way clutch support   17 Deflector plate for torque converter   18 Impeller (in converter housing)   19 Stator   20 Turbine   21 One-way clutch for stator   22 2nd gear brake band   23 Valve body   24 Oil strainer   25 Driving shell   26 Large planet pinion   27 Large sun gear   28 1st and reverse brake band   29 Bearing flange

7:2 Maintenance

The outside of the unit should be kept clean and accumulations of mud and dirt prevented. Quite considerable amounts of heat are generated in the unit and if dirt is allowed to build up it will form an insulating layer which can cause the unit to overheat in high ambient temperatures.

Oil level:

This should be checked every 10,000 km (6000 miles) and also it is advisable to check it before a long run. The dipstick is shown at **C** and the filler tube at **D** in **FIG 7:5**. Run the car until the transmission has reached its normal operating temperature and then stand it on level ground. **Leave the engine idling with N selected and the handbrake applied.** Withdraw the dipstick **C** and wipe it clean with a lint-free cloth or piece of leather. Reinsert the dipstick, press it fully home and immediately withdraw it. If the level is low, top it up to the high mark on the dipstick with Automatic Transmission Fluid. The difference between the high and low marks on the dipstick is .4 Litre (.7 pint). All Automatic Transmission Fluids (ATF) with the Dexron test mark are suitable and it will be found that the majority of mineral oil produced by well-known manufacturers willl be suitable.

Draining:

The old ATF should be drained out of the unit at 30,000 km (18,000 miles) intervals and the unit refilled with fresh fluid. The drain plug **E** is shown in **FIG 7:6**. **The oil will flow more easily if it is warm but take care not to scald the hands if the unit is at its normal operating temperature, as the oil is then very hot.** Not all the old fluid can be drained out as some will remain in the torque converter and it is for this reason that less fluid is required to refill the unit after draining than when it has been dismantled.

When all the oil has drained out take out the bolts that secure the sump and remove the sump. Clean the oil strainer with clean fuel and then air dry it. The sump is refitted in the reverse order of removal but it is most advisable to use a new gasket. **Make sure that absolute cleanliness is observed.** Tighten the sump securing bolts to a torque load of 1 kg m (7 lb ft).

The unit will take approximately 3 to 4 Litres of ATF to refill it. At first fill it with only 2.5 Litres (4.4 Imp pints, 5.3 US pints) of ATF. Pouring in ATF will be easier if a clean funnel and length of extension hose are used. Start the engine and move the selector lever to each position in turn. The level of oil should now be just sufficient to touch the bottom of the dipstick at this stage. Take the car

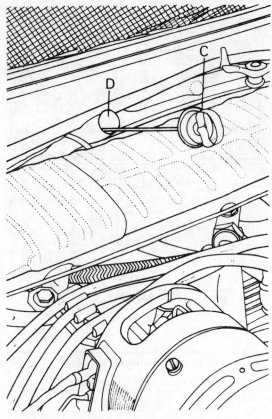

FIG 7:5 The combined filler tube and dipstick

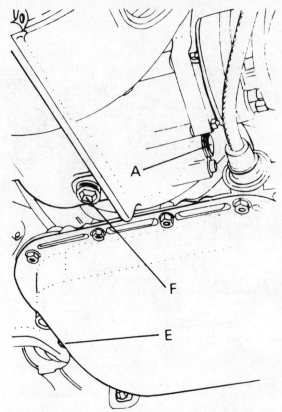

FIG 7:6 The transmission drain plug **E**, the differential drain plug **F** and the differential filler and level plug **A**

for a run to warm up the transmission and then with the engine idling top up to the correct level as described earlier.

Differential unit:

The drain plug is shown at **F** and the combined filler and level plug at **A** in **FIG 7:6**. The level should be checked every 10,000 km (6000 miles) and if it is low it should be topped up to the bottom edge of the filler orifice with Hypoid SAE.90 oil (SAE.80 in arctic climates).

The oil need not be drained at regular intervals, but only for repairs, change of grade or to ensure that only one brand of oil is used. If the differential is drained it will only require 1 Litre (1.75 pint) of oil to refill it and the oil can be pumped in slightly faster than on the manual transmission unit without the danger of the oil flowing back before the unit is full.

7:3 Operation

This section gives the method of use of the automatic transmission system and its limits.

The selector positions are shown in **FIG 7:7** and each position is dealt with under the appropriate heading.

Position P:

This position is for when the car is stationary and will remain so for some time. When this position is selected a mechanical device locks the gearbox and prevents the rear wheels from turning. The device should be able to hold the car on hills but it should not be used in place of the handbrake but only as assistance in holding the car with the handbrake applied. **Do not select P while the car is moving.**

Position R:

This is equivalent to the normal reverse on a mechanical gearbox and should be used as such. **This position should not be selected when the car is moving forwards.**

Position N:

This is equivalent to the normal neutral on a mechanical gearbox. This position should be selected when the car is stuck in traffic jams or stationary for long periods, as the transmission will overheat if the car is held stationary in drive by using the brakes. A safety switch isolates the starter motor in all other selections so that the engine can only be started when N is selected. If N is accidentally selected while the car is moving, lift the foot off the accelerator and wait until the engine is idling before re-selecting drive.

Position D:

This is the normal forward drive selection. The gearbox will automatically select the correct gear out of the forward range of three which is appropriate for the road speed and throttle position.

Position 2:

This acts in the same way as the D position but top gear is isolated and the gearbox does not change up into it. This selection is best for winding roads where it is desirable not to allow the unit to change up into top and it can also be used for travelling downhill where engine braking is required. If the selector is moved back from D the unit will immediately downshift into second gear and for this reason the selection should not be made above road speeds of 100 kilometre/hr (60 mile/hr). Note that to prevent the engine from overspeeding the selector must be moved up into D at this road speed when accelerating.

Position 1:

This selection locks the gearbox into first gear only and it will not upshift at all. **Care must be taken not to exceed a road speed of 60 kilometre/hr (37 mile/hr) in this selection.** It should be noted that this gear is lower in ratio than reverse and it is therefore better to climb steep hills or ramps forwards. This selection should also be used for going down very steep hills so as to have the maximum engine braking. If the selector is moved down from 2 to 1 do not do so above a road speed of 60 kilometre/hr (37 mile/hr). The unit will remain in second gear, unless the throttle pedal is depressed, until the road speed has dropped to 30 kilometre/hr (18 mile/hr) and only then will it downshift into first so the brakes may be needed to slow the car in this speed range.

Starting:

Select N and then operate the starter motor. On models fitted with fuel injection the accelerator pedal should be pushed down and held down until the engine starts, irrespective of the temperature of the engine or outside air. When the engine is running hold the car with the brakes to prevent it creeping and select a drive gear, with the engine at idling. Release the brake and smoothly depress the accelerator pedal. If the engine stalls reselect N before attempting to start the engine. To stop the car release the accelerator and depress the brake. The car may be held on the brake at traffic lights, while a drive selection is still made.

Do not allow the left foot to attempt to operate the brake as a clutch. For this reason it is better to use the handbrake to hold the car when moving off, rather than the footbrake.

The engine **cannot** be started by towing the car and selecting a gear.

Kick-down:

A resistance will be felt at full throttle position and if the pedal is pressed a little harder it will go down into the position where the kick-down switch operates. Provided that the road speed is within limits the gearbox will automatically downshift a gear and stay in this lower gear until either the maximum road speed for that gear is reached or the throttle pedal is released. The kick-down

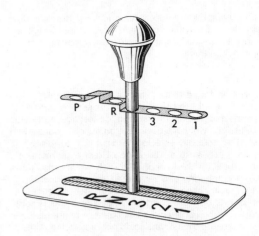

FIG 7:7   The selector lever positions

is used for maximum acceleration, such as when overtaking. If the road speed is below approximately 90 kilometre/hr (56 mile/hr) the gearbox will downshift into second and if the road speed is below approximately 55 kilometre/hr (34 mile/hr) it will downshift into first when the kick-down is operated. The maximum speed before upshift is approximately 60 kilometre/hr (37 mile/hr) for first and 95 kilometre/hr (60 mile/hr) for second.

Towing:

Provided that the transmission is sound and correctly filled with oil and fluid, the car may be towed for a limited distance at a limited speed. The maximum speed for towing is 50 kilometre/hr (30 mile/hr) and the maximum distance is 50 kilometres (30 miles). If the distance exceeds the limit given then the car should either be towed with its rear wheels clear of the ground (use ropes to tie the steering in the straight-ahead position) or else the drive shafts should be removed.

Note that the car cannot be tow or push started.

7:4 Removal and servicing

The removal of the unit follows the same lines as removing the manually operated gearbox. In addition to the operations for the manual gearbox the vacuum pipe from the manifold and the electrical leads from the kick-down switch must also be disconnected. The torque converter is secured to the engine flywheel by bolts and these can be removed in turn, after the cover has been taken off, by rotating the engine and flywheel until the appropriate bolt is at the bottom. It is advisable to mark the engine flywheel and torque converter with paint spots so that they will be reassembled in the original alignment.

Road test:

The owner is not the best person to carry out a road test unless he has had recent experience of driving a similar model with an automatic transmission that is known to be in good order. The road test is best left to a trained fitter who will be able to diagnose faults more readily.

Special equipment is used for checking the operating pressures of the hydraulic system. The owner himself will be so used to faults and idiosyncrasies that he may no longer notice them.

Servicing:

It will be found that even in a VW agency not every fitter will be allowed to dismantle or service automatic transmissions. Those fitters who do service automatic transmissions will have been sent on special courses and most likely specially selected. Apart from skill they will also have access to a full range of test equipment and special tools. In the face of all this the owner has not a hope of competing and he should give in gracefully. If faults appear, check that the routine maintenance has been carried out (see **Section 7:2**) and if this is satisfactory take the car directly to an agent. A minor fault can rapidly turn into a major one so do not press on regardless. Do not remove the gearbox and take that in separately as no effective diagnosis can then be made. It is far better that the agency carries out a minor adjustment than that the owner should blunder around blindly and possibly cause expensive damage.

7:5 Fault diagnosis

This section is not given so that the owner can carry out rectification. It is only given so that the owner will have some idea of the possible cause and it should be noted that this section is nowhere near fully comprehensive and that one symptom can be caused by a variety of faults.

(a) Overheating

1 Incorrect fluid level
2 Dirt insulating casing or blocking air vents
3 Brake bands incorrectly adjusted
4 Stator one way clutch locked in engaged position (rare fault)

(b) Noisy operation

1 Check 1 in (a)
2 Incorrect fluid used in transmission
3 Incorrectly adjusted selector mechanism
4 Defective oil pump

(c) Incorrect shift speeds

1 Check 3 in (b)
2 Governor valve sticking or defective

(d) Poor acceleration

1 Check 3 and 4 in (a)
2 Stator one way clutch slipping

(e) Excessive creep when drive engaged

1 Engine idling speed too high

CHAPTER 8

REAR SUSPENSION AND DRIVE SHAFTS

8:1 Description
8:2 The dampers
8:3 The drive shafts
8:4 The road springs

8:5 Wishbone and hub assembly
8:6 Rear suspension carrier
8:7 Fault diagnosis

8:1 Description

A general view of the complete rear suspension, drive shafts and power unit is shown in **Chapter 6, FIG 6:1**.

Each road wheel is independently mounted using a trailing offset wishbone. A coil spring is mounted between each wishbone and the frame of the car to take the weight of the vehicle and sealed telescopic dampers are mounted concentrically inside the springs to control the suspension movement.

Drive shafts with two homokinetic joints per shaft transmit the drive from the final drive unit to the rear wheel hubs.

On some models a stabilizer bar (anti-roll bar) inter-connects the two wishbones. The stabilizer reduces body roll on corners and also improves the road holding.

The components of one rear suspension are shown in **FIG 8:1**.

8:2 The dampers

Each damper is a sealed telescopic unit which has a double action. Internal stops in each damper limit the maximum downward movement of the suspension. The damper cannot be repaired if it is defective.

Different grades of damper can be fitted in case the car is going to be used in extreme conditions. The standard and heavy-duty dampers are non-adjustable but for extreme conditions fit adjustable Koni dampers.

Removal:

Jack up the rear of the car to give sufficient access room. Make sure that the wishbone is supported, as the damper limits the maximum suspension movement.

Remove the nut and bolt arrowed in **FIG 8:2** from underneath the car. From inside the car, peel back the trim at the luggage shelf and remove the cover, as shown in **FIG 8:3**, to expose the upper attachments. Remove the attachment nut, holding the damper by the flats on the end of the threaded portion. Take off the cupwasher, rubber bush and spacer sleeve. Compress the damper and remove it from under the car.

Install the damper in the reverse order of removal. Before installing the damper check the condition of all the rubber bushes, renewing them if they are worn or perished. The attachment to the body should be tightened to a torque of 22 lb ft (3 kg m) and the attachment to the wishbone 43 lb ft (6 kg m).

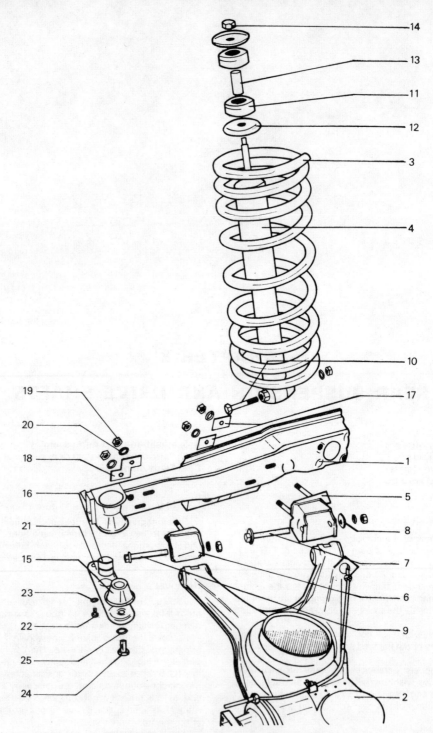

FIG 8:1 The components of the rear suspension

Key to Fig 8:1   1 Rear axle carrier   2 Suspension (wishbone) arm   3 Coil spring   4 Shock absorber   5 Inner suspension arm bracket   6 Outer suspension arm bracket   7 Eccentric bolt   8 Eccentric washer   9 Bolt   10 Bolt   11 Shock absorber rubber bush   12 Dished washer   13 Spacer sleeve   14 Self-locking nut   15 Rubber bush for rear axle carrier   16 Rubber bush for rear axle carrier   17 Mounting plate   18 Mounting plate   19 Nut   20 Spring washer   21 Coverplate   22 Screw   23 Lockwasher   24 Screw   25 Spring washer

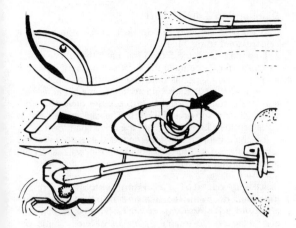

FIG 8:2 The damper attachment to the wishbone

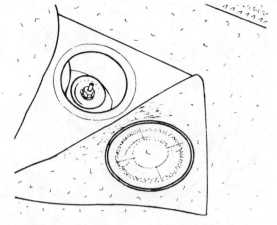

FIG 8:3 The damper attachment to the body

Testing:

The average life of a damper is around 36,000 miles so consideration should be given to renewing them after this mileage. **When renewing dampers for general wear, always renew them in axle sets and preferably renew all four dampers at the same time.**

Bouncing the suspension by hand and checking the time taken for the oscillations to die down is a very rough test, but there are now machines coming into service which carry out this test with extreme accuracy and give a trace of the rebound curve, so that the condition of the dampers can be determined without removing it from the car.

Continuous pitching after passing over a disturbance in the road is an indication of defective dampers.

Once the unit has been removed from the car, check its physical condition. Renew the damper if the body is dented or the ram bent, or there are fluid leaks.

Mount the damper vertically in the padded jaws of a vice and start to pump it with short strokes about the midpoint. Gradually increase the length of the strokes until they reach the full travel of the damper. If there are pockets of no resistance or unequal resistance, or if the damper operates with odd noises, it is defective. **This test will only detect a damper that is actually**

defective and even if the unit passes the test this **is no guarantee that it is operating at full efficiency.** This test should be carried out on new dampers or those that have been in storage for some time as it ensures that all air or gases are bled to the top of the fluid.

8:3 The drive shafts

A drive shaft and its components are shown in **FIG 8:4**. The constant velocity (homokinetic) joints may be dismantled for cleaning and lubricating purposes but if there is excessive radial play the complete joint must be renewed.

A typical attachment is shown in **FIG 8:5**. Before removing the drive shafts, thoroughly clean the area so that dirt cannot fall into or enter the joints when they are freed. Remove the socket-headed bolts that secure the joints to the transmission and rear hub. Tilt the shaft and remove it from the car.

Once the shafts have been removed, fit plastic bags over each joint and secure them with rubber bands (to prevent dirt from entering the joint.) Blank off the transmission and hub for the same reason.

Install the drive shaft in the reverse order of removal using new lockwashers and lockplates. Tighten the socket-headed screws to a torque of 32 lb ft (4.6 kg m).

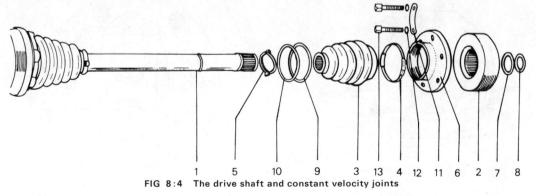

FIG 8:4 The drive shaft and constant velocity joints

Key to Fig 8:4   1 Drive shaft   2 Constant velocity joint   3 Seal   4 Hose clip   5 Clip   6 Cap   7 Dished washer   8 Circlip
9 Ring   10 Ring   11 Lockplate   12 Lockwasher   13 Socket head screw

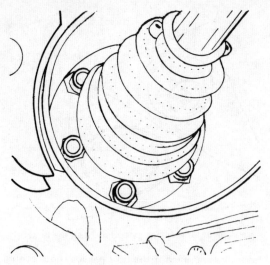

FIG 8:5 Typical drive shaft attachment

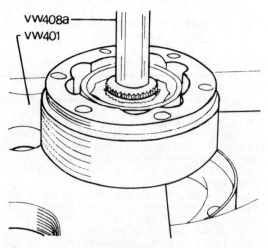

FIG 8:6 Pressing the shaft out of the constant velocity joint

Dismantling a drive shaft:

A press is required to remove and refit the constant velocity joint to the shaft.

Free the clips 4 and 5 then pull back the rubber seal 3. Hold the joint 2 square to the shaft and drive off the cap 6 from it, using a suitable drift. Remove the circlip.

Support the constant velocity joint on a suitable plate and use a suitable mandrel to press the drive shaft out of the joint, as shown in **FIG 8:6**. The seal and remaining parts can then be slid off from the drive shaft itself.

Tilt the inner portion of the joint and press it out of the race as shown in **FIG 8:7**. Remove the balls, align the groove of the hub with that of the cage, and remove the hub from inside the cage.

All the parts of a constant velocity joint are matched on manufacture and must not be interchanged with equivalent parts. For this reason take great care not to intermix parts of different joints but store them separately.

Reassembling a drive shaft:

Clean all the parts in suitable solvent, taking care not to interchange parts of the constant velocity joints. Check the splines on the shafts and hub for wear or defects. Check the balls and the faces against which they operate for wear, scores or pitting. Renew the complete constant velocity joint it defects are found.

Fit the hub back into the cage and press the balls back into position. Align the assembly as shown in **FIG 8:8** and press the cage firmly so that the parts are refitted. Check that the joint articulates fully and freely by hand.

Slide new seals, clips and parts back onto the drive shaft. Note that the dished washer 7 is inserted between the ball hub of the joint and circlip for models fitted with automatic transmission, but fitted between hub and shoulder on the shaft for models with manual-shift transmission.

Support the other end of the shaft on a beam or block of wood and use a tubular mandrel to press the constant velocity joint back onto the splines of the shaft. Install the circlip to secure the joint, making sure that the circlip is fully and squarely seated in its recess.

Pack approximately 2 ozs (60 grammes) of lithium-based grease between the cap and joint and then pack

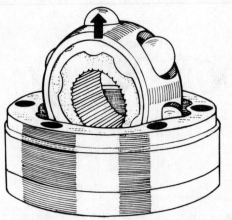

FIG 8:7 Dismantling the constant velocity joint

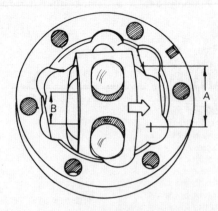

FIG 8:8 The correct alignment of the parts when assembling the constant velocity joint

another 1.2 ozs (30 grammes) of grease into the open end of the joint. Make sure that the grease is packed so that it enters the joint and that no grease is allowed on the faces where the cap contacts the joint or seal.

Press back the cap and secure the seal with new clips. Squeeze the seal by hand so that the grease is forced into the joint.

If the shaft assembly is not to be installed immediately, wrap the joints in plastic bags to prevent dirt from entering or grease leaking out.

8:4 The road springs

Raise the rear of the car onto chassis stands and take the weight of the suspension with a small jack under the wishbone. Remove the road wheel. This will be easier if the road wheel nuts are slightly slackened before raising the car but there should be no difficulty even with the wheel off the ground, as a gear can be engaged and the handbrake applied to lock the wheel.

Disconnect the drive shaft as described in the previous section. Remove the lower damper attachments, shown in **FIG 8:2**.

Carefully lower the jack under the wishbone until the spring has extended sufficiently for its pressure to be released so that the spring can be lifted out.

Install the spring in the reverse order of removal, after checking it for defects or weakening.

8:5 Wishbone and hub assembly

Eccentric bolts mount the wishbones to their attachment brackets while the brackets themselves attach through slotted holes to the rear axle carrier. These adjustments allow the track width to be altered. The track angle can also be altered by turning the eccentric bolts for the attachment of the inner arm of the wishbone to its bracket. **Such adjustments should not be carried out by the owner but should be set by a VW agent using optical equipment.**

It is essential that the positions of the brackets and the set of the eccentric bolts are marked before the suspension parts are removed and that the parts are adjusted to the same settings on reassembly. Once major work has been completed it is advisable to take the car to a VW agent for checks on the suspension geometry.

Removal:

Jack up the rear of the car and place it securely on chassis stands. Remove the road wheel.

Remove the damper (see **Section 8:2**) and remove the drive shaft (see **Section 8:3**). Lower the jack under the wishbone and remove the road spring as described in the previous section.

Disconnect the flexible brake hoses connecting the metal line on the wishbone to the body line (see **Chapter 11**). Empty the hydraulic system by pumping fluid out of a bleed screw on a wheel cylinder and be prepared for a small amount of spillage. Disconnect the handbrake cable from the wheel brake.

The wishbone can now be removed, either by taking out the pivot bolts arrowed in **FIG 8:9** (the third arrow points to the lower damper attachment) or by removing the four nuts arrowed in **FIG 8:10** which secure the wish-

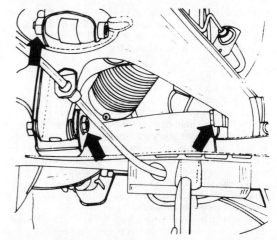

FIG 8:9 The eccentric bolts securing the wishbone to its brackets

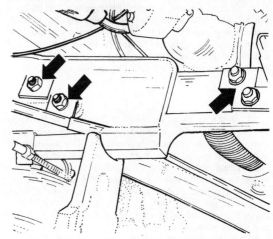

FIG 8:10 The nuts securing the brackets to the carrier

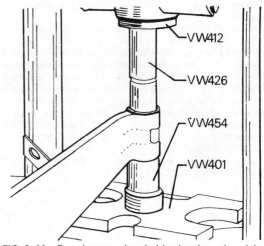

FIG 8:11 Pressing new bonded bushes into the wishbone

bone brackets to the carrier. If the wishbone is freed from the brackets, mark the position of the offset of the eccentric bolts. If the brackets are removed from the carrier, mark the positions of the brackets.

Dismantling:

Disconnect the brake line from the wheel cylinder and free the clips so that the pipe can be removed.

Remove the attachment brackets, if they are still fitted. Check the eccentric bolts for wear or damage. Examine the bonded rubber bushes in the ends of the wishbone arms. If the bushes are worn, press or drive them out, taking great care not to damage the wishbone. New bushes should be pressed back into place, preferably using the tools shown in **FIG 8:11**. **Do not use grease on the bushes** and if lubrication is needed to remove or refit them, use soft soap or water.

Note that the rear wheel hub assembly can be dismantled with the wishbone in place, after removing the drive shaft and road wheel.

Remove the brake drum, after taking out its two countersunk securing screws. Remove the large nut and pull out the wheel shaft. Undo the bolts securing the bearing retainer and carefully drive off the brake backplate and retainer using a rubber or plastic-faced mallet. Drift out the oil seal. Remove flange, bearing races and spacer. The bearing cups can be drifted out, but take care not to interchange the parts of the bearings.

Assembly:

Check the bearings for wear or defects. The bearings should be washed by rotating them under clean solvent until all dirt and grease is removed. Dry them with compressed air but hold them so that they cannot spin. Oil the bearings with thin oil and fit them back into the outer cups. Apply firm hand pressure and oscillate the bearing backwards and forwards. Roughness can be caused by specks of dirt but if the bearing is perfectly clean and still rotates roughly, both bearings should be completely renewed.

Clean the remainder of the parts, noting that it is advisable to renew the oil seals. Use rags or newspaper to remove most of the grease and dirt and then wash with solvent.

Drive the outer ring of the inner bearing back into place. Work grease liberally into the rollers of the inner bearing race and fit the race back into position. Pack a little extra grease around the outside of the bearing and drive the oil seal back into position. Pack 1 oz (30 grammes) of grease into the bearing housing and press the spacer back into position. Drive the outer ring of the outer bearing into position. Liberally grease the inner race of the outer bearing and fit that back into position. Pack a little extra grease around the outside of the bearing and drive in the outer grease seal. Install the brake backplate, bearing retainer and new O-rings. Tighten the bolts for the bearing retainer to a torque of 43 lb ft (6 kg m).

Fit the shaft, with a new O-ring and lockplate, ar tighten the attachment to a torque of 65 to 80 lb ft (9 11 kg m). It is advisable to check the torque required turn the shaft and if the torque exceeds 1.45 lb ft (kg cm) with the shaft attachment tightened to the low limit, install new bearings or spacer.

Refit the brake drum and brake pipe.

Installation:

The wishbone assembly is installed in the reverse ord of removal. Discard the old self-locking nuts and use ne ones on reassembly. All the attachments are tightened a torque of 61 lb ft (8.5 kg m) but **the nuts for th eccentric bolts should not be fully tightened unt the car is back on the ground.** This ensures that th rubber bushes are set into their normal working positio and are not under excessive strain.

Refit the road spring and damper in the reverse ord of removal. Connect up the flexible brake hose and blee the rear brakes (see **Chapter 11**), also connect up th handbrake cables and adjust the handbrake as necessar

Pack a little extra grease into the drive shaft consta velocity joints and check them for wear before installir the drive shaft.

8:6 Rear suspension carrier

This can only be removed after the complete power ur (engine and transmission) has been removed. Instructior for removing the power unit are given under the trans mission removal sections, as the power unit must k removed before the transmission can be separated fro the engine.

Remove both rear wishbone assemblies, as well a road springs and dampers, as described earlier.

Remove the coverplates and take out the carrier.

The carrier is installed in the reverse order of remova tightening its attachments to a torque of 14 lb ft (2 kg m Before installing the carrier, check the condition of th damping rings and rubber bushes, renewing them if the are perished or worn.

8:7 Fault diagnosis

(a) Noisy operation

1 Worn or defective rubber bushes and damping ring
2 Defective damper or defective damper attachments
3 Defective constant velocity joints
4 Defective wheel bearings
5 Insufficient lubricant

(b) Poor handling or excessive tyre wear

1 Check 1 and 2 in (a)
2 Incorrect suspension geometry
3 Weak or broken road spring
4 Damaged or distorted components

CHAPTER 9

FRONT SUSPENSION AND HUBS

9:1 Description
9:2 Maintenance
9:3 Wheel hubs
9:4 The stabilizer (anti-roll bar)
9:5 Suspension ball joint and control arm

9:6 The suspension strut
9:7 The suspension carrier
9:8 Suspension geometry
9:9 Fault diagnosis

9:1 Description

A view of the front suspension and steering unit is shown in **FIG 9:1**. Both wheels are independently sprung, the weight of the car and road shocks being taken by suspension struts. The struts are made up of the damper and the coil spring, and are attached to the bodywork at the upper end. A steering knuckle pivots about the lower end and the knuckle carries the stub axle, about which the wheel hub rotates on two opposed tapered bearings.

A T-shaped carrier is mounted on the body of the car and the control arms pivot in brackets on the carrier, using bonded rubber bushes. The ball joint of the suspension strut is attached to the outer end of each control arm. A radius arm, mounted between control arm and carrier, takes the fore-and-aft loads on each control arm.

An anti-roll bar interconnects the control arms, transferring load from an outside wheel to the inside one on corners, thus reducing body roll and improving roadholding.

The components of the suspension are shown in **FIG 9:2**.

9:2 Maintenance

Apart from routine tyre checking, the only maintenance required is to remove the wheel hubs and repack the bearings with clean grease at intervals of 30,000 miles (50,000 kilometres). The hubs must be removed, cleaned, checked and repacked. **It is not sufficient to remove the grease cap and pack extra grease around the outer bearing** as this may force dirt into the outer bearing while the inner bearing may be on the point of running dry.

9:3 Wheel hubs

The components are shown in **FIG 9:2**.

Removal:

Jack up the front of the car and remove the road wheels. Note that the wheel attachments should be slackened slightly before raising the front of the car, otherwise there will be difficulty in undoing them because the wheels will spin freely.

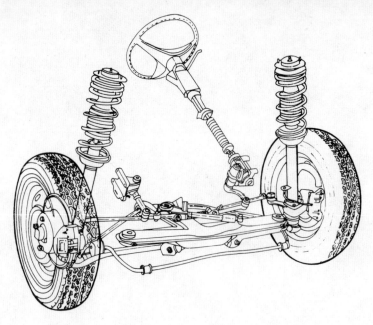

FIG 9:1   The steering and front suspension assemblies

Disconnect the flexible hoses to the metal brake lines on the caliper. Remove the two bolts securing the caliper to the suspension and slide the caliper off the brake disc. Take care not to allow brake fluid to spill onto the brake pads during this operation. Fuller instructions on removing the calipers are given in **Chapter 11**.

Prise off the grease caps (hub caps) from the wheel hubs. Slacken the socket-headed clamp screw 6 on the special nut 5. Undo the special nut using a spanner as shown in **FIG 9:3**. Remove the washer fitted under the nut.

Grasp the disc and pull the hub assembly firmly off from the stub axle, collecting the inner race of the outer bearing 8 as it comes free and not allowing it to drop out.

Cleaning and examination:

Remove the oil seal 11 and take out the inner race of the inner bearing 10.

Wipe away surplus grease and dirt with a piece of rag and then use solvent to remove the remainder. Wash the bearing races separately by rotating them in a bath of clean solvent, such as fuel or paraffin, and then dry them with compressed air (holding them so that they do not spin in the air blast).

Lubricate the bearing races with thin oil and press them back into their outer cones. Apply firm pressure and rotate the bearing by hand. If the bearing is perfectly clean but still feels rough, it is defective. Similarly the bearings are defective if the operating faces are worn, scored, pitted, or discoloured.

If a bearing is defective, renew both bearings complete. Drive out the old outer cones from the hub using a suitable drift and drive the new cones fully and squarely back into place.

Check the operating faces of the brake disc for excessive scoring or damage, either machining them or fitting new hub assemblies if the scores are deep. The surface of the disc should be wiped over with a solvent such as methylated spirits to remove any grease or finger marks before installing the brake caliper.

Assembly and adjustment:

Work grease liberally into the rollers of the race of the inner bearing and smear the cone with grease. Fit the inner race back into position and squarely drive in a new oil seal to secure it in position. Spread grease evenly around on the inside of the hub. Slide the hub assembly back into position on the stub axle. Smear grease on the cone of the outer bearing and work grease liberally into the race of the outer bearing, then fit the race back into position. Install the washer and nut.

Spin the hub and tighten down the adjusting nut until there is a definite resistance to rotation on the hub. This ensures that the bearings are preloaded and pulled fully into place. Slacken back the nut again.

Install the brake caliper, connect up the flexible hose, and bleed the front brakes (see **Chapter 11**).

Refit the road wheel but leave one attachment bolt out. Fit the bracket VW.769 in place of the omitted attachment bolt and fit a DTI (Dial Test Indicator) to the bracket so that its stylus rests vertically on the end of the stub axle, as shown in **FIG 9:4**. Adjust the nut until the end play on the bearings is correct at .001 to .0025 inch (.03 to .06 mm). Provided that the bearings do not operate noisily at the larger clearance it is permissible to increase the end float as far as .005 inch (.12 mm). Tighten the socket-headed clamping screw to a torque of 7 to 9 lb ft (1 to 1.3 kg m). Check that the adjustment is still correct. When

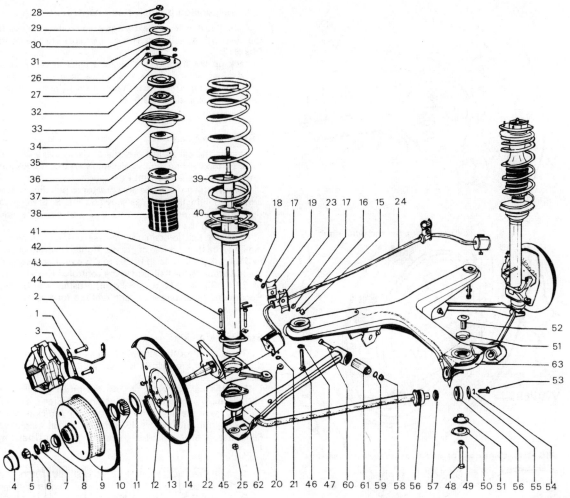

FIG 9:2 The components of the front suspension

Key to Fig 9:2   1 Lockplate   2 Screw   3 Caliper   4 Hub cap   5 Wheel bearing locknut   6 Socket head screw   7 Thrust washer   8 Outer wheel bearing   9 Brake disc   10 Inner wheel bearing   11 Oil seal   12 Screw   13 Spring washer   14 Splash shield   15 Nut   16 Spring washer   17 Washer   18 Screw   19 Stabilizer clamp   20 Nut   21 Spring washer   22 Stabilizer mounting   23 Rubber bush   24 Stabilizer   25 Self-locking nut   26 Self-locking nut   27 Washer   28 Self-locking nut   29 Dished washer   30 Friction ring   31 Damping ring   32 Support plate   33 Friction shell   34 Suspension strut bearing   35 Seat for spring   36 Rubber stop for shock absorber   37 Retaining ring for protective tube   38 Protective tube   39 Coil spring   40 Coil spring damping ring   41 Damper   42 Screw   43 Lockwasher   44 Steering knuckle   45 Ball joint   46 Screw   47 Lockwasher   48 Screw   49 Lockwasher   50 Seat for damping ring   51 Damping ring for front axle carrier   52 Spacer sleeve   53 Screw   54 Spring washer   55 Damping ring plate   56 Radius rod clamping ring   57 Locating ring for radius arm   58 Nut   59 Spring washer   60 Screw   61 Track control arm bush   62 Track control arm   63 Front axle carrier

making the adjustments, spin the hub after every alteration of the position of the adjusting nut.

Refit the grease cap, after wiping it clean (**without filling it with grease**). Refit the remaining wheel attachment after removing the DTI and bracket. Fit the wheel trim into place after lowering the car and fully tightening the wheel attachments.

9:4 The stabilizer (anti-roll bar)

The components are shown in **FIG 9:2** and the attachments on one side to the control arm and frame are shown in **FIG 9:5**.

Jack up the front of the car and remove the road wheels. Make sure that both suspensions are at the same height so that the stabilizer is not in torsion. Remove the nuts securing the stabilizer mountings to the control arms. Remove the nuts and bolts securing the clamps to the bracket on the frame and remove the stabilizer.

Install the stabilizer in the reverse order of removal. Make sure that the rubber bushes and stabilizer mountings are in good condition, renewing them if they are perished or worn. Tighten the nuts securing the mountings to the control arms to a torque of 22 to 25 lb ft (3 to 3.5 kg m) and the nuts for the clamps to the frame to 29 to 32 lb ft (4 to 4.5 kg m).

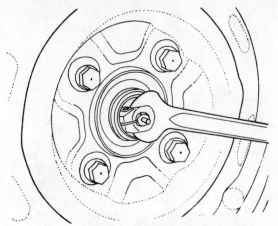

FIG 9:3   The adjusting nut for the wheel hub

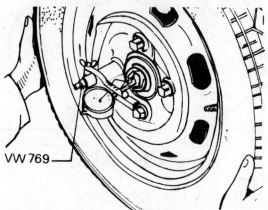

VW 769

FIG 9:4   Checking the end float of the hub bearings

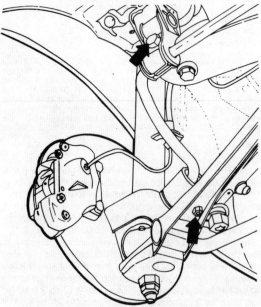

FIG 9:5   The stabilizer attachments

9:5 Suspension ball joint and control arm

A suitable two-legged extractor is required for removing the suspension ball joint. The components are shown in **FIG 9:2**.

Jack up the front of the car and place it on chassis stands. Remove the road wheel to give access room. Disconnect the stabilizer from the control arm by removing the lower nut arrowed in **FIG 9:5**.

Suspension ball joint:

Prepare the car as just described. Use a piece of wire to tie up the steering knuckle assembly so that it does not slide off the suspension strut.

Remove the nut and use an extractor to pull the control arm off from the ball joint, as shown in **FIG 9:6**. Remove the three bolts arrowed in **FIG 9:7** and slide the ball joint off from the strut.

Refit the ball joint in the reverse order of removal, making sure that it is free of grease. Tighten the three bolts to a torque of 39 to 46 lb ft (5.5 to 6.5 kg m) and tighten the nut securing the ball joint to the control arm to a torque of 28 to 32 lb ft (4 to 4.5 kg m) —using a new nut. Reconnect the stabilizer bar and refit the road wheel.

Steering knuckle:

The removal of the steering knuckle is very similar to the removal of the suspension ball joint, with additional work.

With the car prepared, remove the brake caliper and hub assembly as described in **Section 9:3**. Free the outer tie rod from the lever on the steering knuckle after removing the nut, preferably using a special extractor. Fuller details of steering ball joints are given in **Chapter 10**.

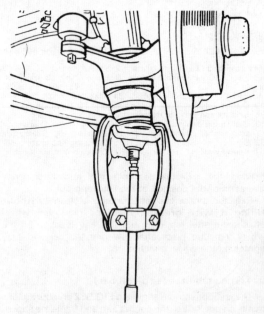

FIG 9:6   Freeing the control arm from the ball joint

Remove the suspension ball joint as described just previously. Slide the steering knuckle off from the suspension strut.

If it is suspected that the knuckle has been damaged or has become distorted, it should be checked using a suitable vernier and steel straightedge. Remove the disc brake shield and clamp a rigid straightedge across the mounting face. Use the vernier to measure the distance between the inside edge of the straightedge and the furthest face of the bore for the steering ball joint in the lever, as shown in **FIG 9:8**. The correct dimension should be 5.208 to 5.230 inch (132.3 to 132.6 mm).

Examine the stub axle for wear, scores or cracks. Put a square onto the dust shield mounting face and use a vernier to measure the dimension between the parallel portion of the stub axle and the square, as shown in **FIG 9:9**. Repeat the check at three positions around the stub axle and if there is a variation greater than .010 inch (.25 mm) the stub axle is distorted.

The steering knuckle is installed in the reverse order of removal. Install the hub assembly and set the correct end float. Note that the brakes will require bleeding.

Control arm and radius arm:

Prepare the car as described earlier. Remove the nut and free the control arm from the ball joint as shown in **FIG 9:6**. Do not remove the three bolts arrowed in **FIG 9:7** unless the ball joint is also going to be removed.

Remove the pivot bolt and its nut that secures the inner end of the control arm to the carrier. Remove the bolt that fits into the end of the radius arm and secures the radius arm to the carrier. Lift out the control arm and radius arm assembly.

Before installing the assembly, check the rubber bushes and renew them if they are worn or perished.

The assembly is installed in the reverse order of removal and the pivot nut as well as the radius arm securing bolt are both tightened to a torque of 58 to 65 lb ft (8 to 9 kg m).

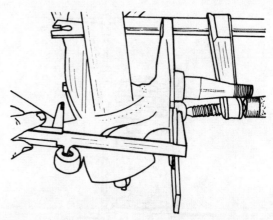

FIG 9:8 Checking the steering lever on the knuckle assembly

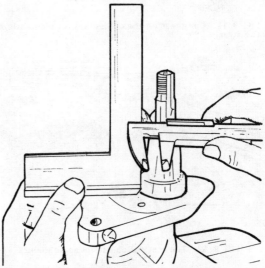

FIG 9:9 Checking the stub axle on the knuckle assembly

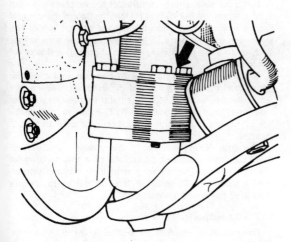

FIG 9:7 The ball joint and steering knuckle attachments

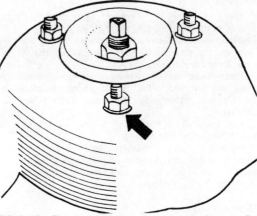

FIG 9:10 The suspension strut upper attachments. Do not slacken the centre nut while the strut is fitted to the car

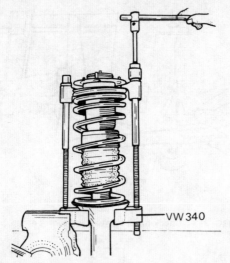

FIG 9:11 Compressing the coil spring for dismantling the strut

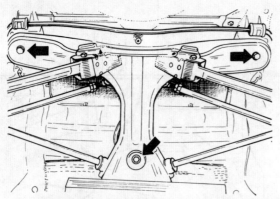

FIG 9:12 The suspension carrier attachments

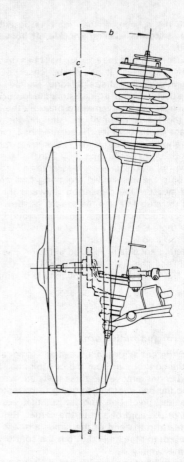

FIG 9:13 The suspension geometry angles

Key to Fig 9:13   a Camber   b Steering pivot angle
c Steering roll radius

9:6 The suspension strut

Removal:

Jack up the front of the car and disconnect the control arm from the suspension ball joint, as described in the previous section. Disconnect the outer tie rod from the lever on the steering knuckle. Disconnect the flexible hose for the brake caliper.

From inside the luggage compartment, remove the three nuts arrowed in **FIG 9:10. Do not slacken the centre nut otherwise the road spring will be released.**

Take the strut out from under the car and lay it on the bench for further dismantling.

Install the strut in the reverse order of removal, using three new self-locking nuts and tightening them to a torque of 14 lb ft (2 kg m). Bleed the front brakes before installing the road wheel.

Dismantling:

With the unit on the bench, remove the brake caliper, hub assembly, ball joint and steering knuckle as required.

Use a suitable spring compressor to compress the road spring, as shown in **FIG 9:11**. Hold the flats of the damper with a spanner and undo the central nut on top of the strut. Remove the parts 26 to 38 inclusive, shown in **FIG 9:2**, release the pressure on the road spring, and take off the road spring.

Check all the parts for wear or damage, including the spring and damper. Though of different appearance, the front damper is checked in a similar manner to the rear one (see **Chapter 8, Section 8:2**) Rumbling when the car is moving is a further indication of a defective front damper.

The strut is reassembled in the reverse order of dismantling, using the compressor to take the pressure of the road spring. Use a new self-locking nut and tighten it to a torque of 51 to 61 lb ft (7 to 8.5 kg m) before removing the spring compressor.

9:7 The suspension carrier

The carrier is attached by slotted holes to the frame. Sideways movement of the carrier allows the camber angles to be equalized between the two suspensions.

For this reason, mark the position of the carrier before removing it. Once it has been installed it is advisable to have the suspension geometry checked by a VW agent.

Removal:

Jack up the front of the car and place it on chassis stands. Remove the front road wheels. Remove the stabilizer (see **Section 9:4**). Free both control arms from the strut ball joints as shown in **FIG 9:6**. Disconnect the steering damper from the carrier.

Support the carrier and remove the three bolts arrowed in **FIG 9:12**. Remove the carrier complete with the control arms and then take off the control arms on the bench.

Installation:

Check all the damper rings and renew them if they are perished or worn. If the carrier has been removed because of accident damage, take it to a VW agent for checks.

Fit the carrier back into place and tighten its three attachment bolts finger tight. Move the carrier laterally until the previously made marks align and then tighten the bolts to a torque of 39 to 46 lb ft (5.5 to 6.5 kg m).

The remaining parts are then connected in the reverse order of dismantling.

9:8 Suspension geometry

The various suspension angles are illustrated in **FIGS 9:13** and **9:14**. The geometry is set by the design of the suspension and, except for equalizing the camber angles between the front wheels, no adjustments are possible. The method of equalizing the camber, after slackening the carrier attachment bolts, is shown in **FIG 9:15**.

Special equipment is required for checking the suspension geometry and the owner should leave such work to a VW agent. If the geometry is found to be incorrect, parts should be carefully examined for damage or distortion. Excessive wear at pivot points can be another cause of incorrect geometry but this type of fault can be repaired by the owner.

Steering geometry is dealt with in the next chapter, but again it will be found easier to leave the work to an agent.

9:9 Fault diagnosis

(a) Wheel wobble or tramp

1 Unbalanced wheels and tyres
2 Incorrect or uneven tyre pressures
3 Loose wheel attachments
4 Defective steering
5 Incorrectly set or defective hub bearings
6 Defective damper
7 Damaged or distorted suspension components

(b) Excessive pitching or 'bottoming'

1 Weak or broken road springs
2 Defective dampers

(c) Excessive rolling on corners

1 Check (b)
2 Broken stabilizer

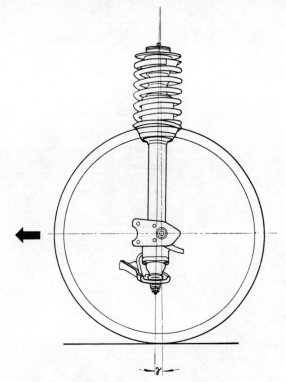

FIG 9:14   The castor angle. This angle is not adjustable

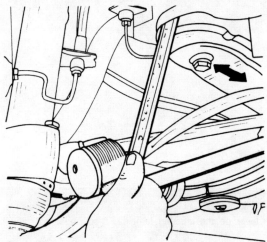

FIG 9:15   Equalizing the camber angles between the front suspensions by moving the carrier sideways

(d) Rattles or rumbles

1 Check 3, 5, 6 and 7 in (a) and also check (c)
2 Worn damping rings or suspension bushes
3 Worn stabilizer bushes

(e) Excessive tyre wear

1 Check 1, 2, 5 and 7 in (a), check (b) and also 2 in (d)
2 Fast cornering, hard acceleration and sharp braking.

CHAPTER 10

THE STEERING SYSTEM

10:1 Description
10:2 Maintenance
10:3 Steering ball joints
10:4 Steering linkage components

10:5 The steering column
10:6 The steering unit
10:7 Steering geometry
10:8 Fault diagnosis

10:1 Description

The relation of the steering system to the front suspension is shown in **FIG 9:1** of **Chapter 9**.

A safety steering column is fitted which is designed to collapse under heavy impact and prevent injury to the driver. The column is fitted with a telescopic portion which should move downwards in a controlled manner. **No repairs can be carried out to this portion and if it has partially collapsed because of mishandling or accident, new parts must be fitted.**

A recirculating ball type steering box is fitted. The steering worm is attached to the column by a coupling so that it rotates with the steering wheel. The worm rotates in adjustable bearings in the case and the ball nut runs up and down on the spiral threads of the worm. The motion is transmitted to the drop arm shaft which carries a Pitman arm (drop arm) splined to the end. The arm then operates the linkage shown in **FIG 10:1** to turn the steering knuckles on the front suspensions.

10:2 Maintenance

The steering box is filled with grease on assembly and does not require routine lubrication. Similarly the ball joints are sealed and do not require routine lubrication.

However, at regular intervals check the ball joints for wear and their gaiters for splits or tears. Wear will show up as play when the steering is turned, so watch the linkage while an assistant turns the steering wheel.

The ball joint gaiters must be renewed before they are fully split, otherwise dirt will enter the ball joint and cause rapid wear. If the gaiter has actually split, it is advisable to install a new ball joint as dirt cannot be flushed out. When renewing gaiters, pack a little extra clean grease into the ball joint.

10:3 Steering ball joints

The steering linkage parts are shown in **FIG 10:1** and it can be seen that an integral ball joint is fitted at either end of the centre tie rod (track rod) for attachment to the Pitman and idler arms. The outer tie rods are fitted with ends containing integral ball joints, which are threaded into the tubes of the outer tie rod. The inner ball joints secure the outer tie rods to the centre one and the outer ball joints secure the tie rods to the steering levers on the suspension knuckle.

If a centre tie rod ball joint is defective the complete centre tie rod must be renewed. If an outer tie rod ball joint is defective it can be removed from the tie rod and a

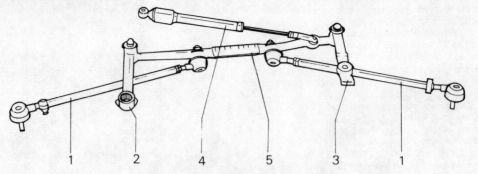

FIG 10:1 The steering linkage assembly

Key to Fig 10:1 1 Side tie (track) rod   2 Pitman (drop) arm   3 Idler arm   4 Steering damper   5 Centre tie (track) rod

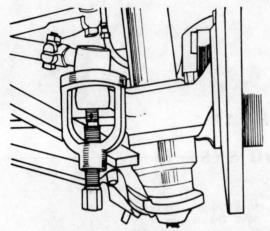

FIG 10:2 Freeing a steering ball joint

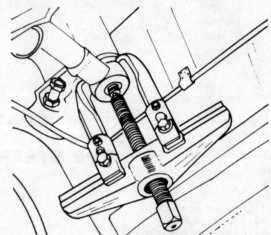

FIG 10:3 Freeing the idler arm

new end screwed back into place. If, on the outer tie rods, the number of turns required to remove the old end are counted and the new end fitted back by the same number of turns then the front wheel alignment will not be lost.

The ball joint pin has an accurately machined tapered portion which fits into a mating taper on the other member and the two tapers are then drawn tight by use of a nut. When it comes to freeing the ball joint it is found that the tapers seem to have welded together. The safest method of freeing the ball joint is to remove the nut and then press the pin out with an extractor as shown in **FIG 10:2**. Tap lightly on the side of the lever while applying pressure on the pin by tightening the bolt of the tool.

If an extractor is not available, do **not** hammer on the end of the threaded portion of the pin. The ball joint will suffer damage by this method. Instead leave the nut on the last few threads and lay a block of metal on one side of the tapered eye. Pull the ball joint firmly apart and then hammer with a copper mallet on the side of the eye opposite to the block of metal. The tapers will quickly free and the nut will prevent the parts flying apart, with possible injury or damage.

10:4 Steering linkage components

It is advised that the complete linkage be removed from the car and the individual components renewed with the assembly on the bench.

Disconnect the outer tie rods from the steering levers on the knuckles, using the extractor shown in **FIG 10:2** after removing the splitpin and nut. Disconnect the damper from the suspension carrier. Remove the nut that secures the idler arm to the pivot bolt of the idler bracket and free the arm using an extractor, as shown in **FIG 10:3**. Remove the nut that secures the Pitman arm to the shaft of the steering box and remove the Pitman arm in a similar manner to removing the idler arm. There is no need to mark the Pitman arm as it can only be fitted in one position because of the wide splines arrowed in **FIG 10:4. Under no circumstances try to hammer the Pitman arm free from the steering box shaft,** as shocks will be transmitted up the shaft and cause internal damage to the steering box. The complete linkage can now be removed from the car.

The assembly is installed in the reverse order of removal. When fitting the idler arm to the idler pivot bolt, use a new nut, hold the bolt with an Allen key and tighten to a torque of 28 to 32 lb ft (4 to 4.5 kg m). Tighten the nut that secures the Pitman arm to the shaft to a torque of 65 to 80 lb ft (9 to 11 kg m) and stake the nut to lock it. The ball joint nuts are tightened to a torque of 22 lb ft (3 kg m) before locking them with new splitpins and tighten the steering damper to carrier attachment to a torque of 28 to 32 lb ft (4 to 4.5 kg m).

Once the linkage has been fitted it is most advisable to check the front wheel alignment.

The parts of the steering linkage can be dismantled using suitable extractors to free the ball joints. When removing the Pitman arm (or idler arm) from the centre tie rod it may be necessary to use a press, as shown in **FIG 10:5**. The components of the steering linkage are shown in **FIG 10:6**.

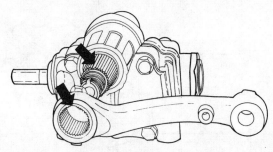

FIG 10:4   The master splines for the Pitman arm

Steering damper:

Check the body for dents or damage and check that the ram is straight and not bent. Make sure that there are no fluid leaks. If any such defect is found, discard the damper and install a new one.

Exercise the damper through its full range of movement and check that there is even resistance to motion in both directions, with no pockets of weak or no resistance.

The attachment of the damper to the centre tie rod is tightened to a torque of 28 to 32 lb ft (4 to 4.5 kg m).

Idler assembly:

It is not necessary to remove the complete linkage in order to service the idler.

Hold the pivot bolt 7, shown in **FIG 10:6**, with an Allen key and remove the self-locking nut 1. Free the idler arm 2 from the bolt using an extractor as shown in **FIG 10:3**.

Take out the plastic protectors and undo the four bolts 5 which secure the bracket to the frame so that the bracket can be removed. The bolt 7 and bush 9 can then be driven out of the bracket and new parts pressed into place.

Install the bracket assembly in the reverse order of removal, tightening the bolts 5 to a torque of 28 to 32 lb ft (4 to 4.5 kg m). Do not forget to install the plastic protectors and do not forget to use a new self-locking nut to secure the idler arm to the pivot bolt.

The bolts 3 on the bracket are supplementary steering stops and they should be adjusted until there is a gap of .12 inch (3 mm) between them and the idler arm at full lock, as shown in **FIG 10:7**.

General examination:

The examination of the ball joints and their gaiters has already been dealt with in **Section 10:2**.

If the tie rod tubes, idler arm or Pitman arm are distorted or bent, renew the defective part. **Do not under any circumstances try to straighten bent parts of the steering linkage.**

Occasionally take some time and check that all attachments are tight and secure as well as being correctly locked. This also applies to the attachments of the steering column and steering box.

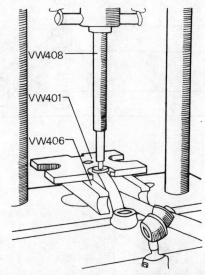

FIG 10:5   Freeing the Pitman arm from the centre tie rod

10:5 The steering column

The column components are shown in **FIG 10:8**, and the attachments are shown in **FIG 10:9**.

Steering wheel:

Remove the horn push parts to expose the nut securing the steering wheel to the column. Take off the nut and remove the washer. Try to free the steering wheel from the splines by gently rocking the rim. If this method fails, a suitable extractor must be used to withdraw the steering wheel from the splines. **Banging or hammering may cause damage to the telescopic portion of the shaft.**

Once the nut has been removed and before the steering wheel is taken off, make aligning marks across the column shaft and hub of the steering wheel so that the wheel will be installed back correctly into the straight-ahead position.

Install the steering wheel in the reverse order of removal and tighten the nut to a torque of 36 lb ft (5 kg m). A few drops of Loctite on the threads will ensure that the nut does not work loose in service.

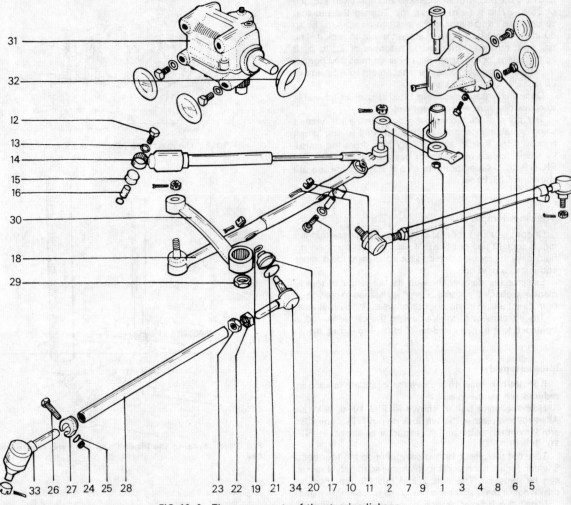

FIG 10:6 The components of the steering linkage

Key to Fig 10:6   1 Self-locking nut   2 Idler arm   3 Screw   4 Nut   5 Screw   6 Spring washer   7 Mounting bolt   8 Idler arm bracket   9 Idler arm bracket bush   10 Splitpin   11 Castellated nut   12 Screw   13 Lockwasher   14 Steering damper   15 Damper rubber bush   16 Sleeve for bush   17 Screw   18 Centre tie rod (track rod)   19 Rubber boot sealing ring   20 Rubber boot   21 Steel ring for boot   22 Nut   23 Tapered ring   24 Nut   25 Spring washer   26 Screw   27 Clip for tie rod (track rod)   28 Tie rod tube   29 Pitman arm (drop arm) nut   30 Pitman arm (drop arm)   31 Steering gear   32 Seal for steering gear   33 Tie rod (track rod) end   34 Tie rod (track rod) end

Removing the steering column:

Disconnect the battery (under the front seat) before starting work

Remove the steering wheel. Disconnect the earth wire for the horn. Disconnect both multi-pin connectors from the switch. Fit the ignition key and turn it to the 'Drive' position. Remove the socket-headed screws securing the lower end of the column to the steering coupling. Similarly remove the socket-headed screws securing the switch and column support. Remove the column assembly complete with the switch.

Remove the circlip and slide the shaft out of the switch assembly. Renew the shaft if it is bent or if the collapsible portion is the slightest bit damaged (cracked or collapsed).

When fitting the parts, install the shaft assembly first (with the closed sides of the column plate pointing forwards and the plate correctly located between the pedal mounting).

Attach the column tube lightly to the switch assembly and slide the complete assembly down the column until the tube is located by the rubber ring. Tighten all attachments finger tight and check that the column is not strained but aligns accurately. Secure the shaft with the circlip. Move the switch in its slotted holes until there is a gap of .08 to .12 inch (2 to 3mm) between the switch and hub of the steering wheel, when the wheel has been installed, and make sure that the direction indicator switch is in the central position. The attachment screws are all tightened to a torque of 7 lb ft (1 kg m) and the screws to the coupling are tightened to a torque of 14 lb ft (2 kg m).

Reconnect the horn earth wire, multi-pin connectors and the battery. Check that the horn and direction indicators operate correctly.

10:6 The steering unit

Removal:

The unit is shown in **FIG 10:6** and the coupling between the unit and steering column in **FIG 10:8**.

Remove the nut securing the Pitman arm to the shaft and pull off the arm with a suitable extractor (leaving the arm attached to the steering linkage). Remove the two socket-headed screws securing the two-arm flange 38 to the coupling 33 and remove the clamp bolt 39 that secures the flange to the wormshaft. Turn the wormshaft to its fullest extent and remove the two-arm flange. Take out the plastic protectors, undo the attachment bolts and remove the unit from the car.

The unit is installed in the reverse order of removal. Before fitting the unit, check the rubber seal in the partition, to see that it is correctly in place and not damaged, and smear it lightly with glycerine or suitable rubber lubricant. Set the unit to the straight-ahead position and also set the steering wheel so that the spokes are level, to ensure that the coupling is correctly connected. Tighten the coupling attachments to a torque of 14 lb ft (2 kg m) and tighten the unit attachment bolts to a torque of 28 to 32 lb ft (4 to 4.5 kg m).

Dismantling:

Wash down the outside of the unit before starting work. The components of the unit are shown in **FIG 10:10**.

Remove the four bolts 5 securing the lower part of the housing 7 to the upper part. Remove the lower part and its gasket, then wipe out the grease from inside the casings.

Slacken and remove the locknut 9 then turn the adjusting screw 14, arrowed in **FIG 10:11**, in a clockwise direction so that it passes down through the upper housing and the Pitman shaft 15 and its associated parts can be removed. Hold the Pitman arm in the padded jaws of a vice, press down on the thrust washer 11, and remove the lockring 10 so that the parts can be removed from the Pitman shaft.

Slacken and remove the locknut 16 and undo the adjuster 17, preferably using the special tool VW.278a as shown in **FIG 10:12**. Tap the housing onto a piece of wood or the palm of the hand to dislodge the bearing parts.

Make up two shells, out of aluminium or suitable metal, which are 30 mm long. Fit these shells in place on the worm and partially unscrew the worm so that the nut and worm assembly can be removed as shown in **FIG 10:13**, with the shells holding the balls in place.

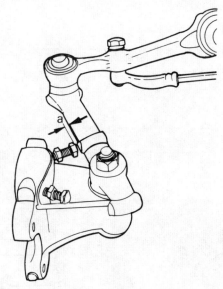

FIG 10:7 Setting the supplementary steering stops

Ball nut and worm:

These should not be dismantled unnecessarily. Wash the assembly in clean fuel and lubricate it with thin oil. Check that the worm rotates freely in the nut, without stiffness or binding **(taking care not to allow the balls to escape).**

Only if the worm turns stiffly or roughly should the unit be dismantled. Similarly the unit must be completely dismantled and reassembled if some of the balls have escaped. All the parts, including the balls, are matched on assembly and individual parts are not obtainable as spares. **This means that if only one ball is lost, the complete unit must be renewed.**

Lay a pad of cloth into the bottom of a container (such as a washing up bowl) and dismantle the unit over this. The pad of cloth will ensure that the balls do not bounce as they drop out. Remove the screw 24, with its lockplate 23 and the clamp 25. Pull out the ball return guides 26 so that the balls 27 in them fall into the container. Turn the nut over and rotate the wormshaft backwards and forwards until the remainder of the balls have fallen out. Pull out the wormshaft from the nut.

Clean the parts and check them for wear or damage. Pay particular attention to the spiral grooves of the wormshaft, checking them most carefully for indentations or any other damage. It is worthwhile using a magnifying glass to check the parts.

Count the balls (total of 58) and divide them into two equal amounts of 29 balls in each group. Fit the wormshaft back into the nut. Feed the balls from one group into one spiral as shown in **FIG 10:14** turning the shaft to guide them in. When as many balls as possible have been fitted, press back one half of the ball return guide into the nut and fill it with the remainder of the balls in the group. Fit the other half of the return guide. Fill the other spiral in a similar manner and then refit the clamp 25 to hold the guides in position. Use a new lockplate and tighten the bolt 24 to a torque of 7 lb ft (1 kg m).

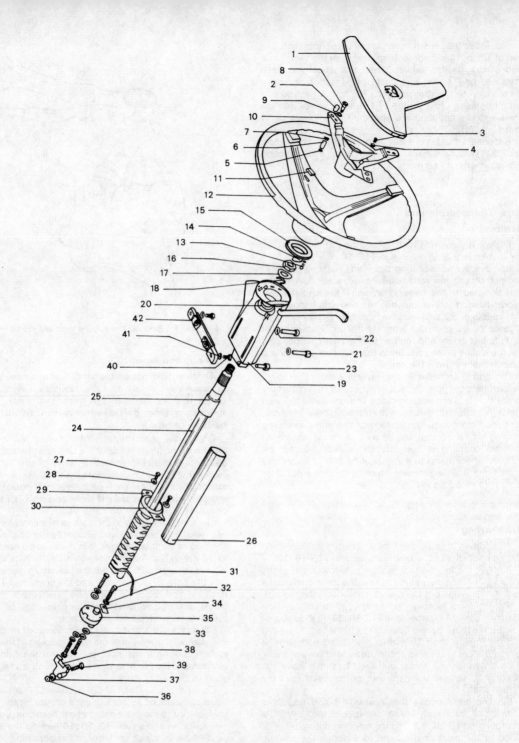

FIG 10:8 The components of the steering column

Key to Fig 10:8 1 to 11 Horn push assembly 12 Steering wheel 13 to 15 Cancelling ring parts 16 Nut 17 Washer 18 Circlip 19 Switch 20 Bearing 21 and 22 Socket-headed attachment bolts and washers 23 Clamp bolt 24 Column shaft assembly 25 Thrust washer 26 Column tube 27 to 30 Support ring and attachments 31 to 39 Steering coupling components 40 to 42 Attachment bracket parts

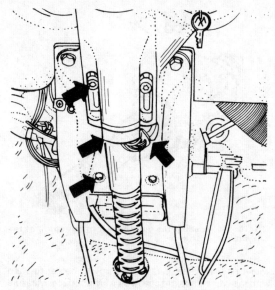

FIG 10:9   The steering column attachments

Assembly and adjustment:

Clean all the parts thoroughly. Discard old seals and gaskets, fitting new ones on reassembly. Check the worm-shaft bearings and renew them if they are worn or defective.

Refit the worm and ball nut assembly to the upper housing, using the made-up shells **A** shown in **FIG 10:13**, and then turn the wormshaft so that it holds the balls securely in place.

Install the lower bearing assembly, smear the threads of the bearing adjuster with sealing compound and tighten it down in the housing to fully press the bearings into place. Slacken back the adjuster slightly and fit the lock-nut 16 loosely into place. Fit a suitable torque wrench onto the wormshaft and tighten down the adjuster until the torque required to turn the wormshaft is correct at 1.5 to 2.0 kg m (2.0 to 2.5 kg m with the seal 22 fitted). Tighten down the locknut to hold the adjuster in position and check again that the torque required to turn the worm-shaft is still within limits. Install the wormshaft seal if this has not already been done.

Fit the adjuster screw 14, spring 13, sleeve 12 and thrust washer 11 back into the Pitman shaft 15. Press down on the thrust washer with a screwdriver and fit a new lockring 10 to secure the parts. Fit the adjusting screw back into the upper housing and turn it in an anticlock-wise direction to fit the shaft assembly back into place. Turn the screw until it reaches the stop and then turn it clockwise by a $\frac{1}{4}$ turn. Make sure that the socket on the shaft locates correctly on the ball nut.

Fill the housing with 250 cc of grease. Install a new oil seal into the lower housing and bolt the lower housing back into place using a new gasket. Tighten the attachment bolts to a torque of 28 to 32 lb ft (4 to 4.5 kg m).

Fit the torque wrench to the wormshaft and set the Pitman arm adjusting screw so that the torque required to turn the wormshaft is a maximum of 8 kg m with minimum play. Tighten the locknut and check that the torque has not altered.

The unit is now ready for installation.

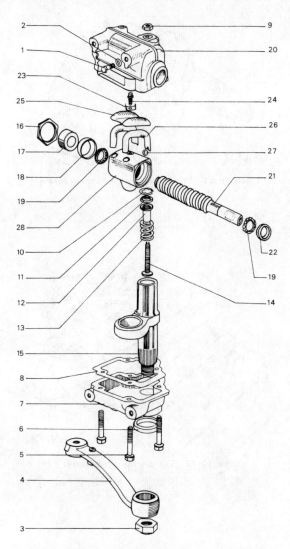

FIG 10:10   The components of the steering unit

Key to Fig 10:10   1 Screw   2 Spring washer
3 Nut for Pitman (drop) arm   4 Pitman (drop) arm
5 Screw and washers   6 Seal for Pitman (drop) arm shaft
7 Lower part of housing   8 Housing gasket
9 Adjusting screw locknut   10 Lockring   11 Thrust washer
12 Thrust sleeve   13 Spring   14 Adjusting screw
15 Pitman (drop) arm shaft   16 Adjuster locknut
17 Worm adjuster   18 Bearing outer race   19 Bearing cage
20 Case upper part   21 Steering worm   22 Worm seal
23 Lockplate   24 Screw with shoulder   25 Clamp for ball
guides   26 Ball return guides   27 Ball   28 Ball nut

10:7 Steering geometry

The front wheel alignment (toe-in) should be checked after major repairs or if one wheel has been 'kerbed' hard. Incorrect alignment will cause rapid tyre wear, leaving one edge of the tread worn to a characteristic feathered edge.

The owner can set the correct alignment, but a trammel must be made up to measure the distance between the

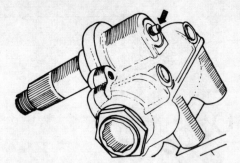

FIG 10:11   The Pitman arm adjusting screw

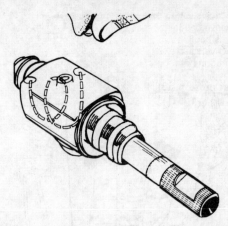

FIG 10:14   Feeding the balls back into one spiral of the ball nut

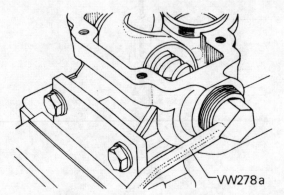

FIG 10:12   The wormshaft adjuster

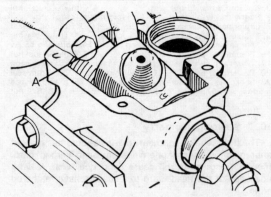

FIG 10:13   Removing the wormshaft and ball nut, using made-up shells **A** to keep the balls in place

wheel rims at wheel centre height. Roll the car forward with the wheels straight ahead on a level surface. Measure the distance between the wheel rims at wheel centre height and at the front of the wheels. Mark the rims at the points where they were measured with chalk and then push the car forwards until the marks are again at wheel centre height but at the rear (so that the wheels have turned exactly a half revolution). Again measure the distance between the wheel rims and the difference between the two dimensions gives the actual alignment. Note that the car must be pushed forwards only while taking measurements. If the alignment is incorrect, slacken the clamps and taper rings on both track rods and either shorten or lengthen each rod by the same amount to bring the setting within limits.

The whole operation is fraught with difficulties and inaccuracies and it is far simpler to take the car to a VW agent, who will check using special gauges and make the settings accurately.

It is just possible to check the steering lock angles using bits of string, long straightedges and protractors but again the VW agent can do the checks quickly, simply and accurately using special gauges.

10:8 Fault diagnosis

(a) Wheel wobble or tramp

1 Unbalanced wheels and tyres, incorrect tyre pressures
2 Slackness in steering linkage
3 Worn or slack hub bearings
4 Defective steering damper
5 Defective dampers or suspension strut assembly

(b) Wander

1 Check 1, 2, 3 and 5 in (a)
2 Front and rear suspensions out of line (body deformed)
3 Weak dampers or coil springs in suspension struts

(c) Heavy steering

1 Check 5 in (a)
2 Very low or uneven tyre pressures
3 Faulty steering unit adjustments

4 Defective steering unit components
5 Defective ball joints
6 Wheels badly out of alignment
7 Defective steering damper
8 Steering column bent or assembled under strain.

(d) Lost motion

1 Check 2 in (a); 3, 4 and 5 in (c)
2 Loose steering wheels or worn splines

3 Pitman arm loose on shaft
4 Defective steering coupling
5 Steering unit attachments loose

(e) Pulls to one side

1 Check 5 in (a); 2 in (b); 2 and 6 in (c)
2 Brake binding
3 Defective or damaged rear suspension
4 Defective or damaged front suspension

CHAPTER 11

THE BRAKING SYSTEM

11 :1 Description
11 :2 Maintenance
11 :3 Flexible hoses
11 :4 The front disc brakes
11 :5 The rear drum brakes
11 :6 The master cylinder

11 :7 Brake pressure limiter valve
11 :8 Bleeding the brakes
11 :9 Handbrake cables
11 :10 Pedal assembly
11 :11 Fault diagnosis

11 :1 Description

Disc brakes are fitted to the front wheels and drum brakes are fitted to the rear wheels. All models are fitted with a tandem master cylinder which ensures that the rear drum brakes are hydraulically independent from the front disc brakes.

When the brake pedal is pressed, hydraulic pressure is generated by the master cylinder and this pressure is led to the wheel brakes through a system of pipes and flexible hoses, shown in **FIG 11 :1**. Also shown in the figure are the components of the tandem master cylinder and the rear wheel cylinders. If there is a leak in one of the hydraulic systems the rear piston in the master cylinder will contact the front one and push it forwards mechanically, or if there is a failure in the other half of the system the front piston will move forwards until it is stopped by the end of the cylinder, allowing pressure to be built up normally by the rear piston. Pedal travel will be longer if one half of the system fails and overall braking efficiency will be reduced but the part of the system that is operating will still function at full efficiency.

A separate mechanical linkage is used to apply the rear brakes for parking.

A pressure-limiting valve is fitted into the rear brake circuit and this valve ensures that at high pedal pressures the maximum pressure to the rear brakes is limited, preventing the rear wheels from locking.

Two shoes, with friction material bonded to them, are fitted in each rear brake. One end of each shoe pivots in an adjuster, so that wear of the linings can be taken up, while the wheel cylinder fits between the other ends of the shoes. When hydraulic pressure is applied to the wheel cylinder the piston moves outwards, forcing the shoes into contact with the revolving brake drum. Return springs ensure that the shoes move away from the drum when the hydraulic pressure is released.

The disc brake has two pistons mounted in the cylinder which move together when hydraulic pressure is applied. The pistons then press the brake pads into contact with the revolving brake disc, clamping it and giving retarding action. The seals around the pistons provide both the self-adjustment and the withdrawal action for the brake. When the piston moves, the seal distorts slightly and when the pressure is released the seal returns to its normal shape, pulling the piston back slightly (giving clearance between pad and disc). If the gap between the pad and disc is excessive, the piston will slide through the seal until it takes up the excess and the distortion of the seal then acts normally to withdraw the piston slightly.

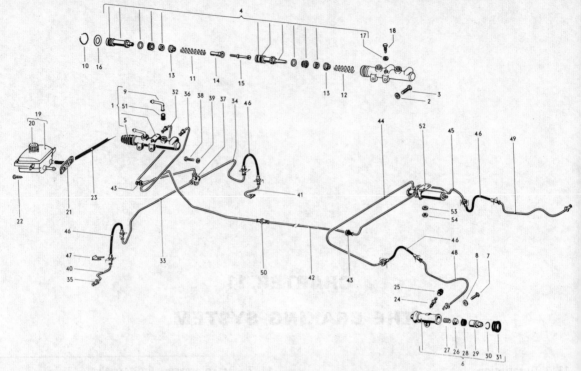

FIG 11:1   The components and lines of the braking system

Key to Fig 11:1   1 Tandem master cylinder (dual-line)   2 Lockwasher   3 Bolt   4 Repair kit for master cylinder   5 Rubber boot   6 Rear wheel brake cylinder   7 Bolt   8 Lockwasher   9 Connection elbow   10 Lockring   11 Rear piston spring   12 Front piston spring   13 Spring seat   14 Stop sleeve   15 Stop sleeve screw   16 Stop washer   17 Seal   18 Bolt   19 Tandem master cylinder reservoir   20 Screw cap reservoir   21 Packing   22 Tapping screw   23 Tube   24 Bleed nipple   25 Rubber dust cap   26 Cup expander   27 Spring for cup expander   28 Wheel brake cylinder cup   29 Wheel brake cylinder piston   30 Piston circlip   31 Rubber boot   32 Master cylinder to T-piece front brake line   33 Front left from T-piece to brake hose brake line   34 Front right from T-piece to brake hose brake line   35 Union nut   36 Brake line from master cylinder to connecting piece   37 Brake lines T-piece   38 Bolt   39 Lockwasher   40 Front left from brake hose to brake caliper brake line   41 Front right from brake hose to brake caliper brake line   42 Brake line from connecting piece to brake pressure limiting valve   43 Grommet for brake and clutch pressure lines in rear floor panel   44 Rear left from pressure limiting valve to brake hose brake line   45 Rear right from pressure limiting valve to brake hose brake line   46 Front and rear brake hose   47 Bracket for brake hose   48 Rear left from brake hose to wheel brake cylinder brake line   49 Rear right from brake hose to wheel brake cylinder brake line   50 Brake lines connecting piece   51 Plug for master brake cylinder   52 Brake pressure limiting valve   53 Lockwasher   54 Nut

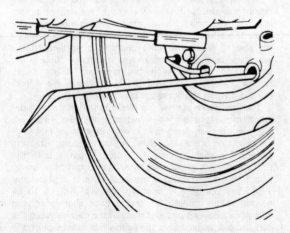

FIG 11:2   Adjusting the rear brakes, a screwdriver can be used in place of the tool shown

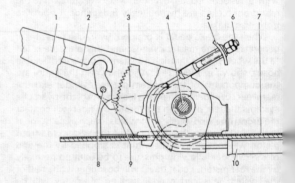

FIG 11:3   The handbrake lever and handbrake adjustment point

Key to Fig 11:3   1 Handbrake lever   2 Pawl rod   3 Ratchet segment   4 Lever pin   5 Cable compensator   6 Brake cable   7 Frame   8 Pawl pin   9 Pawl   10 Cable guide plate

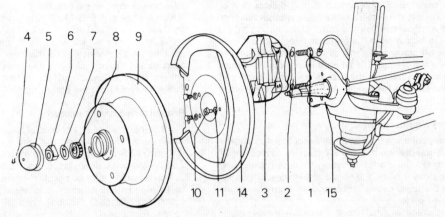

FIG 11 : 4   The disc brake major components

Key to Fig 11 : 4   1 Caliper mounting bolt   2 Lockplate   3 Brake caliper   4 C-washer   5 Hub cap   6 Clamp nut   7 Thrust washer   8 Hub bearing   9 Brake disc   10 Securing bolt   11 Spring washer   14 Splash shield   15 Steering knuckle

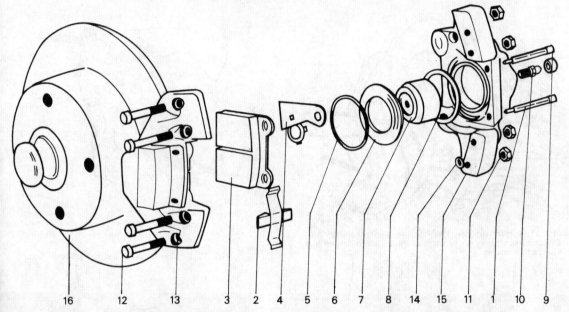

FIG 11 : 5   The brake caliper components. Do not separate the halves of the caliper unnecessarily

Key to Fig 11 : 5   1 Brake pad retaining pin   2 Tensioning spring   3 Brake pad   4 Piston retaining plate   5 Clamp ring   6 Seal   7 Dust cap   8 Rubber seal   9 Dust cap   10 Bleeder valve   11 Hexagon nut   12 Cheese head screw   13 Caliper outer half   14 Seal   15 Caliper inner half   16 Brake disc

11 : 2 Maintenance

Fluid level:

Check the level of the fluid in the translucent hydraulic fluid reservoir. The level will slowly fall as the disc brake pads wear but this is normal. Wipe the top clean before removing the cap and topping up the reservoir. Use only ATE Blue fluid or a fluid that meets specification SAE.70.R3.

At intervals of 18 months, empty the system and refill and bleed it using fresh fluid, or take the car to a VW agent so that the amount of moisture in the fluid can be checked.

Adjustments:

The disc brakes are self-adjusting in use. However, **if the disc brakes have been removed or dismantled the brake pedal must be pumped hard several times after the parts have been installed.** This ensures that any excessive clearance is taken up and the brakes are correctly set for operation.

The method of adjusting the rear drum brakes is shown in **FIG 11 : 2**. Remove the sealing plug from the backplate and jack up the rear of the car. Fit the tool to the teeth of one adjuster and rotate it until the shoe is in firm contact with the brake drum. Slacken back the adjuster two or three clicks until the wheel rotates freely without binding. Repeat the adjustment on the other shoe, noting that it will have to be turned in the opposite direction, and then adjust the other rear brake in a similar manner. Lower the car back to the ground. The lining thickness on the shoes can be checked through the hole in the brake drum and new shoes must be fitted when the old linings have worn down to .1 inch (2.5 mm).

Handbrake adjustments:

Normally adjusting the rear wheels should automatically adjust the handbrake. If there is excessive movement of the handbrake lever after adjusting the rear brakes, first check carefully through the handbrake linkage. Check for seized or damaged cables and check for worn clevis pins or damaged parts.

If the linkage is satisfactory, excessive movement is due to cable stretch. Jack up the rear of the car so that the wheels are clear (with the rear brakes correctly adjusted). Pull back the dust cover at the base of the handbrake lever to expose the cable adjusters, one of which is shown in **FIG 11 : 3**. Apply the handbrake lever by three notches and adjust the cables until both wheels can just be rotated by hand, with the same pressure required on each wheel. Pull the lever on a further two notches and check that the rear wheels are locked. Fully release the handbrake and check that the rear wheels rotate freely without the brakes binding.

Preventative maintenance

All linings should be checked at regular intervals. New shoes must be fitted when the linings have worn down to .1 inch (2.5 mm) and new pads must be fitted when the linings have worn down to .08 inch (2 mm).

Fluid should either be checked or renewed at intervals of 18 months and at intervals of three years the system should be drained, flushed through with methylated spirits (denatured alcohol) and all the components removed and dismantled. Renew all seals and gaskets and check components for wear before reassembling the system, filling, and bleeding with fresh hydraulic fluid.

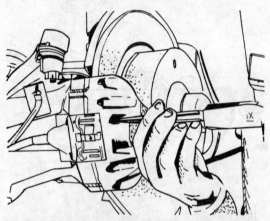

FIG 11 : 6 Driving out the friction pad retaining pins. Check direction as on some models, pins are driven outwards to remove

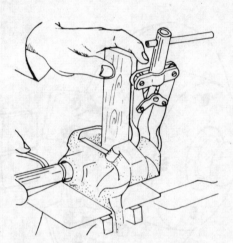

FIG 11 : 8 Removing a caliper piston

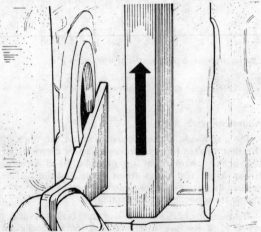

FIG 11 : 7 Checking the position of the piston cut-out with a gauge

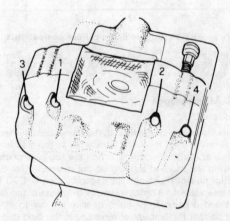

FIG 11 : 9 The sequence for tightening the caliper bolts

Hydraulic fluid is poisonous and acts as an effective paint remover. Old fluid makes a useful substitute for penetrating oil but make sure that it is stored in clearly marked containers so that it cannot be accidentally poured back into the system.

Use only fresh fluid from sealed containers for filling or topping-up the system. The fluid is hygroscopic and will absorb moisture if exposed to the air. Never return fluid directly from bleeding into the reservoir (preferably discard it).

At regular intervals check the metal lines for dents or corrosion. Renew lines which are defective otherwise they may fail under the stress of heavy braking. At the same time examine the flexible hoses for chafing or perishing, noting that their safe maximum life is 5 years and that they should be renewed after this time.

The only solvents that are safe to use with the seals of the hydraulic system are methylated spirits, special cleansing fluids or brake fluid itself. Any other solvent will attack the material of the seals. If metal parts are cleaned with any other solvent, they should be swilled with methylated spirits before assembly of the components to ensure that all traces of other solvent have been removed.

11:3 Flexible hoses

As has already been stated, the hoses should be renewed after five years when their safe life is finished.

If a hose is found to be blocked, try to clear it with compressed air and if this fails discard the hose and fit a new one. Poking through with wire will damage the inner lining.

When removing or installing a flexible hose take great care not to twist or strain the flexible portion. Hold the hose hexagons with a spanner and undo the union nut securing the metal line, using another spanner. Free the clip and pull the hose out of the bracket. Install the hose in the reverse order of removal. Make sure that the hose will not foul on any adjacent part when the steering or suspension moves through its full range.

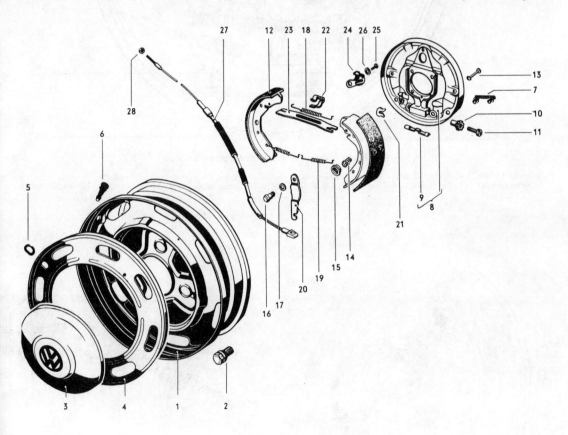

FIG 11:10 The components of the rear brake (drum not shown)

Key to Fig 11:10   1 Wheel disc   2 Wheel securing bolt   3 Hub cap   4 Rim embellisher   5 Grommet for valve hole   6 Rubber valve   7 Sealing bridge for backplate   8 Rear brake backplate   9 Leaf spring for adjusting device   10 Brake shoe adjusting nut   1 Brake shoe adjusting screw   12 Brake shoe with lining   13 Brake shoe steady pin   14 Spring for steady pin   15 Spring seat   6 Fulcrum pin for handbrake operating lever   17 Spring washer   18 Upper brake shoe return spring   19 Lower brake shoe return spring   20 Handbrake operating lever   21 C-washer for fulcrum pin   22 Spring clip for connecting link   23 Connecting link   4 Brake cable bracket   25 Bolt   26 Lockwasher   27 Handbrake cable   28 Nut

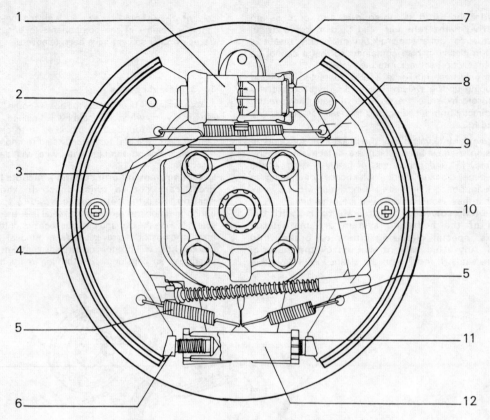

FIG 11:11   The rear brake correctly assembled

Key to Fig 11:10   1 Cylinder   2 Brake shoe with lining   3 Upper return spring   4 Spring with cup and pin   5 Lower return spring
6 Adjusting screw   7 Backplate   8 Connecting link   9 Lever   10 Brake cable   11 Adjusting nut   12 Anchor block

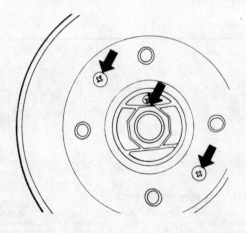

FIG 11:12   Drum attachments

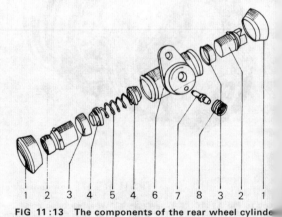

FIG 11:13   The components of the rear wheel cylinder

Key to Fig 11:13   1 Boot   2 Piston   3 Cu
4 Cup expander   5 Spring   6 Cylinder bod
7 Bleeder valve   8 Dust cap

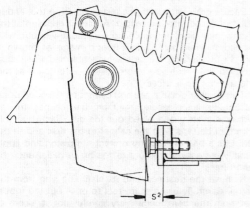

FIG 11:14   Adjusting the brake pedal stop

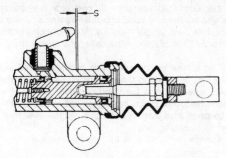

FIG 11:15   Adjusting the brake pedal pushrod

11:4 The front disc brakes

The main components of the disc brake are shown in **FIG 11:4**, and the components of the caliper in **FIG 11:5**.

Renewing friction pads:

The pads must be renewed when the lining material has worn down to .08 inch (2 mm). Factory replacement pads should be fitted and the owner must not attempt to bond new linings onto the old pads.

Jack up the front of the car, after slackening the road wheel attachments, and remove the front road wheels.

Use a suitable drift to drive out the pad retaining pins as shown in **FIG 11:6**. The figure actually shows the pins for a 1600 model but the method is still the same. Remove the tensioning spring and draw out the old pads. A special pair of tongs is made for the task but a piece of strong cord passed through the holes in the lugs and pulled on with the aid of a piece of wood will do just as well.

If the pads are to be used again, mark them for position so that they will be installed back into their original positions. **If the linings are excessively worn or contaminated with oil or grease, new pads must be fitted.**

Use a small brush (such as a bottle brush) and methylated spirits to clean out the piston and recesses in the caliper, followed by compressed air to dry the parts. Check the piston seal and if it is defective or brittle the caliper must be removed for further servicing.

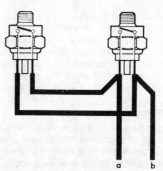

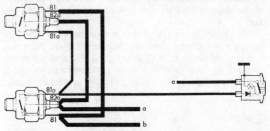

FIG 11:16   The connections for the standard brake light switches

FIG 11:17   The connections for the brake light switches with failure warning light

Key to Figs 11:16 and 11:17   a—to terminal 15
b—to brake lights

Press the pistons back into the caliper. Fluid will be returned to the reservoir during this operation and it may be necessary to syphon some out to prevent it from overflowing. If it is found that one piston starts to move out as the other moves in, if the special piston returning tool is not used, open the bleed screw on the caliper so that surplus fluid is ejected and there is no pressure build-up in the caliper.

Install the new piston retaining plates (supplied with the kit) after checking that the piston is correctly positioned. There is a cut-out in the flange of the piston and this allows the pad to tilt very slightly, reducing brake squeal. The cut-out should be located at an angle of 20 deg. and a gauge is made for the task, as shown in **FIG 11:7**. Special tongs are made for rotating the piston if it is not correctly aligned.

Fit the linings back into place, install the new tensioning spring, and drive the retaining pins back into place with light taps of a hammer.

Pump the brake pedal firmly several times before using the car, to take up the clearance.

Check the clearance between pads and disc before installing the road wheel. The correct clearance should be .002 to .008 inch (.05 to .2 mm). If the car has not been used for some time, or it is found that there is excessive pedal travel even after the system has been bled and the brakes adjusted, it is possible that the piston is sticking in the seal. If the clearance is excessive, remove one pad at a time and fit a block of wood $\frac{1}{4}$ inch (6 mm) thick in its place. Apply heavy pressure on the brake pedal to move the piston out and then press the piston fully back into the bore. Repeat this operation several times, making sure that the master cylinder reservoir does not overflow, and then install the brake pad. Remove the other brake pad and repeat the operation all over again on the other side piston. If this fails to prevent a piston sticking the caliper must be removed for further examination.

Caliper removal:

Jack up the car and remove the road wheel. Attach a length of rubber or plastic tube to the bleed nipple, after removing the rubber dust cap, open the bleed nipple and pump the brake pedal until the system is empty.

Disconnect the hydraulic lines from the caliper, taking care that no fluid spillage falls onto the brake linings. Remove the brake pads as described earlier.

Remove the two attachment bolts securing the caliper to the steering knuckle and slide the caliper off from the disc.

The caliper is installed in the reverse order of removal, using a new lockplate and new bolts, tightening them to a torque of 58 to 65 lb ft (8 to 9 kg m). Fill and bleed the front braking system after the linings have been installed. Pump the brake pedal hard several times and refit the road wheel.

Brake disc:

The disc and front wheel hub are one integral unit. The removal and installation of the unit are dealt with in **Chapter 9, Section 9:3**. Note that it will be necessary to remove the caliper as well.

Check the operating faces of the disc for deep concentric scores or any radial scoring. If cracks are found in the disc it must be renewed but light scoring can be removed by grinding, provided that the minimum disc thickness of .41 inch (10.5 mm) is not reached. The disc must be renewed if it has worn down to a thickness of .39 inch (10 mm).

The build-up of friction material and dirt on the disc can be removed by soaking with trichlorethylene and scrubbing gently with worn emerycloth.

Install the hub assembly and set the correct bearing float. Mount the DTI (Dial Test Indicator) on the suspension so that its stylus rests vertically against the outer operating face of the disc and near to the outer edge. Rotate the hub slowly and check the maximum run-out of the disc. If the run-out exceeds .008 inch (.2 mm) a new hub and disc assembly must be fitted.

Wipe down the disc operating faces using a suitable harsh solvent to remove all grease and finger marks before installing the brake caliper.

Caliper servicing:

Remove the caliper as described earlier. **Do not separate the halves of the caliper. As there are seals fitted between the caliper halves, the caliper must only be cleaned with methylated spirits otherwise the seals will fail.**

Pressure is required to remove the pistons and as soon as one piston has been removed, pressure will blow out and the other piston cannot be removed. The solution is to service one piston at a time, though the other piston can be removed if a flat piece of metal and piece of thick rubber are clamped over the open bore to seal it.

Secure one piston with the piston pressing tool and fit a pad of wood into the caliper. Apply air pressure at the inlet to the caliper and the piston will be driven out, with the pad of wood protecting it from damage, as shown in **FIG 11:8**. Service the side which has had the piston removed then remove the other side piston so that this side too can be serviced.

If a piston sticks in place and cannot be removed using reasonable air pressure, reattach the caliper to the hydraulic system and bleed out the air. Clamp the free piston, or better still fit the caliper to the disc and fit the pad. Use a pad of wood to protect the piston and apply steadily increasing pressure to the brake pedal until the piston frees.

Remove the dust seal and its clamping ring from the piston. Carefully use a sharp tool to prise out the rubber seal from the bore, being very careful not to score or mark the bore. Check the bore for wear, corrosion or scores. Dust marks or very light corrosion may be removed using a plastic pot scourer but if the damage is deeper a complete new caliper must be fitted. Check the chromed surface of the piston for damage and renew the piston if required.

Wet a new piston seal with hydraulic fluid and fit it back into its recess in the bore, using only the fingers, and make sure that it is fully and squarely seated. Press the piston back into place, **taking great care not to allow it to cock and jam in the bore.** Fit the new dust shield and its clamping ring.

Service the other side in a similar manner.

Caliper dismantling:

The two halves of the caliper must only be separated if there are fluid leaks between them, and even then it is recommended that a new caliper is fitted.

Progressively slacken the four nuts securing the caliper halves and separate the two halves.

Thoroughly clean the caliper parts and check the mating faces for damage.

Fit the halves together, using new O-rings between them, and bolt them together using new nuts and bolts. Note that the shorter pair of bolts is fitted outermost. Tighten the nuts in the order shown in **FIG 11:9** to a torque of 7 lb ft (1 kg m). Make sure that the halves are correctly aligned and tighten the nuts, again in order, to a torque of 14 lb ft (2 kg m).

11:5 The rear drum brakes

The components of a drum brake are shown in **FIG 11:10**. The correct assembly of the drum brake is shown in **FIG 11:11** and though this figure is actually for a 1600 model the details of the brake are typical.

Brake drum:

The attachments of the drum are shown in **FIG 11:12** Slacken off the brake adjusters and take out the two countersunk screws securing the drum. Pull off the drum assisting it with light blows from a copper mallet if it sticks.

Hang the drum on a wooden handle and tap it with light metal tool. If the note is flat the drum has a crack in it and must be rejected, fitting a new drum on assembly.

Check the drum for scores. Provided that the drum is not cracked and the linings are not excessively worn the drum may be refitted. When it comes to relining the brakes, discard the scored drum and install a new one. If the drum is also cracked or the shoes require relining, install a drum on reassembly, as well as relining the brakes.

A lightly scored drum may be skimmed out in a lathe, provided that it is mounted on a flange and not in a chuck. The maximum diameter to which the drum may be skimmed out is 9.283 inch (249.5 mm). Oversized linings must be fitted with a skimmed out drum.

Degrease the operating face of the drum with a suitable harsh solvent before refitting the drum.

Relining the brakes:

New or exchange shoes must be fitted if the old linings are worn down to a minimum thickness of .1 inch (2.5 mm), or if they are contaminated with oil or grease.

Always renew the shoes in axle sets to maintain the braking balance. Do not attempt to clean contaminated linings either by use of solvents or baking as the linings will be damaged by any treatment effective enough to remove all the contaminant. Do not attempt to bond or rivet new linings into place but use factory exchange shoes which have had the linings correctly secured and then ground to shape.

1 Jack up the rear of the car and remove the road wheel and brake drum. Slacken off the handbrake cable adjustment and free the cable from the lever in the wheel brake.

2 Grip the outer washer of the shoe steady assembly with a pair of pliers and hold the pin with a finger at the back of the backplate. Press in the washer against the spring and turn it through 90 deg. so that the T-head of the pin can be passed through the slot in the washer and the washer removed. Take off the spring and withdraw the pin from the rear of the backplate. Remove the steady assembly for the other shoe in a similar manner.

3 Slacken off both the adjusters as far as they will go. Thread a length of cord around one end of one shoe and pull the shoe out of its slot. Repeat on the other three ends of the shoes and then remove the return springs. Remove the shoe without the handbrake lever first and then remove the remaining shoe. Do not press the brake pedal when the shoes have been removed.

4 Clean all the metal parts using a stiff brush and air line. Methylated spirits may be used to remove greasy deposits, but take great care not to allow solvent onto the linings.

5 Check that the adjusters rotate freely in their threads and lightly lubricate all pivot and bearing surfaces with white zinc-based grease or equivalent special brake grease. **Do not allow grease onto the linings and also avoid touching them with dirty or oily hands.**

6 Install the new shoes, together with new return springs, in the reverse order of removal. Use the piece of cord to pull the shoes into position and do not forget to install the shoe steadies. Check the operation by gently pulling on the handbrake cable and have an assistant very lightly press down on the brake pedal so that the shoes just start to move.

7 Before refitting the brake drum, tap the shoes into position so that they are concentric. Once the drum is in place, refit the road wheel and then adjust the rear brakes first, followed by the handbrake cables, before lowering the car back to the ground.

Wheel cylinder:

The parts of the wheel cylinder are shown in **FIG 11 :13**. The brake drum and brakes shoes must be removed before the wheel cylinder can be taken off the brake backplate.

Disconnect the metal pipe by undoing the union nut, after emptying the rear brake system through a bleed nipple. Remove the bleed screw and take out the attachment bolt so that the unit can be removed.

Remove the rubber boots 1 and pull out the pistons 2. The seals 3, expanders 4, and spring 5 can then be removed from the body.

Discard the seals, fitting new ones from a service kit on assembly. Wash the parts in methylated spirits and check the bore of the body. If the bore is at all pitted, worn, scored or corroded renew the complete assembly. Do not attempt to polish the bore with abrasive.

Use the parts supplied in a service kit when reassembling the unit. Wet one cup seal with hydraulic fluid and fit it back into the bore, **taking great care not to bend or damage the lips of the seal.** Fit the expander, spring and other expander from the opposite end of the unit and then **carefully** install the other seal, after wetting it with hydraulic fluid. Fit the pistons back into place, after lightly lubricating them with hydraulic fluid or brake grease, and fit the new rubber boots into position.

Install the wheel cylinder in the reverse order of removal. Refit the shoes and drum then bleed the rear brake hydraulic system.

11 :6 The master cylinder

Removal:

Syphon out the fluid from the reservoir and empty both brake systems through bleed nipples on the front and rear brakes.

Remove the front floor covering and disconnect the hoses connecting the master cylinder to the reservoir, by gently pulling out the elbow connectors and plugs from the master cylinder. Disconnect the metal lines by undoing the union nuts. Have rags handy to catch any spillage.

Disconnect the electrical wires from the brake light switches, labelling them if need be to ensure correct connections on reassembly.

Pull back the rubber boot, take out the two attachment bolts and remove the master cylinder from the pedal support bracket.

Installation:

Guide the pushrod on the pedal into the master cylinder and loosely secure the master cylinder in place with the two bolts. Slacken the locknuts on the pushrod and shorten it to a length of approximately $3\frac{3}{4}$ inch (95 mm). Push the master cylinder firmly towards the pushrod and tighten its attachment bolts to a torque of 58 to 65 lb ft (8 to 9 kg m).

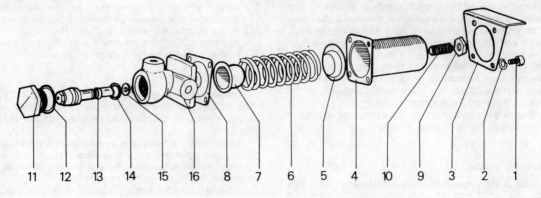

FIG 11:18 The components of the brake pressure limiter valve

Key to Fig 11:18 1 Socket head capscrew 2 Lockwasher 3 Bracket 4 Spring housing 5 Spring plate 6 Spring 7 Thrust cap 8 Gasket 9 Nut 10 Adjusting screw 11 Plug 12 Seal 13 Piston 14 Seal 15 Cup 16 Regulator body

Wet the sealing plugs with a little hydraulic fluid and press them and the hose elbows back into the body. Reconnect the metal lines. Reconnect the electrical wires to the switches.

Adjust the pedal stop, shown in **FIG 11:14**, until the dimension S2 is correct at .96 inch (24.5 mm). Adjust the length of the pushrod until the dimension S, shown in **FIG 11:15**, is correct at .040 inch (1 mm) when the pedal is in the released position. The actual clearance cannot be measured so check the pedal free play by hand instead. The dimension **S** is correct when the pedal free play is $\frac{1}{4}$ inch (6 to 7 mm).

Fill the reservoir with fresh brake fluid and bleed both braking systems.

Servicing:

Remove both brake light switches. Refer to **FIG 11:1**. Lightly press the rear piston into the cylinder bore and take out the stop bolt 18, with its copper seal 17. Still pressing the piston into the bore, remove the lock ring 10 and the stopwasher 16. The internal parts can now be shaken or tapped out of the bore of the body.

Dismantle the internal parts and remove all the old seals. Wash all the metal parts in methylated spirits and check them for wear or damage. If the bore of the master cylinder is worn or damaged a complete new unit must be fitted.

Install the new seals into positions after wetting them with clean hydraulic fluid, using only the fingers and making sure that they face in the correct direction and are fully and squarely seated. All the seals except the secondary one for the rear brake piston are interchangeable. Assemble the internal parts and dip them into clean hydraulic fluid.

Insert the parts back into the bore, **taking great care not to bend back or damage the lips of the seals.** Press the piston down into the bore and refit the stop bolt with a new copper seal. Still holding the piston down the bore, fit the stopwasher and lock ring to secure the piston in place.

Check that the pistons return freely under the action of the springs after they have been pressed down the bore.

Refit the brake light switches.

Brake light switches:

Two switches are installed on the master cylinder on all models. On standard models the switches are in parallel so that either brake circuit on its own can operate the brake lights. The circuit is shown in **FIG 11:16**. To test the switches in this case, disconnect the leads from one switch and operate the brakes while an assistant watches the brake lights. Reconnect the leads and repeat the test with the leads disconnected from the other switch. In both cases the brake lights should operate.

On some models a slightly more complicated switching system is fitted and the switches also operate a warning light if one brake system fails. The circuit is shown in **FIG 11:17**. Periodically press in the warning light to check that the lamp has not failed. Check the operation of the switches by opening a bleed nipple on a front brake caliper and pressing down the brake pedal, catching the fluid that escapes from the bleed nipple. With the ignition switched on, the warning lamp should light. Tighten the bleed nipple before releasing the pedal, to ensure that air is not drawn into the system.

If a switch is removed from the master cylinder, drain out fluid first to prevent spillage. Install the switch and tighten it to a torque of 11 to 14 lb ft (1.5 to 2 kg m) then bleed the braking system to which the switch is fitted.

11:7 Brake pressure limiter valve

The location of the valve is shown in **FIG 11:1** and the components in **FIG 11:18**.

Testing:

As a rough test, feel the valve while an assistant applies firm pressure to the brake pedal and then releases it. As the brakes release a click should be felt in the limiter valve.

For full and accurate checks, two high pressure gauges are required. One gauge is fitted in place of a bleed nipple on the front calipers and the other gauge is fitted in place of a bleed nipple on the rear brakes. Bleed the system to remove the air from the gauges. The pressure in the rear brakes can be raised by screwing in the adjuster screw 10

116

or lowered by screwing it out. Note that pressures of up to 1400 lb/sq inch (100 kg/sq cm) are reached in the front brakes and if the pressure in the rear brakes cannot be set to the correct limits, renew or service the valve.

Servicing :

Service kits of parts, including silicone grease, are available and a complete kit should be used every time the valve is dismantled and reassembled.

Disconnect the brake lines from the valve, catching fluid spillage, and take out the bolts securing the bracket to the frame of the car.

Clamp the valve between the jaws of a vice and take out the socket-headed screws 1. Carefully open the vice until the pressure of the spring 6 has been released, and remove the parts from the body. Unscrew the plug 11 and withdraw the piston 13.

Wet the internal parts with brake fluid when fitting the seals and when installing the piston assembly. Tighten the plug 11 to a torque of 80 lb ft (11 kg m). Fit the remainder of the parts and compress them in the jaws of a vice so that the screws 1 can be refitted and tightened to a torque of 7 lb ft (1 kg m). After the valve has been adjusted, seal the adjusting screw with D14 sealing compound to prevent water from penetrating into the spring portion. When assembling the valve, the space **A** shown in **FIG 11 : 19** must be packed with silicone grease.

Bleed the rear brakes after the valve has been installed in the reverse order of removal.

11 : 8 Bleeding the brakes

This is not routine maintenance but it must be carried out when air has entered the hydraulic system, either on dismantling or by allowing the fluid level in the reservoir to fall so low that air is drawn into the master cylinder.

Bleed the brake with the longest pipe run first. The front and rear brakes are hydraulically independent, so only the system which has been disturbed requires bleeding. Obviously if a common component such as the master cylinder has been removed then both brake systems must be bled.

Fluid which has been bled through the system should be discarded. Only if the fluid is perfectly clean may it be used again, after it has been stored for at least 24 hours in a clean sealed container to allow the air to disperse. **Never return fluid directly from bleeding to the reservoir.**

Before starting the operation, fill the reservoir as full as it will go without spillage, using fresh ATE Blue fluid. As the operation progresses, top up the reservoir as required to prevent air from being drawn into the master cylinder.

Attach a length of plastic or rubber tube to the bleed nipple and dip the free end of the tube in a little clean fluid in a glass container.

Open the bleed screw and have an assistant pump the brake pedal. Continue having the pedal pumped until a clear stream of fluid, perfectly free from any air bubbles, comes out of the bleeder tube. If difficulty is found in removing all the air, air may be leaking in around the bleed nipple on the return stroke. In such cases, close the bleed nipple at the end of a pedal stroke and only open it again when slight pressure has been applied to the pedal. Finally close the bleed nipple on a downstroke of the pedal.

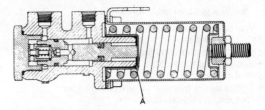

FIG 11 :19   The interior of the cup **A** must be packed with silicone grease on reassembly

If the complete braking system has been dismantled, it may be difficult to remove all the air. In such cases either have the system pressure-bled by a VW agent or bleed the system until safe and effective pedal pressure is obtained. Use the car for a day or so and then bleed the system again (when all the tiny air bubbles will have coalesced into larger ones which are easier to bleed out).

When all brakes have been bled, top up the hydraulic fluid reservoir to the correct level. Have the assistant apply heavy pressure to the brake pedal and check the system for leaks. Refit all the rubber dust covers to the bleed nipples.

11 :9 Handbrake cables

The attachment of the cables to the rear brake is shown in **FIGS 11 :10** and **11 :11** while the attachment to the handbrake lever is shown in **FIG 11 :3**.

Slacken off the adjustment, remove the brake drum and free the cable from inside the rear brake. Free the bracket from the brake backplate. Remove the adjuster nuts and pull the cable rearwards out of the guide.

The cables are installed in the reverse order of removal and the adjustment is then set, after adjusting the rear brakes, as described in **Section 11 :2**.

11 :10 Pedal assembly

The steering column must be removed before the pedal assembly can be removed, or the master cylinder push-rods taken out. Remove the bolts attaching the master cylinders to the bracket assembly but do not disconnect the hydraulic lines to the master cylinders. Remove the attachment screws and take out the assembly.

Install the pedal assembly in the reverse order of removal and then set the pedal stop bolts and pushrod clearances in the master cylinders.

11 :11 Fault diagnosis

(a) Spongy pedal

1 Air in the hydraulic system
2 Fluid leak in the hydraulic system
3 Excessive end float on front hubs
4 Gap between underside of linings and shoes
5 Low fluid level in reservoir

(b) Excessive pedal movement

1 Check 1, 2, 3 and 5 in (a)
2 Excessive lining or pad wear
3 Brakes require adjustment
4 Excessive free play on brake pushrod
5 Defective master cylinder

(c) Brakes grab or pull to one side

1 Wet or oily friction linings
2 Cracked or distorted drum/disc
3 Worn out friction linings
4 Seized handbrake cable
5 Broken shoe return springs
6 Seized wheel cylinder or piston in caliper
7 Uneven tyre pressures or wear
8 Mixed linings or incorrect grades
9 Defective suspension or steering

(d) Brakes bind

1 Check 3 and 5 in (b) and 4, 5 and 6 in (c)
2 Insufficient free play on brake pushrod
3 Seals swollen or perished due to use of incorrect hydraulic fluid

CHAPTER 12

THE ELECTRICAL SYSTEM

12:1 Description
12:2 The battery
12:3 The alternator
12:4 The starter motor
12:5 The wiper motor
12:6 Headlamps

12:7 Relays
12:8 Fuses
12:9 Direction indicators
12:10 Starter switch
12:11 Fault diagnosis

12:1 Description

All the models are fitted with a 12-volt negatively-earthed electrical system, where power is supplied by an engine-driven alternator and stored in a 12-volt lead/acid battery.

Because of its design the alternator has several advantages over a conventional generator. Excitation current is taken through the rotor coils and as the rotor is designed with several poles there is no need to change the direction of current, as on a generator. This gives the alternator its main advantages as the complex commutator is not required (slip rings and brushes being adequate) and the slip rings take only a low current so that their life is longer than the equivalent commutator. The rotor coils can be designed for high rotational speeds as they too are light, taking only a small current. Diodes are required to rectify the AC produced by the alternator to the DC required by the battery. As these only allow current to flow in one direction no cut-out is required, a simple voltage regulator being sufficient.

Do not make or break connections in the charging circuit whilst the engine is running. Do not leave part of the alternator circuit or the battery disconnected with the engine running and the excitation circuit connected. When boost charging the battery or carrying out arc-welding repairs on the bodywork disconnect the charging circuit, as stray induced voltages can damage the alternator components.

A low wattage test lamp and probe leads, or any 0 to 20 voltmeter, may be used to test continuity of circuits or for checking the wiring. Cheap instruments do not measure to the accuracy required when adjusting or checking the performance of components. **For such tests, high grade (preferably moving-coil) instruments must be used.**

Though instructions on servicing the components of the electrical system are given in this chapter it must be pointed out that it is a waste of both time and money to attempt to repair items which are seriously defective, either electrically or mechanically. VW run an exchange scheme and advantage should be taken of this, rather than attempting laborious repairs which may not be successful.

12:2 The battery

The battery not only supplies the heavy current for the starter motor but also stabilizes the voltage in the system. A poor or defective battery will make starting difficult or

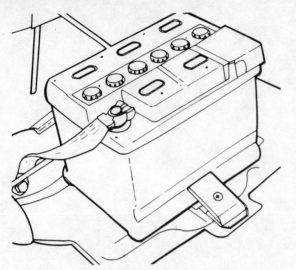

FIG 12:1 The battery location under the front seat

impossible and will also affect the performance of the remainder of the electrical system.

In cold weather the battery loses efficiency while at the same time more demands are made on it. The position of the battery, under the front seat as shown in **FIG 12:1**, does mean that it is partially protected from extremes of outside temperature and at the same time is warmed by the car heater. This position is also good because it gives the battery the smoothest ride and freedom from vibration, which is another cause of battery failure. However, in winter it is often helpful to charge the battery on a trickle charger so that it is always at full capacity. In very cold (arctic) conditions, starting in the morning will be easier if the battery is removed and stored overnight in a warm room.

Maintenance

1 Always keep the top of the battery clean and dry. Wipe away any spillage or electrolyte vented as soon as possible. If the battery surrounds are contaminated with acid the battery should be removed and the area washed with dilute ammonia or baking powder dissolved in warm water. Once the acid has been

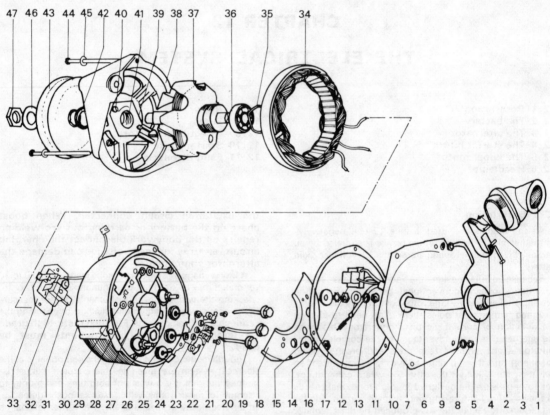

FIG 12:2 The components of the alternator

Key to Fig 12:2 1 Elbow 2 Screw 3 Threaded plate 4 Hose clip 5 Rubber grommet 6 Wiring harness 7 Intake cover 8 Nut 9 Lockwasher 10 Rubber grommet 11 Nut 12 Washer 13 Washer 14 Toothed washer 15 Contact disc 16 Three-pin plug 17 Intake cover gasket 18 Positive diode carrier 19 Positive diodes 20 Cheese head screw 21 Screw for stator winding 22 Diode carrier 23 Diodes 24 Seal 25 Negative diodes 26 Pin for positive diode carrier 27 Screw for brush holder 28 Washer 29 Spring washer 30 Alternator housing 31 Carbon brush 32 Brush retaining screw 33 Brush holder 34 Stator 35 Spring washer 36 Ballbearing 37 Rotor 38 End plate 39 Bearing end plate 40 Screw 41 Drive end bearing 42 Intermediate ring 43 Pulley 44 Housing screw 45 Washer 46 Disc 47 Nut

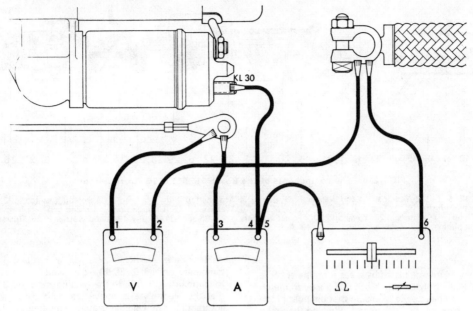

KL 30

FIG 12:3   Checking the alternator output

neutralized the parts should be washed again with plenty of water and once they are dry they should be painted with anti-sulphuric paint.

2. Keep the battery terminals clean and tight. If they are dirty they should be wiped over with a clean cloth or stiff brush. Oxides can be scraped off with a sharp knife or cleaned off with glasspaper. Make sure that galvanic corrosion has not eaten away the connector so that it is providing insufficient contact. Smear the posts and connectors liberally with petroleum jelly (Vaseline) or a suitable proprietary special grease before reconnecting them, as this will help to prevent further corrosion.

3. At regular intervals check the electrolyte level in the cells. Normally monthly checks are sufficient but in hot weather weekly checks may be required. The level should be just above the battery plates in each cell and kept to the mark. **Do not examine the battery with a naked light as the gases given off are explosive. If topping up is required use nothing but pure distilled water.**

Storage:

If the battery has been well maintained short term storage presents no problems. If the battery is to be stored for longer intervals it should be kept in a dry cool room well away from any danger of frost. Coat the terminals and intercell connectors liberally with grease.

At monthly intervals give the battery a freshening-up charge, and then at intervals of three months discharge it down to a cell voltage of 1.8 volts using a suitable lamp, and then recharge it. **Never leave a battery stored in a discharged state as the plates will rapidly sulphate up, ruining the battery.**

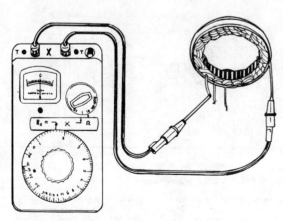

FIG 12:4   Checking the stator for shortcircuits

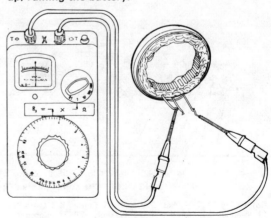

FIG 12:5   Checking the stator for continuity

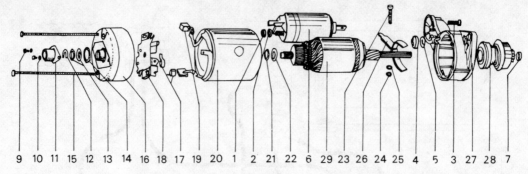

FIG 12:6   The components of the Bosch 311.911.023B starter motor

Key to Fig 12:6   1/2 Terminal nut and washer   3 Bolt   4 Moulded rubber   5 Disc   6 Solenoid switch   7 Retainer
9/10 Screw and washer   11 End cap   12 C-washer   13/14 Washers   15 Through bolt   16 End cap   17 Brush spring
18 Brush holder   19 Brush   20 Yoke   21/22 Thrust washers   23 Pivot   24/25 Pivot nut and washer   26 Operating lever
27 Drive end plate   28 Drive pinion   29 Armature

Testing:

The battery should be tested by measuring the specific gravity of the electrolyte in each cell using a hydrometer. Draw up enough electrolyte to ensure that the float of the instrument is clear of the bottom and side, and then take the reading on the float at eye level. While taking the reading check the appearance of the electrolyte. Electrolyte that appears cloudy or full or specks indicates a defective cell and this will be confirmed if the reading of the cell varies radically from those of the other cells. The specific gravity readings give the following indications:

For climates below 32°C (90°F)

1.270 to 1.290	Cell fully charged
1.190 to 1.210	Cell half-charged
1.110 to 1.130	Cell discharged

Replace spillage with electrolyte of 1.270 specific gravity.

For climates above 32°C (90°F)

1.210 to 1.230	Cell fully charged
1.130 to 1.150	Cell half-charged
1.050 to 1.070	Cell discharged

Replace spillage with electrolyte of 1.210 specific gravity.

The figures are given assuming a standard electrolyte temperature of 16°C (60°F). To convert the actual reading to standard, add .002 to the reading for every 3°C (5°F) that the electrolyte is above standard temperature and subtract for every similar drop in temperature.

The battery may also be tested using a heavy-duty discharge tester pressed firmly into the intercell connectors. A battery known to be low in charge should not be tested by this method. A cell in good condition will maintain a voltage of above 1.6 volts for at least 10 seconds and should be able to keep it up for 15 seconds.

Electrolyte:

Electrolyte should never be added to the battery unless it is to replace spillage or leakage and even then it must be of the correct specific gravity. Mixing electrolyte can be hazardous and it is best to buy it ready mixed. If electrolyte has to be mixed it should be carried out in a glass or earthenware container and the concentrated acid slowly added to the distilled water. **Never, never, add water to acid as the heat will cause the acid to sputter out dangerously.** Allow the mixture to cool and then use a hydrometer to test its specific gravity.

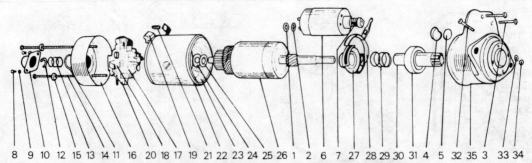

FIG 12:7   The components of the Bosch 003.911.023A starter motor

Key to Fig 12:7   1 Nut   2 Washer   3 Screw   4 Cap   5 Disc   6 Solenoid switch   7 Armature   8 Screw   9 Washer   10 End cap
11 Washer   12 Spring clip   13 Washers   14 Through bolt   15 Washer   16 Cover   17 Brushplate   18 Brush holder   19 Brush
20 Spring   21 Grommet   22 Yoke   23 Coil   24 Washer   25 Washer   26 Armature   27 Operating bush   28 Operating lever
29 Spring   30 Drive shaft   31 Clutch   32 Screw   33 Washer   34 Nut   35 End cap

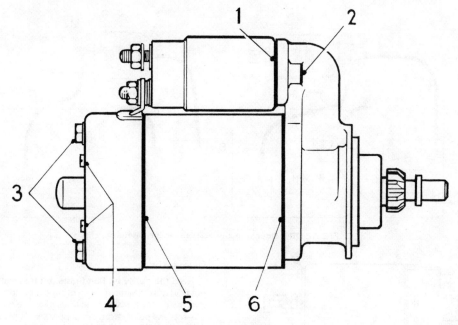

FIG 12:8   Sealing the starter motor after reassembly

Charging:

It will sometimes be necessary to charge the battery from an independent supply. The charging current should ideally be 10 per cent of the battery capacity though boost chargers give a far higher current. A boost charger should only be used in an emergency and only then on a battery known to be in good condition. Charge the battery until it is gassing freely. **Take great care to keep naked lights or sparks away from these gases as they are explosive.**

A poor battery may sometimes be reclaimed by cycling it. Charge the battery fully and then discharge it down to a cell voltage of 1.8 volts, using a lamp that takes the same amount of current as was used for charging. Repeat this cycle of charge and discharge a few times and then charge up the battery ready for use.

12:3   The alternator

The alternator components are shown in **FIG 12:2**. **Take care to carry out the precautions given in Section 12:1.** Another precaution which must be observed is when making connections. **If the circuit is connected with the incorrect polarity, serious damage may result to the alternator.**

Alternator fails to charge:

Test equipment is needed for checking the alternator output and **the methods used for a conventional generator must not be used.**

Without test equipment check the condition and tension of the alternator drive belt (see **Chapter 4, Section 4:4**), adjusting or renewing as required. If the belt is satisfactory, check through all the wires and connections

in the charging circuit. If need be, disconnect wires and use a test lamp and separate supply to check the continuity of wires.

If test equipment is available, disconnect the cable from D+ to terminal 30 on the starter and connect up the circuit as shown in **FIG 12:3**. Use heavy duty cables (at least 6 sq mm cross-sectional area) and make all connections without the engine running. Make sure that all test connections are sound. Start the engine and adjust the rheostat until the ammeter is reading 35 to 38 amps with the engine running at 2000 rev/min. If the alternator and its regulator are satisfactory, the voltmeter will be reading 13.5 to 14.2 volts. If the voltage is not within limits, renew the regulator and repeat the test. If the voltage still is not within limits, check the alternator for defective diodes or other faults.

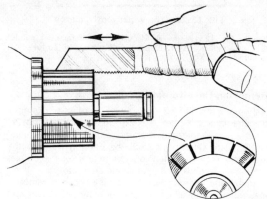

FIG 12:9   Undercutting commutator insulation

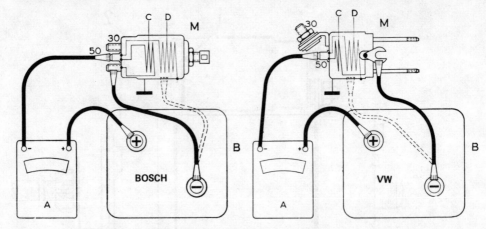

FIG 12:10   Checking the starter motor solenoid

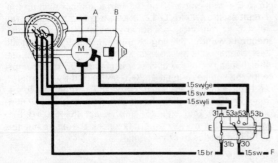

·748+−·004 inch

FIG 12:11   Checking the solenoid protrusion

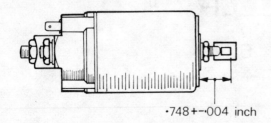

FIG 12:12   The wiper motor circuit

Key to Fig 12:12   **A** Motor   **B** Permanent magnet
C Contact plate   **D** Contacts   **E** Switch   **F** To fuse box,
terminal 15

Removing the alternator:

Remove the oil filter and engine oil dipstick. Remove the alternator drive belt. Take off the engine rear cover-plate and the alternator coverplate. Remove the engine cooling fan. Carefully detach the cooling hose to the alternator, remove the tensioning arm bracket, disconnect the wiring harness, and remove the alternator.

Install the alternator in the reverse order of removal, making sure that all covers are correctly positioned and the drive belt tension correctly set.

Dismantling:

Hold the pulley and undo the nut that secures it. If the nut is very stiff, wrap a piece of rope around the pulley and grip the pulley between the jaws of a vice so that the rope protects the pulley from direct contact. Remove the pulley, using a suitable extractor if required.

Make alignment marks across the housing and front housing so that the tensioning arm will be correctly positioned on assembly.

Use a wire hook to free the brushes from the slip rings and hold them out of the way using the pressure springs on the sides of the brushes. Take out the through-bolts and withdraw the front housing, complete with rotor, from the main housing. A press and suitable plates will be required to remove the rotor and bearing from the front housing, and a suitable extractor will then be needed to pull the bearing off from the rotor shaft. The removal of the bearing need only be done if the bearing is worn or running noisily.

If the wires need to be unsoldered or soldered, use a hot iron of adequate capacity as well as a heat sink. Gripping the wire with pliers will ensure that surplus heat is drawn off into the pliers and not passed to the diodes, which will be damaged by heating.

Assemble the alternator in the reverse order of dismantling, tightening the pulley nut to a torque of 25 to 29 lb ft (3.5 to 4 kg m).

Stator and rotor:

An ohmmeter is required but the rotor can be checked with an ammeter and battery.

Connect the resistance meter across each stator wire in turn and the metal of the stator, as shown in **FIG 12:4**, checking that there is no shortcircuit. Connect the meter between any pair of stator wires and note the reading. Repeat the test between one of the original wires, the method being shown in **FIG 12:5**, and the third wire (again noting the reading). If the stator windings are satisfactory the resistance will be .2 ± .02 ohm. Do not connect a battery directly across the stator wires without some resistance in the circuit as they will take a current of approximately 60 amps on shortcircuit. Failing a meter, the stator can be checked with a 12-volt battery and bulb.

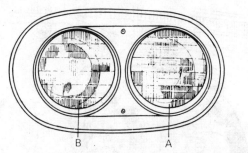

B. INNER HEADLAMP A. OUTER HEADLAMP

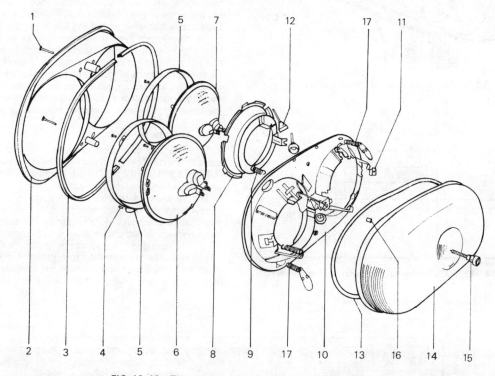

FIG 12:13 The components of a headlamp assembly

Key to Fig 12:13 1 Screw with rubber ring   2 Surround   3 Seal   4 Screw   5 Retainer   6 Low beam insert   7 High beam insert   8 Aiming ring   9 Spring for locator   10 Locator   11 Tapped plate   12 Aiming screw   13 Cover seal   14 Cover   15 Knurled head screw   16 Rubber seal   17 Spring with loop

The bulb must not light when connected between a stator wire and metal of the stator but it must light between each pair of stator wires.

Check the rotor by connecting one probe of the instrument to one of the slip rings and pressing the other probe first against the metal of the rotor (when there should be an infinity reading) and then to the other slip ring when the resistance should be $4 \pm .4$ ohms. An ammeter and battery can be used instead of the ohmmeter as the short-circuit current is small. Connect the battery between the slip rings of the rotor and measure the current with an ammeter in series. If possible connect a voltmeter across the battery to measure the actual voltage. The resistance can then be calculated using Ohm's law (Voltage= Resistance x Current) and the current flow should be in the order of 3 amps when a 12-volt battery is used.

Brushgear:

Renew the brushes if they have reached their minimum length of .55 inch (14 mm) or if the spring pressure is less than 10 to 14 oz (300 to 400 grammes) with the brushes in their normal working position.

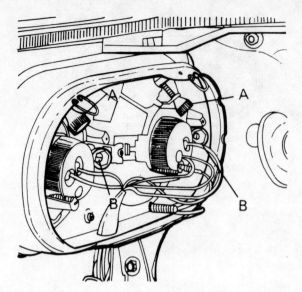

FIG 12:14 The beam adjustment screws

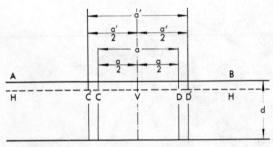

FIG 12:15 Wall markings for setting the headlamp beams

Check the slip rings on the stator. Normally all that is required is wiping over with a piece of cloth moistened with methylated spirits or chloroform. Light burn marks should be polished off with a piece of fine-grade glass-paper. The slip rings only carry a low current so they should not normally burn or wear excessively but if this does occur they may be machined down, provided that the minimum diameter of 1.24 inch (31.5 mm) is not reached.

Diodes:

These are the electrical equivalent of one-way valves and each diode will only pass current in one direction. A defective diode will lower the alternator output and in some cases make it operate noisily.

The diodes can be checked individually after unsoldering their leads (using pliers as a heat sink). Connect up a low-wattage test lamp and 12-volt battery in series, with the free ends of the wires ending in probes. Connect the battery and test lamp across the pin of the diode and its holder then repeat the test but reversing the polarity. The lamp should light with the leads connected in one direction but it should not light when the positions of the leads on the diodes are reversed. If the lamp fails to light at all, check that varnish or insulation on the carrier is not causing poor contact before condemning the diode. If the lamp lights in both directions the diode is defective.

12:4 The starter motor

Three slightly different types of starter motor can be fitted to the car. The two types made by Bosch are shown in **FIGS 12:6** and **12:7**. The other starter is made by VW and is of a very similar construction.

The solenoid is mounted on the starter motor and carries out the dual function of meshing the starter drive and closing the heavy-duty contacts. The solenoid has two windings which are both energized when the starter switch is operated. The windings pull in the plunger which operates the lever to press the drive pinion into mesh with the starter ring teeth on the flywheel. Further movement of the plunger then closes the heavy-duty

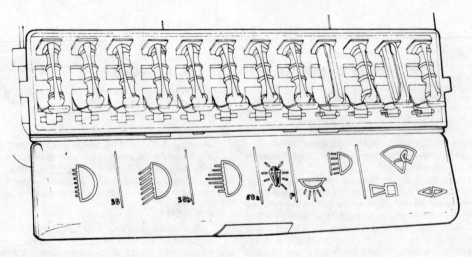

FIG 12:16 The main fuse box

contacts which pass a heavy current through the starter motor. At the same time the pull-in windings of the solenoid are shorted out, leaving the hold-in windings keeping the drive in mesh and the contacts closed.

Starter fails to operate:

1 Check the condition and charge of the battery. Pay particular attention to the cleanliness and tightness of the battery connectors as high resistance here is often a cause of starting difficulties. Make sure that the engine earth strip is in place and good condition as this often gradually deteriorates to make starting difficult.

2 Switch on some lights that can be seen and again try to operate the starter. If the lights go dim then the motor is taking current. A possible cause in this case is that the pinion is jammed in mesh. Select a gear and rock the car backwards and forwards to free the pinion. If this fails then the motor will have to be removed. If the starter motor jams regularly then it is likely that the pinion or flywheel teeth are badly worn. The flywheel teeth can be inspected through the starter motor aperture while slowly turning the engine over. If the pinion is not jammed and the starter motor is taking current without driving the engine then it must be removed and examined for internal defects. Turn the engine over by hand to make sure that the engine itself is not jammed or abnormally stiff.

3 If the lights do not go dim then the motor is taking no current. The starter solenoid operates with a click, so listen for this. If there is no click use a test bulb or voltmeter to check whether current is reaching as far as the solenoid lead. If power is not reaching the solenoid trace back through the circuit, checking with a test lamp, until the fault is found. If the solenoid does operate but the motor takes no current try shorting across the solenoid heavy-duty terminals with a thick piece of metal. The motor now spinning freely indicates that the solenoid contacts are defective and a new solenoid must be fitted. If the motor still does not turn then it must be removed for further examination.

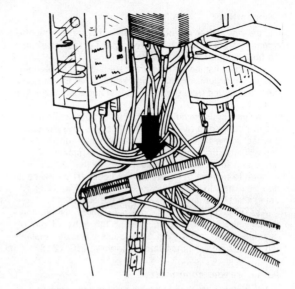

FIG 12:18 The heater supplementary fuse

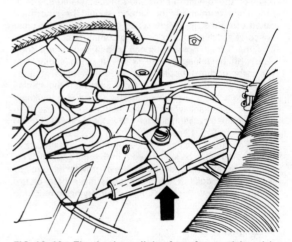

FIG 12:19 The back-up light fuse for models with manual shift transmission

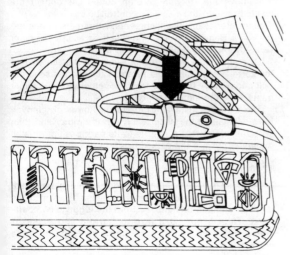

FIG 12:17 The heater main fuse, and heated rear window fuse

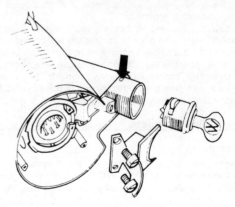

FIG 12:20 The starter switch attachments

Dismantling:

The VW starter motor is slightly different in that the armature shaft is fully supported by the motor itself and no bush is fitted in the flywheel housing.

Generally dismantling requires removal of the solenoid, taking off the end cap and end plate so that the brushes can be removed from the brush holder and then removing the yoke.

The field coils are held in place by the polepieces which are in turn held in place by special screws into the yoke. a wheel screwdriver is required to undo and tighten these screws and once tight they should be staked as an additional lock. For this reason the owner should not attempt to remove or renew the field coils. The field coils can be tested for continuity or shortcircuits while fitted, using a test lamp and battery or suitable meters.

Assemble the motor in the reverse order of dismantling. Sealant should be used to prevent the entry of dirt or moisture. Use sealant VW.D14 at point 1 and use sealant VW.D1a on all the other points shown in **FIG 12 : 8**.

Armature and commutator

Wipe down the segments of the commutator with a piece of lint-free cloth moistened in methylated spirits or fuel. Light burn marks or scoring should be smoothed down using a strip of fine-grade glasspaper. If the wear or scores are deep, skim down the commutator in a lathe. Use the fastest possible speed and a very sharp tool. Finish off by taking a light skim cut using a diamond (or carborundum) tipped tool, or polishing with fine-grade glasspaper can be carried out instead. If the insulation between the segments is undercut, grind a hacksaw blade to the exact width of the insulation and use it to undercut the insulation squarely to a depth of $\frac{1}{32}$ (.8 mm), as shown in **FIG 12 : 9**.

The armature itself cannot be repaired. Shortcircuits in the windings may be suspected if individual segments on the commutator are badly burnt, but a 'growler' is required to check the coils. If the laminations are scored or the shaft bent, renew the armature without trying to machine or straighten it.

Brushgear:

Check that the brushes slide freely in their holders. If the brushes stick, polish their sides on a smooth file and clean the brush holder with a piece of cloth dipped in fuel or methylated spirits.

Renew the brushes if they are worn down to their minimum length. Usually the connectors are brazed into place. Cut the connector so that a short tag remains with the brazing, pass this tag through the loop in the end of the new connector, and solder the new connector into place with a hot iron. Grip the connector with a pair of pliers to prevent solder creeping up the connector and making it stiff.

Renew the brush springs if they are weak.

Solenoid:

The test circuits for checking the current consumption of the solenoid are shown in **FIG 12 : 10**. With the lead connected as shown in the position shown by thick black lines the pull-in windings are checked. The current flow for a Bosch starter motor should be 35 amps maximum, while that for the VW motor should be 30 amps maximum. With the lead connected as shown in the dotted position the holding windings are checked and the current should be a maximum of 11 amps for Bosch solenoids and 12 amps for VW solenoids. If the current is over the limits, the solenoid must be renewed.

Before installing a Bosch solenoid, energize it across a battery and check that the protrusion of the link is correct as shown in **FIG 12 : 11**. If the dimension is not correct ($19 \pm .1$ mm), slacken the locknut and adjust until correct.

Bearings:

Take care not to wash the bushes in solvent as they are impregnated with oil. If the bushes are worn, either fit an exchange starter motor if the motor is generally poor or have new bushes fitted.

12 : 5 The wiper motor

A two-speed wiper motor is fitted as standard and the motor is designed so as to be self-parking. The circuit for the motor is shown in **FIG 12 : 12**. Note that no field coils are fitted and that a permanent magnet is embodied in the cover. Three brushes are used to provide the two-speed operation.

If the motor fails to operate, check carefully through the wiring for breaks or faults. Connect an ammeter in series with the motor, remove the wiper arms so that the motor is not loaded, and check the current consumption. Low current indicates defective brushgear and commutator while high current indicates excessive stiffness in the system or lack of lubrication. Faulty armature windings can also cause a high consumption. At low speed the motor should take 2.5 amps and it should take 3.5 amps at high speed.

Removal:

Disconnect the battery. Take off the cap nuts securing the wiper arms and remove both arms. Take off the cover and unscrew the hexagon bearing nut.

Remove the steering column cover. Disconnect the hoses between the fresh air control box and the vents. Free the clock from its attachments without disconnecting the wires. Remove the lefthand side fresh air and defroster vent, after freeing the hot air hose from the vent.

Disconnect the wiper motor wiring at the switch and the earth lead at the wiper motor. Take out the securing bolt and remove the wiper motor together with the wiper frame. Free the motor from the frame.

The parts are installed in the reverse order of removal. Before installing the wiper arms, run the motor and then switch it off so that it returns to its park position. Install the wiper arms in the parked position.

12 : 6 Headlamps

Either sealed beam units or halogen bulbs are fitted.

The halogen bulbs are separate bulbs fitted into the reflector and can be removed from the luggage compartment. **Take great care not to handle the glass of these bulbs with the bare hand or fingers** as the acids on the skin will etch the quartz of which they are made at the high temperatures at which these bulbs operate.

Sealed-beam units have the filaments sealed into the reflector and the lens sealed to the reflector so that the whole unit acts as a large bulb. Any defect requires renewal of the complete unit, while a crack in the glass will allow air to enter so that the filaments burn out as soon as the lights are switched on.

The components of a unit with sealed units are shown in **FIG 12:13**.

Beam setting

The adjustment screws for the headlights are shown in **FIG 12:14**. It is possible to set the beams using a blank wall or screen. The car must be set at a distance of 5 metres from the wall and pointing squarely at it. Make sure the tyre pressures are correct and put a load of 70 kg at the centre of the rear seat. The wall must then be marked as shown in **FIG 12:15**. V is the vertical and **a** and **a**[1] are the distances between the headlight centres. **AB** is a horizontal line at the same height **d** as the lamp centres and **HH** is drawn 5 cm (2 inch) below **AB**. The inner headlamps are then centred at the crosses formed by the verticals **C** and **D** with the line **AB**. The outer headlamps are adjusted so that the horizontal edge between light and dark lies on the line **HH** and set laterally so that the junction of the horizontal line and **k** line at 15 deg. meets on the intersection of the verticals **C**[1] and **D**[1] with **HH**.

However it will be simpler to avoid all the work and take the car to a VW agent where the beams will be accurately set using special equipment. This will also ensure that the beams are set to meet local state or national state requirements, as these may vary from state to state or country to country.

12:7 Relays

These are used extensively in the electrical system. They can be considered as electrically operated switches. At first sight this may seem odd but they allow the actual control in the car to carry only a low current, with low losses from voltage drop in the wires, and the advantage of requiring only small switches. When the relay is energized by the control, it closes heavy-duty contacts which allow the current to flow to the component to be operated. The relay can be placed in a convenient position ensuring the minimum run of heavy-duty cables.

If a circuit fails to operate, first check that current is flowing through the control wire (using a test lamp or voltmeter). If current is reaching the relay, bridge its heavy-duty contacts with a piece of suitable wire, and if the component or light now operates the relay itself is defective and must be renewed. Before finally condemning the relay, make sure that the power current is reaching the unit and that the component or light operated by the relay (as well as the wiring between relay and components) is satisfactory.

12:8 Fuses

A fuse box is located under the lefthand side dashboard and is shown in **FIG 12:16**. The cover is marked with symbols indicating the circuits that the fuse protects.

Additional line fuses may also be fitted. **FIG 12:17** shows the fuse for the main heater circuit and heated rear window. A fuse in the lefthand side of the engine compartment, shown in **FIG 12:18**, protects the heater from

overheating, while a third fuse shown in **FIG 12:19** is fitted on manual-shift models for the back-up lights.

The fuses are of the continental type and the fuse, which is made from a glass tube with wire inside it, will not fit into the fuse box satisfactorily. Spares may be difficult to obtain so it is most advisable to carry some spare 8 and 16-amp fuses.

The 8-amp fuses are readily identifiable, even in the dark, by the ribs on them.

A minor overload will not normally cause a fuse to blow. Fuses do weaken with age but normally only a fault causes them to blow.

If a circuit fails to operate, or suddenly ceases operation, first check the fuse. If the fuse has blown the wire will be burnt through. Even if the fuse has not blown, make sure that it is making good contact. When a fuse has blown, briefly check through the circuit protected by it for obvious defects and then fit a new fuse. Operate the circuit and check that the new fuse does not blow. If the fuse blows again the circuit must be checked through with care until the fault is found and can be repaired. **Do not fit a fuse of higher rating than called for.** The fuse is designed as the weak link in the circuit and should therefore fail before the wiring, and if a larger rating of fuse is fitted the wiring itself may burn before the fuse blows.

If the fuse lasts for a short time and then blows, there is an intermittent fault in the circuit which will be more difficult to detect. Check carefully through the wiring, looking for frayed insulation which will allow the metal wire to ground under vibration or movement. Some wiring faults can be extremely complicated to trace and in such cases it will be easier to take the car to a VW agent where special meters and test equipment can be used.

It should be noted that, unlike most other cars, the headlamps themselves have fuses in their circuits. Sufficient fuses (total of 4) are fitted to ensure that the lamps will not all fail together and that only one side beam at a time will not operate. This must be remembered if a lamp partially fails as it can be fuse and not filament failure.

12:9 Direction indicators

If these fail to operate correctly, first check the bulbs themselves for blown or defective filaments. If the fuse has blown, the fuel gauge and warning lamps for oil pressure and alternator will also cease to operate, so the fuse can be eliminated if these other circuits function correctly. A blown or defective filament will alter the flash rate and can also make the direction indicators and warning lamp operate in odd ways, and it is also the most likely fault to occur.

If the lamps themselves are satisfactory and the fuse has not blown, renew the flasher unit itself. Handle the flasher unit with care as it it a delicate piece of mechanism and will be damaged irreparably by dropping.

12:10 Starter switch

The starter and ignition switch is mounted on the steering column. It will be necessary to remove the steering wheel and indicator switch before the starter switch can be removed. Make sure that the battery is disconnected before starting work.

Remove the screws and retainer shown in **FIG 12:20**. Fit the key into place and use the key to pull on while depressing the plunger arrowed in the figure with a piece of wire so that the lock cylinder can be removed. Remove the screw and the switch can be drawn out rearwards.

Install the parts in the reverse order of removal.

12:11 Fault diagnosis

(a) Battery discharged

1 Terminals loose or dirty
2 Battery internally defective
3 Shortcircuits in wiring not protected by fuses
4 Alternator not charging
5 Regulator defective
6 Accessories left on for too long with engine not running
7 Insufficient mileage to allow the alternator to charge the battery fully

(b) Battery will not hold charge

1 Low electrolyte level
2 Battery plates sulphated or plate separators ineffective
3 Electrolyte leakage from damaged casing

(c) Alternator output low or nil

1 Driving belt broken or slipping
2 Regulator defective
3 Loose connections or defective wiring
4 Defective diode
5 Excessively worn or dirty brushgear and slip rings
6 Defective rotor or stator coils
7 Mechanical damage or wear in alternator

(d) Starter motor lacks power or will not operate

1 Check 1 and 2 in (a)
2 Battery not at full charge
3 Starter pinion jammed in mesh
4 Defective starter switch
5 Defective starter solenoid
6 Brushes excessively worn or sticking
7 Weak or broken brush springs
8 Commutator excessively worn or dirty
9 Defective armature or field coils
10 Poor engine or battery earth points
11 Starter motor mechanically worn or defective
12 Engine abnormally stiff

CHAPTER 13

THE BODYWORK

13:1 Bodywork finish
13:2 Lubrication
13:3 Seat belts
13:4 Windscreen washer

13:5 The windscreen and fixed glass
13:6 Bonnet locks
13:7 Towing points
13:8 The jack

13:1 Bodywork finish

Cleaning:

The normal operations of washing and waxing, regularly carried out, not only enhance the appearance of the car but also help to protect the car against the ravages of time, grime and weather.

Acids and industrial waste are deposited on the body-work from the air and by rain. If left these deposits will gradually etch the paint, but regular washing removes them. Waxing then fills the pores in the paint, preventing moisture from creeping down to the base metal, and at the same time forms a thin layer which protects the paint from dirt.

VW dealers carry a wide selection of materials for cleaning the car and removing deposits of various types from all surfaces, including upholstery.

Too often the parts of the car which show are cleaned and polished while the underside is totally forgotten. The underside bears the brunt of all the stones thrown up by the wheels as well as collecting mud and salt. The under-side can be washed using a high pressure jet from a hose. Mud and dirt will be softened and easier to remove if the car is stood over a garden sprinkler so that the underside s washed with a steady spray. When the car has been washed underneath, apply the brakes gently several times while driving slowly so that the heat produced dries them out. **Failure to observe this precaution can lead to lack of brakes when they are required.**

Underseal is a thick paint which protects the under-neath of the car from both stones and moisture. However, this can only be really satisfactorily applied to a brand new car, as scrupulous cleaning, preferably with a steam plant, is required to ensure a satisfactory bond. Poor undersealing can be worse than none at all, as stones will chip right through it and moisture will then be trapped between the underseal and body as the underseal lifts.

VW make a special wax protective which is sprayed on to protect the underside. A new coat should be sprayed on at the beginning of winter, after cleaning the underside, so that full protection is afforded against the salt and grit on the roads at this time of year.

Repairs:

Large-scale damage should be left to the experts, as should panel-beating and welding.

Attempts should not be made by the unskilled to dress out dents or creases, as incorrect or injudicious hammer-ing will stretch the metal and make things worse instead

FIG 13:1　The door hinge and check strap lubrication points

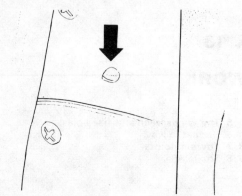

FIG 13:2　The door lock lubrication points

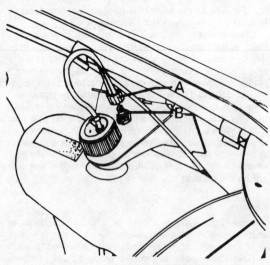

FIG 13:3　The windscreen washer container

of better. By all means attempt to reduce the depth of dent by careful tapping so that less filling will be require

Touch-up kits of paint and spray cans of matchin paint are available and these should be used as require The touch-up kit is supplied with a small brush so th minor scratches and stone chips can easily be touched i A light polish with mild cutting compound or proprieta metal polish after the paint has fully hardened will bler the new and old paint.

For larger areas, use the self-spraying cans. Rememb that the paint fades slightly with age and the new pair while being an exact match for the original, may r longer be a match. The original lustre and colour can b partially restored by removing the upper layer of fade paint with a suitable polish or mild cutting compoun Even so it may well be better to spray a complete panel wing, rather than a patch in the middle which will more obvious.

Before starting to spray a panel or door, remove as muc trim and handles as possible. The work involved will b compensated for by the time taken to mask these par if they are left fitted and the final result will be that muc better. Wash down the area with white spirits to remov wax polish. If silicone-based polishes have been use more drastic treatment is required and special cleanin solutions must be used. If any polish is left, the paint w form 'pop-ups' and craters.

Lightly scuff the area to be sprayed to give a good ke for the new finish. Rub down any rust to bright metal an apply patches of primer over these spots.

Dress out deep dents as far as possible, or consid fitting a new panel if damage is extensive. Use stopp paste or filler paint, as required, to fill the dents an scratches until they are just proud of the surface. Leav to harden thoroughly. Air-drying paste stoppers must b applied in coats, leaving each coat to dry before the ne one is applied, but stoppers with catalytic hardening ma be built up to the required thickness in one go.

Rub down using 400 grade 'Wet and Dry' with plent of clean water. Spend plenty of time and patience at thi stage as effort here ensures a good final appearance Blemishes which are left at this stage will be extremel difficult or impossible to eradicate when it comes t applying the colour coats. If need be, apply further coat of stopper or filler to fill blemishes.

When the rubbing-down has been completed, was with plenty of clean water and leave it to dry. Make check for any marks or blemishes and then give a secon wash to remove slurry that was missed in the first wash

Mask off surrounding areas using masking tape an newspaper. A film of grease smeared over mirrors chrome, or glass will prevent the paint spray from bindinc

Spray the paint evenly onto the area. If a patch is being sprayed, 'feather' the edges by reducing the spray o moving the can slightly faster so that the new pain blends in with the old. For anyone who has not used spray can before it is most advisable to carry out a few trial runs on a piece of cardboard. Do not try to apply th colour in one thick coat, which will most likely sag or run Instead apply at least two thinner coats, sanding dow between coats. If a run or sag does appear, let the pain harden fully and then rub it down with wet and dry befor applying the next coat. A reasonable drying time shoul be left between coats and only light sanding carried out

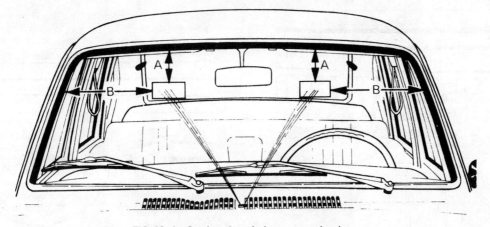

FIG 13:4   Setting the windscreen washer jets

Key to Fig 13:4   a=6 to 8 inch (150 to 200 mm)   b=15 to 19 inch (380 to 480 mm)

When all colour coats have been applied, leave the paint to harden and then remove all the masking. Leave the paint to harden at least overnight, preferably longer, before polishing it with a mild cutting compound. This will remove minor surface blemishes left after spraying and will also remove any spray dust that has settled.

Leave the paint to harden off fully for a period of several weeks before applying any wax polish.

13:2 Lubrication

Servicing and lubrication covers the mechanical components of the car and so often the bodywork is neglected. The body has several hinge points and bearing surfaces, all of which should have their regular attention and lubrication.

Weather seals:

These should either by lightly dusted over with talc or wiped over with a very thin film of glycerine. This treatment will prevent the seals from sticking, or freezing, and give them a longer satisfactory life.

Lock cylinders:

Do not use oil or grease on these. Sprinkle a little powdered graphite over the key and work this in the lock several times.

If the lock freezes in winter, because of water in the lock, do not use force. Heat the key and gently guide it into place. Keep heating the head of the key with a lighter or matches until the ice melts and the lock can be operated. A special lock defreezing agent is made but heating the key if the lock does freeze and covering the lock when washing the car with a hose should be sufficient.

Door hinges and locks:

These should be checked and lubricated every three months at least.

Remove the plastic plugs from on top of the door hinges and fill the wells arrowed in **FIG 13:1** with SAE.30 engine oil. Refit the plastic plugs. At the same time oil the

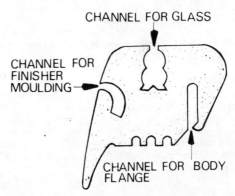

FIG 13:5   Typical cross-section through weatherstrip moulding

CHANNEL FOR GLASS

CHANNEL FOR FINISHER MOULDING

CHANNEL FOR BODY FLANGE

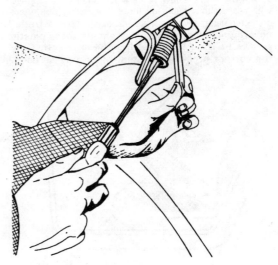

FIG 13:6   Adjusting the bonnet lock bolt

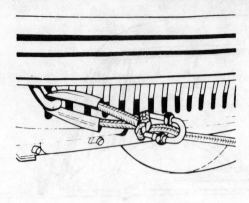
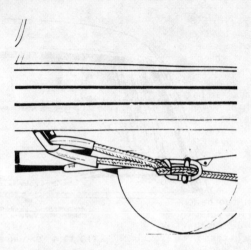

FIG 13:7   The towing eyes on the body

bearings of the rollers for the door check straps, also arrowed in the figure. Have rags handy to catch any spillage and to wipe away surplus oil.

The lock itself is lubricated after removing the plug arrowed in **FIG 13:2**. Inject a few drops of engine oil and refit the plug.

Other points:

Hood locks, hinges for flaps and other bearing surfaces should be lightly greased at intervals to prevent them from becoming stiff. Take care not to apply excessive grease, operate the part a few times to work the grease in and then wipe away surplus lubricant. In all cases, little and regular is far better than a frantic dollop when the parts become stiff.

13:3 Seat belts

Strong points are built into the body for the attachment of seat belts. In the few cases where the car is supplied with seat belts not already fitted, the strong points are protected using cover washers and plastic screws. **Under no circumstances whatsoever should these plastic screws be used for attaching the seat belt. Only the correct high-tensile steel bolts may be used.**

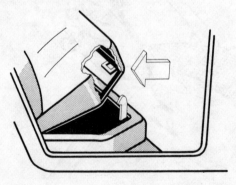

FIG 13:8   Removing the rear seat squab

Provided that the owner takes care not to twist the belts, the fitting of standard three-point belts should present no major problems. Only if the owner is fully competent to carry out a careful, safe, and correct installation should he attempt to fit non-standard or inertia-reel type belts.

A badly fitted seat belt will give a false sense of security and under certain circumstances may be even more dangerous than no belt at all.

13:4 Windscreen washer

A large capacity ($2\frac{1}{2}$ pints, $1\frac{1}{2}$ Litres) windscreen washer operated by air pressure from the spare tyre is fitted as standard.

The spare tyre should be pumped up to a maximum of 42 lb/sq inch (3 kg/sq cm) and this will be sufficient for three to four fillings of the container before the spare tyre needs pumping up again. A valve is fitted which prevents the spare tyre pressure from dropping below 28 lb/sq inch (2 kg/sq cm).

The container and its connecting hose are shown in **FIG 13:3**. To fill the container, unscrew the cap and fill it to the brim. Note that methylated spirits may be used as antifreeze in cold weather and a few drops of liquid detergent will help in cleaning the glass.

When inflating the spare wheel there is no need to remove luggage or reach the spare wheel itself. Unscrew the hose **A** from the valve **B** and inflate the tyre through the valve **B**.

Do not forget to disconnect the hose from the spare wheel when taking out the spare wheel, and note that the screenwash will only operate on the pressure remaining in the container if the spare wheel is flat or its pressure has dropped below 28 lb/sq inch.

Adjustment:

The direction of the jets can be adjusted by inserting needle into the orifice and rotating the jet in its socket. The optimum positions at which the jets should strike the glass are shown in **FIG 13:4**, when the car is stationary. This setting ensures that the jets hit the screen at speed and do not wash the roof or inject into the fresh air grille.

5 The windscreen and fixed glass

All the fixed glass on the body is secured by the same method so instructions for the windscreen apply equally to all the other glass. The windscreen wiper arms should be removed when removing or refitting the windscreen.

If the glass in the windscreen has broken then all the parts must be removed not only from the interior but also from the windscreen defrosting and demisting vents. It may be necessary to partially dismantle the ventilation system to ensure that all glass particles are removed. On models fitted with heated backlights the leads must be disconnected before removing the backlight.

Either safety or laminated glass can be fitted. Safety glass can be tapped into place using a rubber mallet but this must not be done to laminated glass. On all types of glass it is safer to use firm hand or foot pressure and to wrap the hand with thick rags to prevent injury in case the glass does break.

A sectioned view of a typical rubber weatherstrip for the glass is shown in FIG 13:5. Sealant is injected into the grooves around the glass and body flange and it will most likely be found that the weatherstrip is damaged on removal, especially if the glass has been broken. To prevent leaks when the glass has been refitted it is most advisable to use a new rubber moulding on reassembly.

Removal:

If the glass has broken remove all the parts and strip out the weatherstrip. If the glass requires to be removed for other reasons, first take off the trim moulding. Carefully move the covering clips to one side so that the joints between the trim moulding halves are exposed. Lift up one end of the moulding with a blunt screwdriver and pull it out of the weatherstrip. Go round between the glass and weatherstrip with a thin wooden wedge to break the sealant. Have an assistant outside the car to take the glass as it comes free and from inside the car press out the glass with firm pressure from a padded hand or foot, starting at the corners and working around the windscreen. When the glass is out lay it onto a padded clean bench to prevent it from becoming scratched or damaged. Peel out the weatherstrip.

Before refitting the glass check the flange around the body aperture for dents or protrusions. Knock down level with the remainder of the flange and dress out dents with a hammer and block of metal. If the flange is left distorted it will set up stress points in the glass which may cause it to fail in service. Remove all old sealing compound.

Refitting:

Smear the channel for the glass in the weatherstrip with sealing compound and fit the weatherstrip around the glass so that its join is at the centre of the top of the glass.

Make up a short length (70 mm, 3 inch) of 8 mm ($\frac{5}{16}$ inch) diameter tube and slightly flatten one end. Pass one end of a length of cord through this tube and by opening the channel for the trim moulding with the tube lay the cord all round in the channel in the weatherstrip. The cord must be long enough to go all

around the channel. Cross the ends of the cord over at the bottom centre of the windscreen and leave enough cord hanging out to get a firm grip on.

3 Fit the two halves of the trim moulding into the slot in the weatherstrip. Slowly pull on the cord while pressing the moulding into place so that as the cord comes out it lifts the rubber lip of the weatherstrip into place. If necessary lubricate the rubber with water or soft soap. When both halves of the moulding are in place. refit the cover sleeves over the joints.

4 Coat the outer face of the aperture flange and lower corners of the aperture with sealing compound. Run a length of cord around in the channel for the glass in the weatherstrip, leaving sufficient ends hanging out. Have an assistant press the glass and weatherstrip assembly firmly and accurately into position in the aperture, having passed the ends of the cord through the aperture into the car. From inside the car pull steadily on the ends of the cord, vertically to the flange and parallel to the glass, so that as the cord comes out it lifts the lip off the weatherstrip over the flange in the aperture.

5 If there is insufficient sealant in place inject more using a special gun. Wipe away surplus sealant with a cloth moistened in methylated spirits, white spirits or petrol. The cloth must only be sufficiently damp to remove the surplus sealant and care must be taken to ensure that the solvent does not dilute sealant or wash it out from the channels.

13:6 Bonnet locks

Both the luggage compartment and engine compartment lid locks are operated from inside the cars using cables to connect the knob to the cable. The luggage compartment lid is also held by a safety catch which can only be opened while standing at the front of the car.

To renew a cable, remove the lock and coverplate so that the cable can be released from the catch. Pull the cable out through the guide tube. Well grease the new cable with universal grease and slide it back into position through the guide tube. Refit the lock but do not close the lid until the cable is adjusted. The cable should be set so that there is a small amount of free movement before it starts to move the latch.

The tightness of the lock can be varied by screwing the lock bolt in or out as shown in FIG 13:6. If the lid rattles when closed the bolt should be screwed upwards to tighten the lock. If the cover is extremely difficult to close or open, first check that the lock is greased and that the cable is operating satisfactorily. If there is no fault then screw the bolt slightly downwards. Check the adjustment by opening and closing the cover several times.

13:7 Towing points

Towing eyes are built into the bodywork, as shown in FIG 13:7. Since there is one at the front and one at the rear there is no excuse for wrapping tow ropes around the axles or other vulnerable spots.

13:8 The jack

In case the owner has not found the jack supplied with the car, it is clipped into place under the rear seat squab. The method of removing the rear seat squab is shown in

FIG 13:8. When installing the squab, press it well back to make sure that both hooks can engage correctly.

Jacking points are built into the body under the sills and the square portion of the jack is inserted into the square tube.

When using the jack, make sure that the wheels are chocked or the handbrake firmly applied. If possible avoid using the jack on hills. The jack supplied is only designed for raising the car to change a wheel. **It must not be used as a sole means of support when working under the car,** though it can be used to raise the car so that adequate supports can be put into place.

APPENDIX

TECHNICAL DATA

Engine   Fuel system   Ignition system   Clutch
Manual shift transmission   Automatic transmission
Suspension   Steering   Brakes   Electrical
Dimensions and weights   Wheels and tyres
Capacities   Torque wrench settings

WIRING DIAGRAM

FIG 14:1   Volkswagen 411 from 1968

CONVERSION TABLES

HINTS ON MAINTENANCE AND OVERHAUL

GLOSSARY OF TERMS

INDEX

TECHNICAL DATA

Unless otherwise stated the dimensions are given in inches and the figure in brackets is the dimension in millimetres

ENGINE

Type:	Flat-four, with longitudinally split crankcase castings. Four separate cylinder barrels, with one cylinder head for a pair of cylinders
Location:	Longitudinally mounted at rear of car, behind transmission unit
Cooling:	Air cooled, using crankcase driven centrifugal fan
Cubic capacity:	1679cc (102.46 cu inch)
Bore:	3.543 (90)
Stroke:	2.598 (66)
Compression ratio:	
1968	7.8:1
All other years	8.2:1
Firing order:	1—4—3—2
Valve clearances:	.004 (.10) on all valves, engine COLD
Crankshaft:	Four main bearing, forged steel
Bearings:	
Nos. 1, 3 and 4	Aluminium bushes with lead-based bearing material
No. 2	Three layer, aluminium shells
Journal diameter:	
Nos. 1, 2 and 3	2.3609 to 2.3617 (59.97 to 59.99)
No. 4	1.5739 to 1.5748 (39.98 to 40.00)
Crankpin diameter	2.1644 to 2.1653 (54.98 to 55.00)
End float	(Controlled by shims at No. 1, flywheel end bearing)
Normal	.0027 to .0051 (.07 to .13)
Wear limit	.006 (.15)
Bearing clearances:	
Journal to bearing:	
Nos. 1 and 3	.0019 to .004 (.05 to .10) Wear limit (.007 (.18)
No. 2	.0011 to .0035 (.03 to .09) Wear limit .0066 (.17)
No. 4	.0019 to .004 (.05 to .10) Wear limit .0074 (.19)
Crankpin to bearing	.0008 to .0027 (.02 to .07) Wear limit .006 (.15)
Connecting rod side clearance	.004 to .016 (.1 to .4) Wear limit .028 (.7)
Oil seal shoulder	
Outside diameter	2.9487 to 2.9566 (74.9 to 75.1)
Wear limit	2.9290 (74.4)
Camshaft:	Three bearing, cast iron
Bearings	Aluminium shells
Drive	Helical toothed gears from crankshaft
End float	.0016 to .0051 (.04 to .13) Wear limit .006 (.16)
Journal diameter	.9837 to .9842 (24.99 to 25.00)
Drive gear backlash	.000 to .002 (.00 to .05)

Cam followers (tappets):
Diameter of follower
New ...	...	...	...	...	.9432 to .9450 (23.96 to 23.98)
Wear limit ...	...	...	...	...	.9421 (23.93

Bore diameter
New ...	...	...	...	...	.9448 to .9456 (24.00 to 24.02)
Wear limit ...	...	...	...	...	.9467 (24.05)

Pushrod maximum bend	...	...	...	...	.012 (.3)

Crankcase:
... ... Matched magnesium alloy castings

Main bearing bores
Nos. 1 to 3 ...	...	...	...	...	2.7560 to 2.7568 (70.00 to 70.02)
					Wear limit 2.7580 (70.03)
No. 4 ...	...	...	...	...	1.9685 to 1.9696 (50.00 to 50.03)
					Wear limit 1.9701 (50.04)

Camshaft bearing bores	...	...	...	1.0825 to 1.0833

Cylinders:
... ... Grey cast iron

Piston to cylinder clearance
Normal ...	...	...	...	...	.0016 to .0023 (.04 to .06)
Wear limit ...	...	...	...	...	.008 (.20)

Pistons and piston pins:
... ... Fully floating, light alloy with steel inserts

Piston weights
'—' (Brown identification)	...	...	...	16.65 to 16.9 ozs (472 to 480 grammes)
'+' (Grey identification)	...	...	...	16.9 to 17.2 ozs (480 to 488 grammes)
Piston pin diameter ...	...	...	...	.9052 to .9055 (22.996 to 23.000)
Connecting rod bush ...	...	...	...	.9058 to .9061 (23.008 to 23.017)

Piston rings:
... ... Two compression, one oil control

Fitted gap
Upper ...	...	...	...	...	.014 to .021 (.35 to .55)
					Wear limit .035 (.90)
Middle ...	...	...	...	...	.012 to .014 (.30 to .35)
					Wear limit .035 (.90)
Oil control ...	...	...	...	...	.010 to .016 (.25 to .40)
					Wear limit .037 (.95)

Side clearance in piston
Upper ...	...	...	...	...	.0023 to .0035 (.06 to .09)
					Wear limit .0047 (.12)
Middle ...	...	...	...	...	.0016 to .0027 (.04 to .07)
					Wear limit .004 (.10)
Oil control ...	...	...	...	...	.0008 to .0019 (.02 to .05)
					Wear limit .004 (.10)

Cylinder heads:
... ... Light-alloy with inserts

Valve seat width
Inlet ...	...	...	...	...	.070 to .086 (1.8 to 2.2)
					.078 to .098 (2.0 to 2.5)

Valve seat angle
Inlet ...	...	...	...	...	30 deg.
Exhaust ...	...	...	...	...	45 deg.

Rocker assembly
Rocker arm internal bore	...	...	...	.7874 to .7882 (20.0 to 20.2)
				Wear limit (.7890 (20.4)
Rocker shaft diameter	...	...	...	.7854 to .7861 (19.95 to 19.97)
				Wear limit .7865 (19.98)

Valve guides ...	...	...	...	...	Not renewable

Internal diameter
Inlet ...	...	...	...	...	.3149 to .3156 (8.00 to 8.02)
					Wear limit 3.172 (8.06)
Exhaust ...	...	...	...	...	.3543 to .3550 (9.00 to 9.02)
					Wear limit .3556 (9.06)

Valves:
Stem diameter
Inlet ... ... .3125 to .3129 (7.94 to 7.95)
Wear limit .3109 (7.90)
Exhaust ... ... .3507 to .3511 (8.91 to 8.92)
Wear limit .3491 (8.87)
Head diameter
Inlet ... ... 1.4684 to 1.4764 (37.3 to 37.5)
Exhaust ... ... 1.287 to 1.299 (32.7 to 33.0)
Valve to valve guide rock
Normal ... ... .018 (.45)
Wear limit ... ... .035 (.9)

Valve springs:
Test ... ... 1.177 (29.9) at 178 to 205 lb (81 to 93 kg)

Valve timing:
Inlet opens ... ... 4 deg. BTDC
Inlet closes ... ... 39 deg. ABDC
Exhaust opens ... ... 40 deg. BBDC
Exhaust closes ... ... 3 deg. ATDC

Compression test pressure* ... ... (Engine warm, throttle open and sparking plugs removed at starter motor cranking speed)

Normal ... ... 114 to 142 lb/sq inch (8 to 10 kg/sq cm)
Minimum ... ... 100 lb/sq inch (7 kg/sq cm)

*A high test pressure indicates excessive deposits in the combustion chamber.

Lubrication system:
Normal oil pressure at 2500 rev/min ... ... 42 lb/sq inch (3 kg/sq cm)
Minimum oil pressure at 2500 rev/min ... 28 lb/sq inch (2 kg/sq cm)
Normal oil consumption ... ... 1.4 to 2.8 Imp pints (1.7 to 3.4 US pints) per 1000 miles
(.5 to 1 Litre per 100 kilometres)
Pressure switch operates ... ... 2.1 to 6.3 lb/sq inch (.15 to .45 kg/sq cm)

Relief valve springs
Test ... ... 23.4 mm at 11.1 kg (24.4 lb)
21.0 mm at 3 kg (6.6 lb)

FUEL SYSTEM

Type: ... ... Twin carburetter with mechanical fuel pump, or fuel injection system controlled by computer and supplied by electrically driven pump

Fuel pressure:
Mechanical pump ... ... 4.5 lb/sq inch (.3 kg/sq cm)
Electric pump ... ... Regulated to 28 lb/sq inch (2 kg/sq cm)
Idling speed:
Carburetter ... ... 900 rev/min
Fuel injection ... ... 950 +50 rev/min (adjusting up to speed never down from a faster setting)

Carburetter jets:
Standard transmission:

	34 PDSIT-2 (lefthand)	34 PDSIT-3 (righthand)
Carburetter type		
Choke tube	26	26
Main jet	x 135	x 135
Air correction jet	150	175
Slow-running jet	55	55
Float needle valve	1.2	1.2
Float needle valve washer	.5	.5
Float weight	70 gr.	7.0 gr.
Pump delivery	.7 to .9 cc/stroke	.7 to .9 cc/stroke
Throttle valve gap	.8 mm	.8 mm
Distance from injector tube to carburetter top face	12.5 mm	12.5 mm

Automatic transmission:

Choke tube	x 135	x 135
Main jet	150	175
Slow-running jet	55	55
Float needle valve	1,2 mm	1,2 mm
Float needle valve washer	.5 mm	.5 mm
Float weight	7.0 gr.	7.0 gr.
Pump delivery	.7 to .9 cc/stroke	.7 to .9 cc/stroke
Throttle valve gap	.8 mm	.8 mm
Distance from injector tube to carburetter top face	12.5 mm	12.5 mm

IGNITION SYSTEM

Sparking plugs:
Gap	.028 (.7)
Type	Champion L.88 or L.87Y

Ignition coil:
Manual shift	Bosch 021.905.115
Automatic	021.905.205B

Distributor: ... ... Bosch 021.905.205
Points gap: ... ... .016 (.4)
Dwell angle: ... ... 47 to 53 deg.

Ignition timing:
Approximate static or idling	5 deg. BTDC (Black mark)
Accurate	32 deg. BTDC (Red mark) at 3200 rev/min with vacuum hose disconnected

CLUTCH

Type: ... ... Single plate, hydraulically operated
Hydraulic fluid: ... ... ATE Blue (or SAE.70.R3)

MANUAL SHIFT TRANSMISSION

Type: ... ... Fourspeed, synchromesh engagement
Lubricant: ... ... SAE.90 Hypoid for both gearbox and final drive (common supply)

Ratios:
First	3.81:1
Second	2.11:1
Third	1.40:1
Top	1.00:1
Reverse	4.30:1
Final drive	
Early	3.727:1
Later	3.91:1

AUTOMATIC TRANSMISSION

Type:	Hydrodynamic torque converter, threespeed epicyclic gearbox
Lubricant:	
Gearbox	ATF
Final drive	Hypoid oil
Ratios:	
First*	2.65:1
Second	1.59:1
Top	1:1
Reverse	1.8:1
Final drive	
Early	3.67:1
Later	3.91:1

*Use forward for climbing steep ramps or very steep inclines as first is a lower ratio than reverse

SUSPENSION

Type:	Independent on all four wheels, using coil spring and telescopic dampers	
Toe-in:	1 to 3 mm unladen	
Camber:		
Front	1 deg. 15 min. ±20 min. unladen	
Rear	1 deg. ±30 min. unladen	
Wheelbase:	98.4 (2500)	
Front track:	54.2 (1376)	
Rear track:	52.8 (1342)	
Turning circle:	37.3 ft (11.4 metres)	
Wheel bearing end play:	.001 to .005 (.03 to .12)	
Coil springs:	*Front*	*Rear*
Total coils	8	8½
Effective coils	6½	7
Coil diameter	5.08 (129)	5.31 (135)
Wire diameter	.485 (12.35)	.594 (15.1)

STEERING

Type:	Recirculating ball steering box
Ratio:	
Steering box	22.38:1
Overall	19.35:1
Wheel angle at full lock:	
Inner	36 deg. 25 min. ±1 deg.
Outer	32 deg. 40 min. ±1 deg.

BRAKES

Type:	Tandem system, disc brakes on front and drum brakes on rear. All four brakes hydraulically operated by pedal. Rear brakes operated by mechanical linkage for parking
Adjustments:	
Disc brakes	Self-adjusting in service
Drum brakes	Two adjusters per brake
Handbrake	At base of handbrake lever
Fluid:	ATE Blue
Minimum lining thickness:	
Disc brake pads	.08 (2)
Drum brake shoes	.04 (1)

Brake drums:

Diameter ... ... 9.768 +.008 (248.1 +.2)
Skim diameter* 9.803 (249)
Wear limit 9.823 (249.5)
Maximum ovality or taper ... ... .004 (.1)
Maximum runout ... ... .010 (.25)

*Fit oversize linings

Disc brake:

Thickness ... ... .433 —.004 (11.0 —.1)
Refacing thickness ... ... .413 (10.5)
Wear limit ... ... .394 (10)
Runout ... ... .008 (.2) maximum

Brake caliper piston diameter 1.654 (42)
Wheel cylinder diameter: ... ... .874 (22.2)
Master cylinder diameter: ... ... .75 (19.05)

Brake regulator valve:

Regulation begins at ... ... 525 lb/sq inch (37 kg/sq cm)

Test pressures:

Front brakes reading 738 lb/sq inch (53 kg/sq cm)
Rear must read 625 ±28 lb/sq inch (44 ±2 kg/sq cm)
Front brakes reading 1420 lb/sq inch (100 kg/sq cm)
Rear brakes must read 937 ±43 lb/sq inch (66 ±3 kg/sq cm)

ELECTRICAL

Type: ... ... Lead/acid battery, alternator
Voltage and polarity: ... ... 12-volt. Negative earth

Alternator:

Type ... ... Bosch K1 (Regulator Bosch ADN)
Ratio engine/alternator 2.26/1
Maximum current 35-amps

Starter motor: ... ... Bosch or VW
Horsepower ... ... .7 (.8 for automatic)

DIMENSIONS AND WEIGHTS

Overall length ... ... 178.2 inch (4525 mm)—411E
179.2 inch (4553 mm)—411LE
Overall width ... ... 64.4 inch (1635 mm)—411E
64.9 inch (1650 mm)—411LE
Overall height—unladen ... ... 58.5 inch (1485 mm)—All models
Ground clearance ... ... 5.3 inch (135 mm)

Unladen weight:
Two-door saloon ... ... 2248 lbs (1020 kg)
Four-door saloon ... ... 2292 lbs (1040 kg)
Variant ... ... 2590 lbs (1175 kg)

Permissible load:
Two-door saloon ... ... 992 lbs (450 kg)
Four-door saloon ... ... 948 lbs (430 kg)
Variant ... ... 1030 lbs (470 kg)

Permissible total weight:
Two-door saloon ... ... 3240 lbs (1470 kg)
Four-door saloon ... ... 3240 lbs (1470 kg)
Variant ... ... 3626 lbs (1645 kg)

Permissible front axle load:
Two-door saloon ... ... 1477 lbs (670 kg)
Four-door saloon ... ... 1477 lbs (670 kg)
Variant ... ... 1477 lbs (670 kg)

Permissible rear axle load:

Two-door saloon	...	...	...	...	1807 lbs (820 kg)
Four-door saloon	...	...	...	...	1807 lbs (820 kg)
Variant	...	...	...	...	2204 lbs (1000 kg)

Roof load* ... ... 165 lbs (75 kg)
Trailer with brakes** ... ... 1984 lbs (900 kg)
Trailer without brakes** ... ... 1102 lbs (500 kg)

*Check, as local regulations may severely limit use of roof rack.
**Not recommended for earlier models with automatic transmission.

WHEELS AND TYRES

Wheel size: ... ... $4\frac{1}{2}$J x 15

Tyre size:
Sedan (saloon) ... ... 155 SR x 15
Variant ... ... 165 SR x 15

Tyre pressures: ... ... *lb/sq/inch (kg/sq cm)*

	Front	Rear
Sedan		
Normal	20 (1.4)	26 (1.8)
Fully loaded	21 to 23 (1.5 to 1.6)	28 to 31 (2 to 2.2)
Variant		
Normal	18 (1.3)	30 (2.1)
Fully loaded	18 (1.3)	35 (2.5)
Winter tyres	21 (1.5)	38 (2.7)

CAPACITIES

Air cleaner: ... ... .8 Pint, (.45 Litre)

Automatic transmission:
From dry ... ... 10.5 Pints (6 Litres)
After draining ... ... 5.25 Pints (3 Litres)
Final drive ... ... 1.75 Pints (1 Litre)

Engine:
With filter change ... ... 6.125 Pints (3.5 Litres)
No filter change ... ... 5.25 Pints (3 Litres)

Fuel tank: ... ... 11 Gallons (50 Litres)
Reserve ... ... 1.5 Gallons (6 Litres)

Standard transmission:
From dry ... ... 4.375 Pints (2.5 Litres)
After draining ... ... 3.5 Pints (2 Litres)

Steering box ... ... 250 cc
Windscreen washer: ... ... 2.5 Pints (1.5 Litres)

TORQUE WRENCH SETTINGS

Given in lb ft (kg m in brackets)

Engine:

Clutch	18	2.5
Connecting rod nuts	24	3.3
Crankcase nuts and bolts	14	2
Crankcase nuts	17	2.4
Cylinder head nuts	23	3.2
Drive plate (automatic)	61	8.5
Flywheel	90	12.5
Rocker arm nuts	10	1.4
Sparking plugs	25	3.5

Gearbox:

Bearing pin, selector shaft	10	1.4
Cover—bearing	32	4.5
Cover—selector	7	1
Crownwheel	32	4.5
Drive shaft to gear	14	2
Gearbox to final drive	14	2
Oil sump	7	1
Selector forks	14	2
Selector housing	14	2
Reverse light switch	18	2.5

Rear axle:

Bearing cover	43	6
Drive shaft flange	32	45
Wheel shaft and flange	65 to 80	9 to 11

Brakes and clutch:

Master cylinder	58 to 65	8 to 9
Residual pressure valve	14	2
Bleed nipples	3.6	.5 maximum

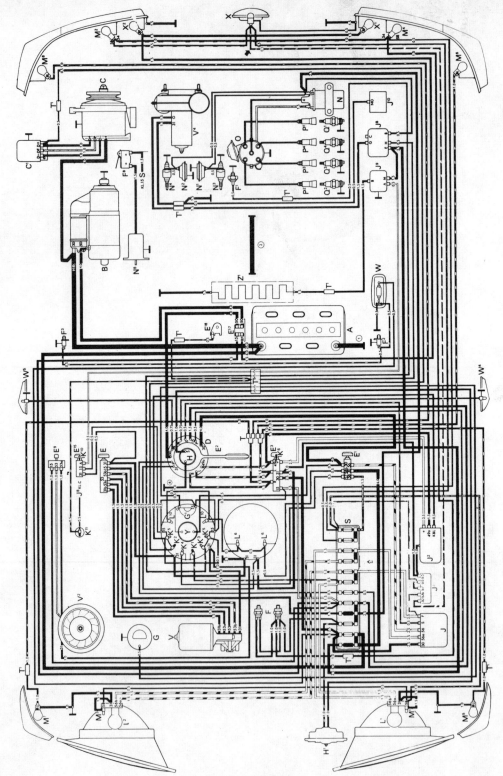

FIG 14:1   Wiring diagram for Volkswagen 411 since 1968

Key to Fig 14:1

A Battery   B Starter motor   C Alternator   C1 Voltage regulator   D Ignition/starter switch in steering column switch   E Windscreen wiper switch
E1 Light switch   E2 Flasher switch and switch for headlamp flasher and dipped lights   E3 Hazard warning lights   E9 Ventilation motor switch   E15 Switch for heated rear window   E16 Heater switch   E17 Starter inhibitor switch and reversing light switch (automatic transmission)   F Brake light switch   F1 Oil pressure switch
F2 Lefthand door contact switch   F3 Righthand door contact switch   F8 Kick-down switch   G Fuel gauge sender unit   G1 Fuel gauge   H Horn operating pad   H1 Horn
J Dipper and headlamp flasher relay   J2 Hazard warning light relay   J3 Parking light relay (if fitted)   J8 Heater booster relay   J9 Heated rear window relay   J10 Safety switch for heater booster   K1 High beam warning light   K2 Alternator charging warning light   K3 Oil pressure warning light   K4 Parking lamp warning light   K5 Flasher warning light   K6 Hazard warning light warning lamp   K10 Heated rear window warning light   K11 Heater booster warning light   L1 Bulb for lefthand headlamp   L2 Bulb for righthand headlamp   L6 Speedometer light bulb   L10 Instrument panel light bulb   M1 Lefthand parking light bulb   M2 Righthand tail and brake light bulb   M3 Righthand parking light bulb   M4 Lefthand tail and brake light bulb   M5 Lefthand front flasher lamp bulb   M6 Lefthand rear flasher lamp bulb   M7 Righthand front flasher lamp bulb   M8 Righthand rear flasher lamp bulb   N Ignition coil   N1 Lefthand automatic choke   N2 Righthand automatic choke   N3 Electromagnetic cut-off valve, left
N4 Electromagnetic cut-off valve, right   N5 Electromagnet   O Ignition distributor   P1 Cylinder No. 1 spark plug connector   P2 Cylinder No. 2 spark plug connector
P3 Cylinder No. 3 spark plug connector   P4 Cylinder No. 4 spark plug connector   Q1 Cylinder No. 1 spark plug   Q2 Cylinder No. 2 spark plug   Q3 Cylinder No. 3 spark plug
Q4 Cylinder No. 4 spark plug   S Fuse box   T Cable adaptor   T1 Single cable adaptor   T5 Push-on connector   V Windscreen wiper motor   V2 Ventilation motor, front   V4 Heater air blower   W Interior light   W4 Lefthand side marker light   W5 Righthand side marker light   X Number plate light   X1 Lefthand reversing light   X2 Righthand reversing light   Y Electric clock   Z1 Heated rear window   1 Battery/body earth strap   2 Gearbox (transmission)/Body earth strap   3 Horn operating pad/steering coupling earth strap

Inches	Decimals	Milli-metres	Inches to Millimetres		Millimetres to Inches	
			Inches	mm	mm	Inches
1/64	.015625	.3969	.001	.0254	.01	.00039
1/32	.03125	.7937	.002	.0508	.02	.00079
3/64	.046875	1.1906	.003	.0762	.03	.00118
1/16	.0625	1.5875	.004	.1016	.04	.00157
5/64	.078125	1.9844	.005	.1270	.05	.00197
3/32	.09375	2.3812	.006	.1524	.06	.00236
7/64	.109375	2.7781	.007	.1778	.07	.00276
1/8	.125	3.1750	.008	.2032	.08	.00315
9/64	.140625	3.5719	.009	.2286	.09	.00354
5/32	.15625	3.9687	.01	.254	.1	.00394
11/64	.171875	4.3656	.02	.508	.2	.00787
3/16	.1875	4.7625	.03	.762	.3	.01181
13/64	.203125	5.1594	.04	1.016	.4	.01575
7/32	.21875	5.5562	.05	1.270	.5	.01969
15/64	.234375	5.9531	.06	1.524	.6	.02362
1/4	.25	6.3500	.07	1.778	.7	.02756
17/64	.265625	6.7469	.08	2.032	.8	.03150
9/32	.28125	7.1437	.09	2.286	.9	.03543
19/64	.296875	7.5406	.1	2.54	1	.03937
5/16	.3125	7.9375	.2	5.08	2	.07874
21/64	.328125	8.3344	.3	7.62	3	.11811
11/32	.34375	8.7312	.4	10.16	4	.15748
23/64	.359375	9.1281	.5	12.70	5	.19685
3/8	.375	9.5250	.6	15.24	6	.23622
25/64	.390625	9.9219	.7	17.78	7	.27559
13/32	.40625	10.3187	.8	20.32	8	.31496
27/64	.421875	10.7156	.9	22.86	9	.35433
7/16	.4375	11.1125	1	25.4	10	.39370
29/64	.453125	11.5094	2	50.8	11	.43307
15/32	.46875	11.9062	3	76.2	12	.47244
31/64	.484375	12.3031	4	101.6	13	.51181
1/2	.5	12.7000	5	127.0	14	.55118
33/64	.515625	13.0969	6	152.4	15	.59055
17/32	.53125	13.4937	7	177.8	16	.62992
35/64	.546875	13.8906	8	203.2	17	.66929
9/16	.5625	14.2875	9	228.6	18	.70866
37/64	.578125	14.6844	10	254.0	19	.74803
19/32	.59375	15.0812	11	279.4	20	.78740
39/64	.609375	15.4781	12	304.8	21	.82677
5/8	.625	15.8750	13	330.2	22	.86614
41/64	.640625	16.2719	14	355.6	23	.90551
21/32	.65625	16.6687	15	381.0	24	.94488
43/64	.671875	17.0656	16	406.4	25	.98425
11/16	.6875	17.4625	17	431.8	26	1.02362
45/64	.703125	17.8594	18	457.2	27	1.06299
23/32	.71875	18.2562	19	482.6	28	1.10236
47/64	.734375	18.6531	20	508.0	29	1.14173
3/4	.75	19.0500	21	533.4	30	1.18110
49/64	.765625	19.4469	22	558.8	31	1.22047
25/32	.78125	19.8437	23	584.2	32	1.25984
51/64	.796875	20.2406	24	609.6	33	1.29921
13/16	.8125	20.6375	25	635.0	34	1.33858
53/64	.828125	21.0344	26	660.4	35	1.37795
27/32	.84375	21.4312	27	685.8	36	1.41732
55/64	.859375	21.8281	28	711.2	37	1.4567
7/8	.875	22.2250	29	736.6	38	1.4961
57/64	.890625	22.6219	30	762.0	39	1.5354
29/32	.90625	23.0187	31	787.4	40	1.5748
59/64	.921875	23.4156	32	812.8	41	1.6142
15/16	.9375	23.8125	33	838.2	42	1.6535
61/64	.953125	24.2094	34	863.6	43	1.6929
31/32	.96875	24.6062	35	889.0	44	1.7323
63/64	.984375	25.0031	36	914.4	45	1.7717

UNITS	Pints to Litres	Gallons to Litres	Litres to Pints	Litres to Gallons	Miles to Kilometres	Kilometres to Miles	Lbs. per sq. In. to Kg. per sq. Cm.	Kg. per sq. Cm. to Lbs. per sq. In.
1	.57	4.55	1.76	.22	1.61	.62	.07	14.22
2	1.14	9.09	3.52	.44	3.22	1.24	.14	28.50
3	1.70	13.64	5.28	.66	4.83	1.86	.21	42.67
4	2.27	18.18	7.04	.88	6.44	2.49	.28	56.89
5	2.84	22.73	8.80	1.10	8.05	3.11	.35	71.12
6	3.41	27.28	10.56	1.32	9.66	3.73	.42	85.34
7	3.98	31.82	12.32	1.54	11.27	4.35	.49	99.56
8	4.55	36.37	14.08	1.76	12.88	4.97	.56	113.79
9		40.91	15.84	1.98	14.48	5.59	.63	128.00
10		45.46	17.60	2.20	16.09	6.21	.70	142.23
20				4.40	32.19	12.43	1.41	284.47
30				6.60	48.28	18.64	2.11	426.70
40				8.80	64.37	24.85		
50					80.47	31.07		
60					96.56	37.28		
70					112.65	43.50		
80					128.75	49.71		
90					144.84	55.92		
100					160.93	62.14		

UNITS	Lb ft to kgm	Kgm to lb ft	UNITS	Lb ft to kgm	Kgm to lb ft
1	.138	7.233	7	.967	50.631
2	.276	14.466	8	1.106	57.864
3	.414	21.699	9	1.244	65.097
4	.553	28.932	10	1.382	72.330
5	.691	36.165	20	2.765	144.660
6	.829	43.398	30	4.147	216.990

HINTS ON MAINTENANCE AND OVERHAUL

There are few things more rewarding than the restoration of a vehicle's original peak of efficiency and smooth performance.

The following notes are intended to help the owner to reach that state of perfection. Providing that he possesses the basic manual skills he should have no difficulty in performing most of the operations detailed in this manual. It must be stressed, however, that where recommended in the manual, highly-skilled operations ought to be entrusted to experts, who have the necessary equipment, to carry out the work satisfactorily.

Quality of workmanship:

The hazardous driving conditions on the roads to-day demand that vehicles should be as nearly perfect, mechanically, as possible. It is therefore most important that amateur work be carried out with care, bearing in mind the often inadequate working conditions, and also the inferior tools which may have to be used. It is easy to counsel perfection in all things, and we recognize that it may be setting an impossibly high standard. We do, however, suggest that every care should be taken to ensure that a vehicle is as safe to take on the road as it is humanly possible to make it.

Safe working conditions:

Even though a vehicle may be stationary, it is still potentially dangerous if certain sensible precautions are not taken when working on it while it is supported on jacks or blocks. It is indeed preferable not to use jacks alone, but to supplement them with carefully placed blocks, so that there will be plenty of support if the car rolls off the jacks during a strenuous manoeuvre. Axle stands are an excellent way of providing a rigid base which is not readily disturbed. Piles of bricks are a dangerous substitute. Be careful not to get under heavy loads on lifting tackle, the load could fall. It is preferable not to work alone when lifting an engine, or when working underneath a vehicle which is supported well off the ground. To be trapped, particularly under the vehicle, may have unpleasant results if help is not quickly forthcoming. Make some provision, however humble, to deal with fires. Always disconnect a battery if there is a likelihood of electrical shorts. These may start a fire if there is leaking fuel about. This applies particularly to leads which can carry a heavy current, like those in the starter circuit. While on the subject of electricity, we must also stress the danger of using equipment which is run off the mains and which has no earth or has faulty wiring or connections. So many workshops have damp floors, and electrical shocks are of such a nature that it is sometimes impossible to let go of a live lead or piece of equipment due to the muscular spasms which take place.

Work demanding special care:

This involves the servicing of braking, steering and suspension systems. On the road, failure of the braking system may be disastrous. Make quite sure that there can be no possibility of failure through the bursting of rusty brake pipes or rotten hoses, nor to a sudden loss of pressure due to defective seals or valves.

Problems:

The chief problems which may face an operator are:
1 External dirt.
2 Difficulty in undoing tight fixings
3 Dismantling unfamiliar mechanisms.
4 Deciding in what respect parts are defective.
5 Confusion about the correct order for reassembly.
6 Adjusting running clearances.
7 Road testing.
8 Final tuning.

Practical suggestion to solve the problems:

1 Preliminary cleaning of large parts—engines, transmissions, steering, suspensions, etc.,—should be carried out before removal from the car. Where road dirt and mud alone are present, wash clean with a high-pressure water jet, brushing to remove stubborn adhesions, and allow to drain and dry. Where oil or grease is also present, wash down with a proprietary compound (Gunk, Teepol etc.,) applying with a stiff brush—an old paint brush is suitable—into all crevices. Cover the distributor and ignition coils with a polythene bag and then apply a strong water jet to clear the loosened deposits. Allow to drain and dry. The assemblies will then be sufficiently clean to remove and transfer to the bench for the next stage.

On the bench, further cleaning can be carried out, first wiping the parts as free as possible from grease with old newspaper. Avoid using rag or cotton waste which can leave clogging fibres behind. Any remaining grease can be removed with a brush dipped in paraffin. If necessary, traces of paraffin can be removed by carbon tetrachloride. Avoid using paraffin or petrol in large quantities for cleaning in enclosed areas, such as garages, on account of the high fire risk.

When all exteriors have been cleaned, and not before, dismantling can be commenced. This ensures that dirt will not enter into interiors and orifices revealed by dismantling. In the next phases, where components have to be cleaned, use carbon tetrachloride in preference to petrol and keep the containers covered except when in use. After the components have been cleaned, plug small holes with tapered hard wood plugs cut to size and blank off larger orifices with grease-proof paper and masking tape. Do not use soft wood plugs or matchsticks as they may break.

2 It is not advisable to hammer on the end of a screw thread, but if it must be done, first screw on a nut to protect the thread, and use a lead hammer. This applies particularly to the removal of tapered cotters. Nuts and bolts seem to 'grow' together, especially in exhaust systems. If penetrating oil does not work, try the judicious application of heat, but be careful of starting a fire. Asbestos sheet or cloth is useful to isolate heat.

Tight bushes or pieces of tail-pipe rusted into a silencer can be removed by splitting them with an open-ended hacksaw. Tight screws can sometimes be started by a tap from a hammer on the end of a suitable screwdriver. Many tight fittings will yield to the judicious use of a hammer, but it must be a soft-faced hammer if damage is to be avoided, use a heavy block on the opposite side to absorb shock. Any parts of the steering system which have been damaged should be renewed, as attempts to repair them may lead to cracking and subsequent failure, and steering ball joints should be disconnected using a recommended tool to prevent damage.

3 If often happens that an owner is baffled when trying to dismantle an unfamiliar piece of equipment. So many modern devices are pressed together or assembled by spinning-over flanges, that they must be sawn apart. The intention is that the whole assembly must be renewed. However, parts which appear to be in one piece to the naked eye, may reveal close-fitting joint lines when inspected with a magnifying glass, and, this may provide the necessary clue to dismantling. Left-handed screw threads are used where rotational forces would tend to unscrew a right handed screw thread.

Be very careful when dismantling mechanisms which may come apart suddenly. Work in an enclosed space where the parts will be contained, and drape a piece of cloth over the device if springs are likely to fly in all directions. Mark everything which might be reassembled in the wrong position, scratched symbols may be used on unstressed parts, or a sequence of tiny dots from a centre punch can be useful. Stressed parts should never be scratched or centre-popped as this may lead to cracking under working conditions. Store parts which look alike in the correct order for reassembly. Never rely upon memory to assist in the assembly of complicated mechanisms, especially when they will be dismantled for a long time, but make notes, and drawings to supplement the diagrams in the manual, and put labels on detached wires. Rust stains may indicate unlubricated wear. This can sometimes be seen round the outside edge of a bearing cup in a universal joint. Look for bright rubbing marks on parts which normally should not make heavy contact. These might prove that something is bent or running out of truth. For example, there might be bright marks on one side of a piston, at the top near the ring grooves, and others at the bottom of the skirt on the other side. This could well be the clue to a bent connecting rod. Suspected cracks can be proved by heating the component in a light oil to approximately 100°C, removing, drying off, and dusting with french chalk, if a crack is present the oil retained in the crack will stain the french chalk.

4 In determining wear, and the degree, against the permissible limits set in the manual, accurate measurement can only be achieved by the use of a micrometer. In many cases, the wear is given to the fourth place of decimals; that is in ten-thousandths of an inch. This can be read by the vernier scale on the barrel of a good micrometer. Bore diameters are more difficult to determine. If, however, the matching shaft is accurately measured, the degree of play in the bore can be felt as a guide to its suitability. In other cases, the shank of a twist drill of known diameter is a handy check.

Many methods have been devised for determining the clearance between bearing surfaces. To-day the best and simplest is by the use of Plastigage, obtainable from most garages. A thin plastic thread is laid between the two surfaces and the bearing is tightened, flattening the thread. On removal, the width of the thread is compared with a scale supplied with the thread and the clearance is read off directly. Sometimes joint faces leak persistently, even after gasket renewal. The fault will then be traceable to distortion, dirt or burrs. Studs which are screwed into soft metal frequently raise burrs at the point of entry. A quick cure for this is to chamfer the edge of the hole in the part which fits over the stud.

5 **Always check a replacement part with the original one before it is fitted.**

If parts are not marked, and the order for reassembly is not known, a little detective work will help. Look for marks which are due to wear to see if they can be mated. Joint faces may not be identical due to manufacturing errors, and parts which overlap may be stained, giving a clue to the correct position. Most fixings leave identifying marks especially if they were painted over on assembly. It is then easier to decide whether a nut, for instance, has a plain, a spring, or a shakeproof washer under it. All running surfaces become 'bedded' together after long spells of work and tiny imperfections on one part will be found to have left corresponding marks on the other. This is particularly true of shafts and bearings and even a score on a cylinder wall will show on the piston.

6 Checking end float or rocker clearances by feeler gauge may not always give accurate results because of wear. For instance, the rocker tip which bears on a valve stem may be deeply pitted, in which case the feeler will simply be bridging a depression. Thrust washers may also wear depressions in opposing faces to make accurate measurement difficult. End float is then easier to check by using a dial gauge. It is common practice to adjust end play in bearing assemblies, like front hubs with taper rollers, by doing up the axle nut until the hub becomes stiff to turn and then backing it off a little. Do not use this method with ballbearing hubs as the assembly is often preloaded by tightening the axle nut to its fullest extent. If the splitpin hole will not line up, file the base of the nut a little.

Steering assemblies often wear in the straight-ahead position. If any part is adjusted, make sure that it remains free when moved from lock to lock. Do not be surprised if an assembly like a steering gearbox, which is known to be carefully adjusted outside the car, becomes stiff when it is bolted in place. This will be due to distortion of the case by the pull of the mounting bolts, particularly if the mounting points are not all touching together. This problem may be met in other equipment and is cured by careful attention to the alignment of mounting points.

When a spanner is stamped with a size and A/F it means that the dimension is the width between the jaws and has no connection with ANF, which is the designation for the American National Fine thread. Coarse threads like Whitworth are rarely used on cars to-day except for studs which screw into soft aluminium or cast iron. For this reason it might be found that the top end of a cylinder head stud has a fine thread and the lower end a coarse thread to screw into the cylinder block. If the car has mainly UNF threads then it is likely that any coarse threads will be UNC, which are not the same as Whitworth. Small sizes have the same number of threads in Whitworth and UNC, but in the $\frac{1}{2}$ inch size for example, there are twelve threads to the inch in the former and thirteen in the latter.

7 After a major overhaul, particularly if a great deal of work has been done on the braking, steering and suspension systems, it is advisable to approach the problem of testing with care. If the braking system has been overhauled, apply heavy pressure to the brake pedal and get a second operator to check every possible source of leakage. The brakes may work extremely well, but a leak could cause complete failure after a few miles.

Do not fit the hub caps until every wheel nut has been checked for tightness, and make sure the tyre pressures are correct. Check the levels of coolant, lubricants and hydraulic fluids. Being satisfied that all is well, take the car on the road and test the brakes at once. Check the steering and the action of the handbrake. Do all this at moderate speeds on quiet roads, and make sure there is no other vehicle behind you when you try a rapid stop.

Finally, remember that many parts settle down after a time, so check for tightness of all fixings after the car has been on the road for a hundred miles or so.

8 It is useless to tune an engine which has not reached its normal running temperature. In the same way, the tune of an engine which is stiff after a rebore will be different when the engine is again running free. Remember too, that rocker clearances on pushrod operated valve gear will change when the cylinder head nuts are tightened after an initial period of running with a new head gasket.

Trouble may not always be due to what seems the obvious cause. Ignition, carburation and mechanical condition are interdependent and spitting back through the carburetter, which might be attributed to a weak mixture, can be caused by a sticking inlet valve.

For one final hint on tuning, never adjust more than one thing at a time or it will be impossible to tell which adjustment produced the desired result.

GLOSSARY OF TERMS

Allen key Cranked wrench of hexagonal section for use with socket head screws.

Alternator Electrical generator producing alternating current. Rectified to direct current for battery charging.

Ambient temperature Surrounding atmospheric temperature.

Annulus Used in engineering to indicate the outer ring gear of an epicyclic gear train.

Armature The shaft carrying the windings, which rotates in the magnetic field of a generator or starter motor. That part of a solenoid or relay which is activated by the magnetic field.

Axial In line with, or pertaining to, an axis.

Backlash Play in meshing gears.

Balance lever A bar where force applied at the centre is equally divided between connections at the ends.

Banjo axle Axle casing with large diameter housing for the crownwheel and differential.

Bendix pinion A self-engaging and self-disengaging drive on a starter motor shaft.

Bevel pinion A conical shaped gearwheel, designed to mesh with a similar gear with an axis usually at 90 deg. to its own.

bhp Brake horse power, measured on a dynamometer.

bmep Brake mean effective pressure. Average pressure on a piston during the working stroke.

Brake cylinder Cylinder with hydraulically operated piston(s) acting on brake shoes or pad(s).

Brake regulator Control valve fitted in hydraulic braking system which limits brake pressure to rear brakes during heavy braking to prevent rear wheel locking.

Camber Angle at which a wheel is tilted from the vertical.

Capacitor Modern term for an electrical condenser. Part of distributor assembly, connected across contact breaker points, acts as an interference suppressor.

Castellated Top face of a nut, slotted across the flats, to take a locking splitpin.

Castor Angle at which the kingpin or swivel pin is tilted when viewed from the side.

cc Cubic centimetres. Engine capacity is arrived at by multiplying the area of the bore in sq cm by the stroke in cm by the number of cylinders.

Clevis U-shaped forked connector used with a clevis pin, usually at handbrake connections.

Collet A type of collar, usually split and located in a groove in a shaft, and held in place by a retainer. The arrangement used to retain the spring(s) on a valve stem in most cases.

Commutator Rotating segmented current distributor between armature windings and brushes in generator or motor.

Compression The ratio, or quantitative relation, of the total volume (piston at bottom of stroke) to the unswept volume (piston at top of stroke) in an engine cylinder.

Condenser See capacitor.

Core plug Plug for blanking off a manufacturing hole in a casting.

Crownwheel Large bevel gear in rear axle, driven by a bevel pinion attached to the propeller shaft. Sometimes called a 'ring gear'.

'C'-spanner Like a 'C' with a handle. For use on screwed collars without flats, but with slots or holes.

Damper Modern term for shock-absorber, used in vehicle suspension systems to damp out spring oscillations.

Depression The lowering of atmospheric pressure as in the inlet manifold and carburetter.

Dowel Close tolerance pin, peg, tube, or bolt, which accurately locates mating parts.

Drag link Rod connecting steering box drop arm (pitman arm) to nearest front wheel steering arm in certain types of steering systems.

Dry liner Thinwall tube pressed into cylinder bore

Dry sump Lubrication system where all oil is scavenged from the sump, and returned to a separate tank.

Dynamo See Generator.

Electrode Terminal, part of an electrical component, such as the points or 'Electrodes' of a sparking plug.

Electrolyte In lead-acid car batteries a solution of sulphuric acid and distilled water.

End float The axial movement between associated parts, end play.

EP Extreme pressure. In lubricants, special grades for heavily loaded bearing surfaces, such as gear teeth in a gearbox, or crownwheel and pinion in a rear axle.

Fade	Of brakes. Reduced efficiency due to overheating.
Field coils	Windings on the polepieces of motors and generators.
Fillets	Narrow finishing strips usually applied to interior bodywork.
First motion shaft	Input shaft from clutch to gearbox.
Fullflow filter	Filters in which all the oil is pumped to the engine. If the element becomes clogged, a bypass valve operates to pass unfiltered oil to the engine.
FWD	Front wheel drive.
Gear pump	Two meshing gears in a close fitting casing. Oil is carried from the inlet round the outside of both gears in the spaces between the gear teeth and casing to the outlet, the meshing gear teeth prevent oil passing back to the inlet, and the oil is forced through the outlet port.
Generator	Modern term for 'Dynamo'. When rotated produces electrical current.
Grommet	A ring of protective or sealing material. Can be used to protect pipes or leads passing through bulkheads.
Grubscrew	Fully threaded headless screw with screwdriver slot. Used for locking, or alignment purposes.
Gudgeon pin	Shaft which connects a piston to its connecting rod. Sometimes called 'wrist pin', or 'piston pin'.
Halfshaft	One of a pair transmitting drive from the differential.
Helical	In spiral form. The teeth of helical gears are cut at a spiral angle to the side faces of the gearwheel.
Hot spot	Hot area that assists vapourisation of fuel on its way to cylinders. Often provided by close contact between inlet and exhaust manifolds.
HT	High Tension. Applied to electrical current produced by the ignition coil for the sparking plugs.
Hydrometer	A device for checking specific gravity of liquids. Used to check specific gravity of electrolyte.
Hypoid bevel gears	A form of bevel gear used in the rear axle drive gears. The bevel pinion meshes below the centre line of the crownwheel, giving a lower propeller shaft line.
Idler	A device for passing on movement. A free running gear between driving and driven gears. A lever transmitting track rod movement to a side rod in steering gear.
Impeller	A centrifugal pumping element. Used in water pumps to stimulate flow.
Journals	Those parts of a shaft that are in contact with the bearings.
Kingpin	The main vertical pin which carries the front wheel spindle, and permits steering movement. May be called 'steering pin' or 'swivel pin'.
Layshaft	The shaft which carries the laygear in the gearbox. The laygear is driven by the first motion shaft and drives the third motion shaft according to the gear selected. Sometimes called the 'countershaft' or 'second motion shaft.'
lb ft	A measure of twist or torque. A pull of 10 lb at a radius of 1 ft is a torque of 10 lb ft.
lb/sq in	Pounds per square inch.
Little-end	The small, or piston end of a connecting rod. Sometimes called the 'small-end'.
LT	Low Tension. The current output from the battery.
Mandrel	Accurately manufactured bar or rod used for test or centring purposes.
Manifold	A pipe, duct, or chamber, with several branches.
Needle rollers	Bearing rollers with a length many times their diameter.
Oil bath	Reservoir which lubricates parts by immersion. In air filters, a separate oil supply for wetting a wire mesh element to hold the dust.
Oil wetted	In air filters, a wire mesh element lightly oiled to trap and hold airborne dust.
Overlap	Period during which inlet and exhaust valves are open together.
Panhard rod	Bar connected between fixed point on chassis and another on axle to control sideways movement.
Pawl	Pivoted catch which engages in the teeth of a ratchet to permit movement in one direction only.
Peg spanner	Tool with pegs, or pins, to engage in holes or slots in the part to be turned.
Pendant pedals	Pedals with levers that are pivoted at the top end.
Phillips screwdriver	A cross-point screwdriver for use with the cross-slotted heads of Phillips screws.
Pinion	A small gear, usually in relation to another gear.
Piston-type damper	Shock absorber in which damping is controlled by a piston working in a closed oil-filled cylinder.
Preloading	Preset static pressure on ball or roller bearings not due to working loads.
Radial	Radiating from a centre, like the spokes of a wheel.

Radius rod	Pivoted arm confining movement of a part to an arc of fixed radius.
Ratchet	Toothed wheel or rack which can move in one direction only, movement in the other being prevented by a pawl.
Ring gear	A gear tooth ring attached to outer periphery of flywheel. Starter pinion engages with it during starting.
Runout	Amount by which rotating part is out of true.
Semi-floating axle	Outer end of rear axle halfshaft is carried on bearing inside axle casing. Wheel hub is secured to end of shaft.
Servo	A hydraulic or pneumatic system for assisting, or, augmenting a physical effort. See 'Vacuum Servo'.
Setscrew	One which is threaded for the full length of the shank.
Shackle	A coupling link, used in the form of two parallel pins connected by side plates to secure the end of the master suspension spring and absorb the effects of deflection.
Shell bearing	Thinwalled steel shell lined with anti-friction metal. Usually semi-circular and used in pairs for main and big-end bearings.
Shock absorber	See 'Damper'.
Silentbloc	Rubber bush bonded to inner and outer metal sleeves.
Socket-head screw	Screw with hexagonal socket for an Allen key.
Solenoid	A coil of wire creating a magnetic field when electric current passes through it. Used with a soft iron core to operate contacts or a mechanical device.
Spur gear	A gear with teeth cut axially across the periphery.
Stub axle	Short axle fixed at one end only.
Tachometer	An instrument for accurate measurement of rotating speed. Usually indicates in revolutions per minute.

TDC	Top Dead Centre. The highest point reached by a piston in a cylinder, with the crank and connecting rod in line.
Thermostat	Automatic device for regulating temperature. Used in vehicle coolant systems to open a valve which restricts circulation at low temperature.
Third motion shaft	Output shaft of gearbox.
Threequarter floating axle	Outer end of rear axle halfshaft flanged and bolted to wheel hub, which runs on bearing mounted on outside of axle casing. Vehicle weight is not carried by the axle shaft.
Thrust bearing or washer	Used to reduce friction in rotating parts subject to axial loads.
Torque	Turning or twisting effort. See 'lb ft'.
Track rod	The bar(s) across the vehicle which connect the steering arms and maintain the front wheels in their correct alignment.
UJ	Universal joint. A coupling between shafts which permits angular movement.
UNF	Unified National Fine screw thread.
Vacuum servo	Device used in brake system, using difference between atmospheric pressure and inlet manifold depression to operate a piston which acts to augment brake pressure as required. See 'Servo'.
Venturi	A restriction or 'choke' in a tube, as in a carburetter, used to increase velocity to obtain a reduction in pressure.
Vernier	A sliding scale for obtaining fractional readings of the graduations of an adjacent scale.
Welch plug	A domed thin metal disc which is partially flattened to lock in a recess. Used to plug core holes in castings.
Wet liner	Removable cylinder barrel, sealed against coolant leakage, where the coolant is in direct contact with the outer surface.
Wet sump	A reservoir attached to the crankcase to hold the lubricating oil.

INDEX

A

Accelerator pump 38
Air cleaner:
    Carburetter type 30
    Fuel injection type 42
Alternator 123
Automatic air cooling 53
Automatic choke 32
Automatic transmission:
    Maintenance 79
    Removal 81

B

Ball joints:
    Steering 97
    Suspension 92
Battery... 119
Beam setting, headlamps 129
Belt tension 56
Big-ends 25
Bleeding:
    Brakes 117
    Clutch 63
Brake adjustments 109
Brake linings 115
Brake master cylinder 115
Brake pads 113

C

Camshaft 25
Capacitor 145
Capacitor, distributor 48
Carburetter:
    Adjustments 38
    Faults 33
    Operation 32
    System 30
Clutch:
    Adjustment 60
    Maintenance 59
    Master cylinder 61
    Removal 23
    Slave cylinder 61
Computer 41
Contact points, distributor 46
Cooling fan 24
Cooling system, engine 53
Crankcase 24
Crankshaft 25
Crankshaft gears 25
Cylinder 20
Cylinder head 18

D

Damper:
    Front 94
    Rear... 83
    Steering 99
Deflector plates 18
Differential 74
Direction indicators 129

Disc brake 113
Distributor:
    Capacitor 48
    Contact points 46
    Drive 49
    Removal 48
    Setting 50
Drive shafts 85

E

Electrolyte 122
Engine:
    Description 9
    Reassembly 26
    Removal 12
Evaporative emission control 29

F

Firing order 48
Flexible hoses 111
Flywheel 23
Friction linings:
    Clutch 64
    Disc brakes 115
    Drum brakes 113
Front hubs 89
Fuel filter:
    Carburetter 30
    Fuel injection system 43
Fuel pump:
    Carburetter 30
    Fuel injection system 43
Fuses 129

G

Gaskets, engine 26
Gearbox:
    Dismantling... 66
    Reassembly 68
Grinding-in valves 19
Gudgeon pins 20

H

Handbrake:
    Adjustment 110
    Cables 117
Headlamps 128
Heater 53
Hub bearings:
    Front 89
    Rear... 87
Hydraulic fluid... 143
Hydrometer test, electrolyte 122

I

Idling adjustments:
    Carburetter 40
    Fuel injection 43
Idling speeds 141
Ignition faults 47
Ignition timing... 50

J

Jet sizes 142

L

Lock:
    Bonnet 135
    Steering 129

M

Main bearings 24
Master cylinder:
    Brakes 115
    Clutch 61

O

Oil cooler 23
Oil filter 15
Oil level:
    Automatic transmission 79
    Engine 16
    Transmission 65
Oil pressure 141
Oil pump 23

P

Pedal clearance:
    Brake 116
    Clutch 60
Pilot jet, electromagnetic 32
Piston ring gaps 140
Piston rings 21
Pistons 22
Pushrods 19

R

Rear axle 83
Rear coil springs 87
Rear dampers 83
Rear hubs 87
Removing:
    Engine 12
    Transmission 65
Rocker assembly 18

S

Seat belts 134
Selector mechanism—automatic transmission... 80
Slow-running adjustments:
    Carburetter 40
    Fuel injection 43
Sparking plugs 50
Specific gravity, electrolyte 122
Stabilizer bar 83, 91
Starter motor 126
Steering column 99
Steering gear unit 101
Steering wheel 99
Suspension:
    Front 89
    Rear... 83

T

Technical data 139
Thermostat 56
Timing:
    Ignition 50
    Valves 25
Torque wrench settings 17, 146
Transmission 65

V

Vacuum control, ignition 45
Valve clearances 19
Valve guides 19
Valves 19
Valve springs 19
Valve timing 25

W

Wheels and tyres 145
Windscreen 135
Windscreen washer 134
Windscreen wiper 128
Wiring diagrams 148

THE AUTOBOOK SERIES OF WORKSHOP MANUALS

Alfa Romeo Giulia
1962 on
Aston Martin 1921-58
Audi 100 1969 on
(Austin, Morris etc.)
1100 Mk. 1 1962-67
(Austin, Morris etc.) 1100
Mk. 2, 1300 Mk. 1, 2,
America 1968 on
Austin A30, A35, A40
Farina
Austin A55 Mk. 2, A60
1958-69
Austin A99, A110 1959-68
Austin J4 1960 on
Austin Maxi 1969 on
Austin, Morris 1800
1964 on
BMC 3 (Austin A50,
A55 Mk. 1, Morris
Oxford 2. 3 1954-59)
Austin Healey 100/6, 3000
1956-68
(Austin Healey, MG)
Sprite, Midget 1958 on
BMW 1600 1964 on
BMW 1800 1964-68
BMW 2000, 2002 1966 on
Chevrolet Corvair 1960-69
Chevrolet Corvette V8
1957-65
Chevrolet Vega 2300
1970-71
Chevrolet Corvette V8
1965-71
Chrysler Valiant V8
1965 on
Chrysler Valiant Straight
Six 1966-70
Citroen DS 19, ID 19
1955-66
Citroen ID 19, DS 19, 20,
21 1966-70
Datsun 1200 1970 on
Datsun 1300, 1600
1968 on
Datsun 240Z Sport
1970 on
De Dion Bouton
1899-1907
Fiat 124 1966 on
Fiat 124 Sport 1966 on
Fiat 125 1967 on
Fiat 500 1957 on
Fiat 600, 600D 1955-69
Fiat 850 1964 on
Fiat 1100 1957-69
Fiat 1300, 1500 1961-67
Ford Anglia Prefect 100E
1953-62
Ford Anglia 105E,
Prefect 107E 1959-67
Ford Capri 1300, 1600
1968 on
Ford Capri 2000 GT,
3000 GT 1969 on
Ford Classic, Capri
1961-64
Ford Consul, Zephyr,
Zodiac, 1, 2 1950-62
Ford Corsair Straight
Four 1963-65

Ford Corsair V4 1965-68
Ford Corsair V4 1969 on
Ford Cortina 1962-66
Ford Cortina 1967-68
Ford Cortina 1969-70
Ford Cortina Mk. 3
1970 on
Ford Escort 1967 on
Ford Falcon V8 1964-69
Ford Thames 10, 12,
15 cwt 1957-65
Ford Transit 1965 on
Ford Zephyr Zodiac
Mk. 3 1962-66
Ford Zephyr V4, V6,
Zodiac 1966 on
Hillman Avenger 1970 on
Hillman Hunter 1966 on
Hillman Imp 1963-68
Hillman Imp 1969 on
Hillman Minx 1 to 5
1956-65
Hillman Minx 1965-67
Hillman Minx 1966-70
Hillman Super Minx
1961-65
Holden Straight Six
1948-66
Holden Straight Six
1966 on
Jaguar XK120, 140, 150,
Mk. 7, 8, 9 1948-61
Jaguar 2.4, 3.4, 3.8
Mk. 1, 2 1955-69
Jaguar 'E' Type 1961 on
Jaguar 'S' Type 420
1963-68
Jaguar XJ6 1968 on
Jowett Javelin Jupiter
1947-53
Landrover 1, 2 1948-61
Landrover 2, 2a, 3 1959 on
Mercedes-Benz 190b,
190c 200 1959-68
Mercedes-Benz 220
1959-65
Mercedes-Benz 220/8
1968 on
Mercedes-Benz 230
1963-68
Mercedes-Benz 250
1965-67
Mercedes-Benz 250
1968 on
Mercedes-Benz 280
1968 on
MG TA to TF 1936-55
MGA MGB 1955-68
MG MGB 1969 on
Mini 1959 on
Mini Cooper 1961 on
Morgan 1936-69
Morris Marina 1971 on
Morris Minor 2, 1000
1952-71
Morris Oxford 5, 6 1959-71
NSU 1000 1963 on
NSU Prinz 1 to 4
1957 on
Opel Ascona, Manta
1970 on
Opel G.T. 1900 1968 on

Opel Kadett, Olympia
993 cc, 1078 cc
1962 on
Opel Kadett, Olympia
1492, 1698, 1897 cc
1967 on
Opel Rekord C 1966 on
Peugeot 204 1965 on
Peugeot 404 1960 on
Peugeot 504 1968-70
Porsche 356a, 356b, 356c
1957-65
Porsche 911 1964-69
Porsche 912 1965-69
Reliant Regal 1962 on
Renault R4, R4L, 4
1961 on
Renault 6 1968 on
Renault 8, 10, 1100
1962 on
Renault 12 1969 on
Renault R16 1965 on
Renault Dauphine
Floride 1957-67
Renault Caravelle 1962-68
Rover 60 to 110 1953-64
Rover 2000 1963 on
Rover 3 Litre 1958-67
Rover 3500, 3500S
1968 on
Saab 95, 96, Sport
1960-68
Saab 99 1969 on
Saab V4 1966 on
Simca 1000 1961 on
Simca 1100 1967 on
Simca 1300, 1301, 1500,
1501 1963 on
Skoda One (440, 445, 450)
1957-69
Sunbeam Rapier Alpine
1955-65
Toyota Corolla 1100
1967 on
Toyota Corona 1500
Mk. 1 1965-70
Toyota Corona 1900 Mk. 2
1969 on
Triumph TR2, TR3,
TR3A 1952-62
Triumph TR4, TR4A
1961-67
Triumph TR5, TR250,
TR6 1967 on
Triumph 1300, 1500
1965 on
Triumph 2000 Mk. 1, 2.5 PI
Mk. 1 1963-69
Triumph 2000 Mk. 2, 2.5
PI Mk. 2 1969 on
Triumph Herald 1959-68
Triumph Herald 1969-71
Triumph Spitfire Vitesse
1962-68
Triumph Spitfire Mk. 3
1969 on
Triumph GT6, Vitesse 2
Litre 1969 on
Triumph Toledo 1970 on
Vauxhall Velox, Cresta
1957 on

Vauxhall Victor 1, 2, FB
1957-64
Vauxhall Victor 101
1964-67
Vauxhall Victor FD 1600,
2000 1967 on
Vauxhall Viva HA 1963-66
Vauxhall Viva HB 1966-70
Vauxhall Viva, HC Firenza
1971 on
Vauxhall Victor 3300,
Ventura 1968 on
Volkswagen Beetle
1954-67
Volkswagen Beetle
1968 on
Volkswagen 1500 1961-66
Volkswagen 1600
Fastback 1965 on
Volkswagen Transporter
1954-67
Volkswagen Transporter
1968 on
Volvo P120 1961-70
Volvo P140 1966 on
Volvo 160 series 1968 on
Volvo 1800 1961 on